Kay's
Life

Kay's Life

The Stories of Kay Conklin

by Kay Conklin

proving
press

Book Design & Production:
Columbus Publishing Lab
www.ColumbusPublishingLab.com

Paperback ISBN: 978-1-63337-882-7
E-Book ISBN: 978-1-63337-883-4

Printed in the United States of America
1 3 5 7 9 10 8 6 4 2

Table of Contents

———————

Foreword

K ay and George Conklin walked into my office at Ohio Wesleyan University on a beautiful April morning. Kay carried a large stack of papers as her husband gave me a nervous but friendly smile.

The 87-year-old woman had a determined look. "Are you John McGory? Someone said I should come talk to you."

"Yes, I am. What can I do for you?" The usual visitors to my office were tired-eyed college students pleading for a break of some kind so two elderly individuals had me baffled.

"I want a book," Kay said as she plunked down the big stack of papers onto my desk with a thud.

This conversation started my wonderful historical journey into a past world of small-town American life.

Kay Conklin personifies the American Dream. She grew up a middle-child of a large farming family that struggled through the Depression, living in seven different homes throughout central Ohio. The early homes had no electricity or running water.

The young woman graduated from high school with no money, car, job, or hopes of going to college. But a determined spirit led her to great things. She got a job as a secretary at Ohio Wesleyan and took one class a semester for 12 years before graduating. The week she graduated she was elected Delaware (Ohio) County Recorder and served four terms.

She succeeded as an elected official, but Kay has one passion. She loves to write. And in 2017, the Delaware Gazette began publishing Kay's first-person articles about her life over the decades in small-town Ohio.

What started off as a one-time opportunity ended up with over 180 articles covering life in Midwest America over the past nine decades. World War II, life in small downtowns, horse farms, family struggles, and America's progress get captured through her thoughtful words.

My job in this was to dictate each article into a digitized format and edit them. I started off thinking it would be a boring task. But soon, the articles brought smiles and tears as her prose brought alive visions of a truly American life.

Kay told me in no uncertain terms on that spring morning that she wanted a book. Now she has one and anyone who reads this will share in her beautiful tales of an American life well lived and told.

—John McGory

Remembering the Big Day Back in 1959

After the past eight years of writing, I am now aware that I may be repeating myself when I write about anything in my life. I have written a lot about my days in the Delaware City School system, as well as about my family. I have also written a lot about my jobs. But today, I am absolutely sure that I have not written anything about getting married 65 years ago.

Just this past Thursday, on January 25th, we spent the day thinking about that day back in 1959 when a lot of people we knew came to the church and watched George and me get married. It was a warm day for January, and there was a big flood going on in the vicinity.

It was 1957 that I first met George at our church, and we ended up getting married there in 1959. And we have continued to go there for the past 65 years. It was a nice wedding with the family members being in the wedding, and a classmate of George's played the organ, and another classmate sang. Our reception was in the basement after the ceremony. We had the usual refreshments that most people had back in the 1950s: wedding cake and punch. As we left the church to go on our honeymoon, someone had just tied a "Just Married" sign and some tin cans onto the back of our car.

Our church hasn't changed too much in the past 65 years. During that time, we have had 21 different ministers, several different organists, all sizes of choirs, several very good Sunday school teachers, and a lot of funerals. Back during the time of our wedding, we had about 90 people coming every Sunday. And we always had a choir wearing their green robes. We also had several women's groups that no longer exist.

When my parents had their 50th wedding anniversary party, I thought they were very old. I don't feel as old as I thought they were back then. There was a big party for them in our brother's home. Our younger daughter was only three years old at the time. She wanted a piece of cake as soon as we got there but was told she had to wait. She still wanted to have a piece, so one of my sisters told her that she couldn't have a piece of the decorated cake on display, but if she went to the kitchen, someone would give her a piece of the sheet cake. The next day when asked about our grandparents' party, she said, "They had two cakes: a lookin' cake and an eatin' cake." That was 50 years ago and we still laugh about it.

Since I have just written about two pieces of cake for my parents' anniversary party, I will tell you another story about two pieces of cake. Last week when we were eating out at Amato's, we had a great pizza and sub. A couple of hours later I was hungry for some dessert, so we stopped downtown for a piece of cake.

It was the middle of the afternoon. No one was in the restaurant but us and the waitress. When we asked what they had for dessert, she said they had only two pieces of cake still in the kitchen. One was chocolate with chocolate icing, and the other was a layered cake with a lot of white icing. So, we ordered them both.

They were great. It was when the bill came that we found that they were $10.00 for each piece. Only because it was our 65th anniversary did we gladly pay the $20 plus tax, and then laughed about it all the way home.

Lost Billfold No Match
for TSA Agent

W hile standing in line recently to go through security at Orlando airport in Florida, I knew we were in trouble when I saw the sick look on my husband's face.

George realized that he had lost his billfold, which meant he didn't have a driver's license and couldn't board our flight home to Ohio.

In desperation, George retraced his steps to the point where our daughter, Cathy, had dropped us off.

The longer George was gone, the more I was certain that nothing positive would come out of our situation - especially given that we had just watched the news about the March 22nd bombing at Brussels airport and knew that security at airports worldwide would be on high alert.

While watching for George, I saw a Transportation Security Administration agent directing some women and noticed his caring, professional manner. I decided that, if we needed help, we should find him.

When George returned, he still had a sick look: his billfold, he said, was "long gone."

We decided to call Cathy to ask her to return to the airport, but we didn't know what we would do without the driver's license or any other identification.

We were fortunate to find the agent I had seen earlier. After we told him our story, he immediately started asking questions and calling us George and Kay - which made us think he was on our side.

The agent told me that, because I had my driver's license and boarding pass, I could go ahead and board. I was in no shape to agree, though, so I stayed put.

Just when we were sure that George would never get on the plane, the agent gave us a glimmer of hope: he said he would call Washington and have someone ask George questions that only he could answer. If he knew the correct answer to every question and passed the security pat-down and X-ray, we could board the plane for home.

Before he finished telling us what he was hoping to do, it was done: the person in Washington was on the line.

The questions came fast, and George answered just as fast. The last question: What is the model car you have before the car you have now?"

When we finally realized that the man was talking about our 1994 Chevy Beretta, the agent looked at us and said, "Follow me."

We followed him through a mass of waiting people until we reached the point of the pat-down and X-ray; George was led off to the right, and I went left. Just before we parted ways with the agent, I asked him for his name, as I wanted to let his supervisor know what a great help he had been.

His name: Daren Diaz.

My husband and I eventually got a "Compliment/complaint Card" to fill out before proceeding to board.

Meanwhile, our daughter had returned to the airport and gone straight to the lost and found.

She explained our situation, was asked a lot of questions, and the airport officials helped her make some phone calls.

Soon, an amazing thing happened: The officials handed George's billfold to Cathy, and everything -Everything! - was still inside.

A JetBlue attendant had found it and turned it in.

Cathy couldn't get to us, so she called George to tell him that she had his billfold and would mail it home.

Thanks to the TSA agent and the JetBlue attendant, George and I smiled all the way home.

Memories of
the Strand Theatre

O n the day before school started in the fall of 1944, my dad and mom moved all my siblings and me to Delaware. There were eight of us inside our two-seater, four-door car. My only memory of the entire trip is when we got to Delaware and passed the Strand Theatre.

I remember saying, "Oh, goody, they have a show in this town." As our dad turned north on Union Street, I watched out the back window until the sign "Strand" was out of sight.

I was about to enter the 3rd grade and knew I would be getting to go to the show because it was within walking distance of our new house. I enjoyed every one of the shows I got to see, but remember being totally bored when the newsreels came on. Mostly because President Truman seemed to talk endlessly about the war that was going on. However, there was always a good cartoon to follow.

Luckily, on Sunday afternoons, after eating dinner and doing the dishes, we could all walk to the Strand to see whatever was on. We seemed to always arrive in the middle of one of the double features, watched to the end of it, then watched the entire next feature, and stayed in our seats until the original first feature came back and saw something that looked familiar. When we were all sure we had seen it to that point, we got up and walked back home. I remember walking forward up the aisle, but my head was always turned backwards to get to see every last second of what was still on the screen.

Those were the days when the Strand had just one theatre and we could sit in the balcony and see what was going on below. We were lucky to get a candy bar because I learned later that not every kid did. Of course, at least one of us always had to use the restroom, and I still laugh about how the ladies' room always reminded me of a cave.

I need to stop using the word "show" (as in "picture show") because, as an adult, I was told that I should call it a "movie." I sometimes still use the word "show" and find myself flinching and waiting to be corrected.

In 1966, a previous owner, George Johnson, and his wife and little son, Chuckie, moved in across the street from us. George worked six days a week, taking off only on Mondays. He always stayed home with Chuckie while his wife, Cindy, and I went to the Strand to see whatever was shown that night. We always sat in the balcony. During that time, the balcony was "off limits" and no one was allowed to sit up there. But Cindy wanted to because that's where she could smoke.

We always got the biggest box of popcorn and made sure we didn't drop any of it on the floor. George popped his own popcorn and made small packets of candy that sold for a price most kids could afford. I have known him to have some patrons hand him a $1.00 bill to pay for their snacks and George handed them back a dollar's worth of change.

In 1994, George and Cindy sold the Strand and moved back to Greece. When his own father was killed in Greece, his mother put her 16-year-old son, George, on a ship bound for the United States. He was alone and didn't know any of the English language. Somehow, he got himself from the New York harbor clear to Chicago, Illinois. While in Chicago, he worked at a theatre that belonged to his uncle. He learned English by paying attention to the movies while cleaning the theatre every day.

We enjoyed getting to know him well during the years he lived across the street from us. When Chuckie got old enough to help with cleaning the Strand, George would throw a big handful of quarters on the floor between the seats and Chuckie would clean up the spilled popcorn and candy wrappers while looking for the money.

As I walked down East Winter Street a couple of weeks ago, I saw the "Stars" being put in place on the sidewalk in front of the Strand. What a great idea for downtown Delaware! While there, I took a second look at the entrance when I remembered the little booth that used to be there to house the employee who sold us our tickets. I've often wondered what it would have been like to have that job and how did they keep warm in the winter?

My thoughts, at this moment, are of wishing I could go back, and just one more time, have Sunday dinner with all my siblings, do the dishes, and walk downtown to see the Strand marquee announcing a double feature that we could sit through like we did in the 50s. Thanks to all the owners and employees who made it possible for everyone to be so well entertained right here in our own hometown of Delaware.

I Miss Eating at the Brown Jug

During the 30 years I was working in downtown Delaware, I ate a lot of lunches at the Brown Jug Restaurant (aka "The Jug").

This was during the years from 1977 until 2008. In the 70s, it was mostly a bar, but it grew into a place that served good meals for the downtown working people.

At first, there were no hostesses, so you hoped to find an empty booth on your own. Everyone in town seemed to want to eat at the same time, so it was always crowded.

After many times of looking for a spot to sit down, we started talking to a woman named Ruthie, who was always eating alone. She invited us to sit with her, and our friendship blossomed from then on.

Soon, other women who worked with us at Ohio Wesleyan University came by., needing a place to sit. By the time we were squeezing six into the booth every day, one of the owners told us that if we were going to eat there every day, he would give us a table of our own, that was near the back. Thus, the "Lunch Bunch" was formed.

The Brown Jug was our "home away from home." Judy was our waitress every day. Once I asked her what she would recommend to eat that day, and she jokingly said: "I don't know. I don't eat here." Once, when I ordered a cheeseburger soup, she told me that I didn't like it the last time I had ordered It. She was right. Too much pepper for me. (I had forgotten that little fact).

Over the years, we had lots of parties during our lunch hours. We always had a cake for everyone's birthday, as well as a special red and green pizza on our last day of work before Christmas. All our families knew where they could find us from noon to 1:00 p.m. If we were needed, they would call the Jug. That was before the days of cell phones.

Everyone always met there when we had our Willis High School class reunions. At our last reunion, we got to sit outside on the new patio at the corner of Sandusky and William streets and watch the lights come on in downtown Delaware.

Close to the end of our years of having lunch there, our Lunch Bunch dwindled down to about four or five, and we no longer needed the table. Some women moved away and others retired. They were the ones who sent mail to the rest of us at the Jug. After everyone had read the cards, we stuck them behind the wooden cut out of the Jug on the wall, to be found in later years.

With their business being so good, we assumed the Brown Jug would be there for a very long time to come. However, much to everyone's surprise, on July 7th, 2008, the Jug had been sold and would be closed as of the next day. So everyone spread the word to come to eat on that last day.

Our first thoughts were on how we were going to miss eating all their special soups and sandwiches and pizzas. But soon, the real loss of the Jug closing set in. We had lost our meeting place and no longer would be seeing all the friends we had made over the past 30 years. No more seeing the owners, Bill Stroud and Ed Wolf. They both had been there almost every day of those 30 years, taking orders, serving, making jokes, and singing "Happy Birthday" as only Ed Wolf could sing it.

No more seeing the downtown business owners who had kept Delaware open during the time the sidewalks and streets were torn up. They met there every Friday noon and also had their own table.

No more seeing those two sweet little ladies who came in just as everyone else was leaving. They were sisters and told me they often came in for an afternoon drink.

No more getting to know the faithful workers who made the Jug our home away from home. Our experience there was a little like TV show "Cheers" - where everyone knew your name.

One of the Jug co-owners, Bill, died. I used to run into the other co-owner, Ed, at Buehler's, but that store is closed now, too. When I run into any of the other Jug patrons, we talk about our days there and how we still miss the life we had.

No more seeing those familiar faces sitting in their same booths, waving to us, as we walk past them on the way to our table in the back every day.

As a wonderful gesture of friendship, a student from OWU sent me a copy of a book about the Brown Jug restaurant. It contains recipes of many of their signature soups and sandwiches. Recently I had a homemade bowl of their wonderful "Poor Man's soup." It was a tasty blast from my past.

I know what we had at the Jug could never be duplicated, but it would be nice for any of the old patrons to have a place to go again. And who knows - maybe run into some of the other old patrons and talk about the good old days and how we all still miss the Jug.

Thanks to the owners - known to us as Red and Ed - and their families, for their hospitality in making our lunches the highlight of our working day in downtown Delaware for all those 30 years.

I Enjoy My Time in
Our Libraries

S pending time in libraries is one of my favorite things to do. I am fortunate to be living just one block from our library in Ashley.

When I moved here, there was already a small library on the main street in town. Over the years, it has grown by having a new addition in 1981, and then another edition in 1991. I was on the library board over the time these additions were built. That's probably why I often refer to it as "another room in my house." While growing up in the Delaware City Schools, I always went to the Carnegie library on North Sandusky Street in Delaware. I often stopped on my way home from school to use their encyclopedias to help with my homework.

Due to Delaware County's growth, and having insufficient parking spaces, a new library was built on East Winter Street where an Albers grocery store used to be. I remember hearing the story that in order to afford to build it, they used one of the walls from the original Albers store as part of the building. That was done to be able to get a tax break by saying it was part of an old building, not a brand new one. A couple of months ago, I visited the Delaware Library and with the help of the director, we think we found that very wall.

I was fortunate to get to spend an hour in the Delaware Library recently and I enjoyed every minute of its quiet hustle and bustle. My first decision was to read the front page of one of the newspapers on display. When I'd had enough of reading about how bad a shape the world's in, I walked through the children's section and looked at the titles and covers of all their new books. While there, I noticed a couple of mothers with small children checking out books. For the very first time, I saw a self-check-out place where the little three-and-four-year-olds were checking out their own books! I know I'm behind in today's technology, but now I find that I'm even behind some three-and-four-year-olds.

Gone are the days of looking for jobs in the "want ads" of newspapers. Now you have to get on your computer. If you need one, the library has a whole room of computers for you to use. Back in the day, "want ads" were divided into two categories: one for male jobs, and the other for female jobs. The world has changed a lot since then.

When it was getting time for me to leave, a lady at the copy machine wanted to show me her family pictures she had just copied. That's when I found out that the library has a copy machine that will produce color pictures. Good to know!

As my waiting time was about to end, I decided to wait in the area between the double doors. This is where they keep the books that are for sale. They charge $1.00 for hardbacks and $0.50 for paperbacks. They have a beautiful wall there of stained glass artwork of children reading books. Thanks to the Don and Eleanor Byerly family for financing this beautiful entryway.

If I have any extra time, I usually pick out one of their sale books to take home with me. I recently found out that you really can't judge a book by its cover. Due to the fact that I was in a hurry, I took the first book that had a cover that interested me. When I got home, I found out that the above quote really is true.

I was on the board of trustees at the Ashley Wornstaff Memorial Library for 30 years. During that period of time, in addition to the experience of building on the 1981 and 1991 editions, I learned where the real money comes from to fund such a wonderful place. I also learned about the jobs of all the employees who keep the doors open six days a week. And, most interesting of all, I learned that the Chesley Wornstaff family donated the funds so the original part of this library could be built back in 1928, in memory of their son, Albertus.

Just today, an interesting fact was added to my knowledge of our Ashley library. I was told by one of the librarians that it was haunted! They have a visiting ghost with the name of Mildred, who has been a patron and loved cats. She liked to read magazines and has been seen by at least three employees. And I think I was told that she was seen in the vicinity of the magazines. And also - something about seeing a lot of cats in the basement.

Just when I thought I'd finished this story about libraries, I found a picture of that wall from the Albers store that was used in the building of the Delaware library! I had left it in the box I used for stories I had already written. I recognized it from seeing the St. Mary's Church in the background.

Our First Racehorse
Tango Tag

D id you know that if you raised your hand at a certain time and place and an auctioneer yells, "Sold!" it can totally change your life forever? That's what happened when my husband, George, raised his hand at the Delaware County Jug Sale during fair week of 1966.

In a split second he went from a regular guy, minding his own business, to owning a beautiful yearling filly that came with nothing but her name. Her name was Tango Tag.

At that moment, we didn't own a farm, or a truck, or a trailer, or a barn, or even a big bucket to use to give her a drink of water. After all, this was George's very first racehorse he ever owned. Please don't think he had completely lost his mind because he knew he could get a stall for her at the same place where his grandfather, Charlie Norris, trained his horses in Plain City. And then later, moved it closer to home to be trained at the Morrow County Fairgrounds.

There were only 68 yearlings, to be sold as racehorses, in the state of Ohio in 1966. Tango Tag was number 64. This year of 2016, approximately 500 yearlings, to be sold for racehorses, will be sold in Ohio. Usually only one out of every 10 yearlings ever get to the races. Tango's first win was at the Union County Fair, and she took a lifetime record at Scioto Downs in 2:04.

I have always called George an owner, trainer, driver, slave, with an emphasis on slave because he always had done everything by himself. He even had to do his own shoeing after an incident when the blacksmith had shod our horse at a wrong angle, which would be equivalent to having to walk with a child's block under your toes.

As with a lot of horses, their names often come from the names of their sire and dam. As for Tango, her sire was "Tag Me" and her dam was "Laffango." Tango started racing as a 2-year-old then raced again as a three-year old, and won her first race at Marysville as a four-year-old. She also won at Scioto Downs in 2:04 in 1970. We have the picture to remember it by.

As a six-year-old, Tango had to give up racing because of a stress fracture. She then became a broodmare. Her first foal was a filly we named "Georgia Kay" who would have been a very good racehorse for a long time, but she had to be put down as a three-year old because of a racing injury. That happening was a very big loss. Tango's next foal was named "Sweet Georgia Kay" and she outdid her mother in that she won at Scioto Downs in 2:03.

We bought our farm in 1973. By that time he had other horses to train. The farm had just a cow barn on the property and George made it over into a horse barn. Over a period of years, George built a racetrack, another horse barn with 22 stalls, an indoor arena, and an outdoor arena. Of course, a lot of fences had to be built with the many gates that keep the horses where they belong.

When one of our other horses became ill, our vet was not able to treat it, so he told us to take him to the Ohio State University for diagnosis. Luckily, they determined what was wrong and sent the horse home with the prescription. The amount needed was 420 pills. Two weeks of pills every morning and every night. They had to be crushed, mixed with water, put in a syringe and squirted down the horse's throat. The pharmacist said there was a problem with that number of pills.

He asked George if he knew what the pills would cost. George said he didn't. He was told that the price would be $850. So, George asked if it came in a generic brand. The pharmacist said, "That's the generic brand."

And, that the non-generic brand would cost $1080. When George told him the pills were for a horse, the pharmacist said he hadn't noticed that the prescription had come from a vet at OSU. At that time, the pharmacist said that these same pills are also taken by humans.

However, while the horses will be taking 30 pills a day, the humans will be taking only one pill a day. For the above number of pills, humans will pay $1080, while a bottle of 500 of the very same pills for the horses will only cost $37.50. The pharmacist told us that there are a lot of medications that are used by both humans and horses, not just the one we wrote about here. And that the difference in prices are just as high for humans and as low for animals.

Tango Tag died very unexpectedly when she was only eight years old. She had died in the night and George found her in her stall the next morning. She is buried at our farm. In memory of her, we have a big sign that was on the front of her stall door at the Jug Sale when George bought her exactly 50 years ago this week. We have saved Tango Tag's stall sign, and all of our win pictures because, after all, she was our very first racehorse.

The Things I
Have Lost

T here are definitely lots of things that I have lost in my lifetime. Last year I had a loss that was very unusual. Not many people have had their own car totaled while it is sitting in their own garage. But I did.

While I was a passenger inside the car that caused the accident, I watched as my new white Chevy Malibu was being crunched up the back and shoved into the barrels that were stored inside the garage in front of the car. I saw the center beam of our garage fall to the right of me with electric wires coming down as well. As the wrecker dragged my car away, I heard my husband George say, "Take a good look because you'll never see that car again."

The insurance company notified us that the car was totaled. The police chief said he had never written up a report on a car being totaled while in its own garage.

Our other car, a 1994 aqua Chevy Beretta, still runs. It was in perfect shape, inside and out. I even talked about putting it in an antique car show when it was old enough. But that idea went by the wayside when George started using it as a farm truck. Now we don't take it out on the highway because the bottom has a severe rust problem and might fall apart any day.

People speak in terms of losing their loved ones when they die. In my case I have lost parents, grandparents, aunts, uncles, cousins, and in-laws. Right now, all six of my siblings are living and, when I add up all our ages, we are a total of 564 years old and range in age from 72 to 91. We have been in each other's lives all of our lives.

Years ago, I saw a quote on a man's hat that read, "Of all the things I've lost, I miss my mind the most." Needless to say, those words have stuck with me ever since. I just finished reading "Still Alice" by Lisa Genova. It is a novel about a 50-year-old woman having early onset of Alzheimer's Disease. It is so well written that you can imagine what Alice was going through as she was losing her memories.

Things most people lose seem to be their car keys, glasses and cell phones. I once read a statistic about how much time in our lives we spend looking for things we have lost. The total was measured in months! We always hang our keys together in one place. At least this way, we haven't ever lost our car keys. But we did lose our car.

As for me personally, I have lost some of my good eyesight, as well as some of my hearing. And when I look in the mirror, I am always reminded that my hair is no longer dark brown. I often think about the memories I would have lost had I not started keeping a journal when I was 33 years old. I wish I had been encouraged to keep one during my growing-up years. I would love to be able to read about what all went on while I was moving in and out of 13 different houses with my six siblings and our mom and dad.

I started this article about things I have lost, but now I will add the things that have disappeared from my house. This list includes a nice white summer dress, a TV remote, an open jar of Mayo from the refrigerator, a black velvet dressy dress, and an opal ring to name a few. A lot of times you don't know something has gone until you go to get it, and it isn't there.

That's what has happened at our farm. Things that turned up missing including electric saw, a log chain, a couple of axes, a 50-foot tape measure, an electric fan and, recently, several hay hooks. Just when it was time to make hay, George had to go out and try to find three new ones.

It wasn't until his third farm supply store that he finally found the three he needed. Having to do this running around meant he lost at least two hours of sunshine. (You know you have to make hay when the sun shines!)

So, what do I consider as my biggest loss? It's definitely not my car! It's the loss of the members of my family and old friends. A lot of the memories of the time I spent growing up with them are gone now. Since I am nearing the time when I may be losing more and more of my memories, I have begun to write more and more in my journals.

My sister, Ann, once said that when I get really old, she imagines that George will sit down and read my journals to me. What a thought! But it's a good thought and I don't want to lose it.

My First Day of School

My first day of school, as a college student at Ohio Wesleyan University was a long time coming. I hadn't been in a classroom since high school, which was 23 years earlier.

I knew that if you are a full-time employee of the university, you can take one class each semester for free. So, I applied and was hired to be the secretary in the education department, beginning in January 1977.

I signed up for my first class to be that fall semester. Each semester is 15 weeks long with two semesters a year. I filled out lots of forms, which even included my parents' name and address. I was given a catalog of all the classes to choose from. It's big stuff when you can open the catalog and choose the class that you will be giving your life over to for the next 15 weeks.

I chose to take speech. In this class, you spend your time writing speeches on topics of your own choice, giving speeches, and listening to other students in the class giving their speeches. The professor was there to give his opinions and suggestions on how to do a better job.

Since it was fall semester and the Delaware County Fair was going on, I chose for my first speech to be about the Little Brown Jug race.

One of the rules is to relate your speech to your audience. Give them a reason to want to listen to you. I began my first speech with these words to the other students in the class: "After you have graduated from OWU, for the rest of your life, people will ask you where you went to college. In your case, you will say OWU in Delaware Ohio. With that said don't be surprised if some people over the years say to you 'Delaware Ohio, that's where the Little Brown Jug is raced, isn't it?' After all this particular race is well known in the world of harness racing. It brings in people, and racehorses, from all over the United States and Canada. You don't want to sound dumb and say you don't know anything about such a big race, so I'm going to tell you all about it, so you can have an educated answer that may impress someone, like maybe, a future boss."

By the end of that sentence, the big football players in the back of the class sat up straighter and seemed to pay attention to the rest of my speech. I explained where the huge purse of winnings comes from for the winner of the Jug. I told them about the payments that have to be made when the Jug "hopeful" is a yearling, and another when he is a two-year-old and again as a three-year old, and finally you pay a big starting fee for the day of the race. In 2015, the total purse was $677,000 and there were 46,000 people attending the race.

I explained that only three-year old pacers can enter. Not trotters, just pacers. Then I explained the difference between trotters and pacers. It also helps to know why this big race is being held at a County Fair, and not some big raceway. It's because the Delaware County Fair racetrack is the fastest track around. It just so happens that when the track was built, the men who were in charge of the job, knew what they were doing.

I added that it's always the third Thursday afternoon in September, so go out to the fairgrounds on Pennsylvania Avenue and you may see some records being broken.

I knew those football players in the back of the room liked my speech because when I finished, they clapped.

When I had taking one class every semester for about eight years, I was asked if I had a plan worked out so that, at some point, I could graduate. When I looked into the requirements for graduation, I found if I took a couple of science classes, a foreign language, and got a few more credits, I could graduate in the spring of 1988. Could I really sign up for science classes and survive? The worst would be taking a foreign language at my age. I had long ago passed my prime to be learning to speak another language.

But I did it. I graduated on Mother's Day in May 1988. It took me a total of 11 years of taking one class a semester, as well as a few summer school classes, to meet all the requirements to walk across the stage and have the president of the university hand me my diploma.

And just a note to let you know what happened because I filled out the form when they asked for my parents' name and address. When that first class ended, my mother asked me why she got a bill for $4 from OWU. When I looked, it was my grade for my speech class. I had made a 4.0. I was 41 years old, and they sent my first OWU grade card to my mom.

My Schoolmate's Name
Was Norma Jean

S omewhere in my past, I had read that when washing windows, you should use newsprint to dry them. Just wad it up in a ball and you won't have streaks or smears. So, on a day of cleaning my front porch, I took out several sections of the Sunday paper in preparation for the task at hand. My storm door has a lot of different panes of glass, so I knew lots of newsprint would be needed.

I don't know what I'd been thinking when I realized I was throwing away pictures of persons who had recently passed. In a split second, I had picked up the paper and wadded it up to use to dry off the windows I was washing. I had even gotten a good look at one of the women on the one of the pages. How would I feel if someone had taken my picture to dry their windows? Not something I had ever thought about before.

There was something familiar about one of the pictures that I had already tossed away, but I couldn't remember what it was. So, I decided to dig through the trash to find the picture of that particular woman. Would I even recognize which one she had been, now that the paper was all wrinkled, torn, and wet? I had to spread what was left to the page out in the sun so I could get a good look. And, sure enough, there she was.

First thing I noticed was her smile. And when I looked at her name, I saw that her first name was Norma Jean. That was what I had noticed. Her name was an unusual name from my high school. My goodness, I was friends with a girl named Norma Jean. Could that Norma Jean be the same Norma Jean I had gone to high school with? Next, I looked to see what year she had been born. It said 1936. That was when I was born.

The Norma Jean I knew was one year ahead of me at school, but it still could be her. Quickly my eyes went to see where she was from. She was from Delaware OH. Me, too. And just as quickly, I noticed her parents' names and saw that she wasn't the Norma Jean I had known after all.

What had come over me that I would want to dig in the trash to find out more about her in the first place? Am I now identifying with a woman dying because she is my age? All I can think of right now is that I have stepped over the invisible line in life from when you stop collecting things and start getting rid of things.

I've always heard that everyone has a story. After doing a quick read of the other information about her, I saw she had worked at the Pro Football Hall of Fame and later went on to be a small business owner. She was survived by a husband of 58 years and had lots of children, grandchildren, and great grandchildren. However, as I read further, I saw that she was preceded in death, not only by her parents, but by a sister, a son and a granddaughter. Now when I look at that picture of her, I saw that the smile wasn't as sparkling as I first thought it was. Everyone has sadness in their lives, but with the loss of a sister, a son and a granddaughter, I felt that her life probably had a lot of sadness, too.

I spent the rest of the afternoon cleaning my porch and thinking about why I felt so bad to have used this picture of Norma Jean to dry my windows. I knew then that I wanted to write a story about finding Norma Jean's picture. I tried to smooth out the paper so I could cut out the picture to go with the future story. Later, I realized that I have a picture of the other Norma Jean in my 1953 Delhi. How many girls do you suppose were named Norma Jean back in 1936? Those two women couldn't have been named for the well-known Norma Jean (Marilyn Monroe), because Marilyn Monroe was only 10 years old when these Norma Jeans were born.

When I finished cleaning my porch, I sat back, put up my feet and thought about the whole subject of obituaries being printed. I have often heard it said that the only reason some people take their local paper is so they can read the obituaries. Often, I try to guess how old the person was from the picture that goes with the listing. Men in military uniforms are usually in their 80s and 90s now.

Women's hairdos usually give away their age, as does having the person look directly into the camera or be looking off to the side. It's always sad to see a child's picture. And sometime a much younger picture is used. That would be my choice.

One thing I've learned from all of this, is that the next time I'm drying windows with newsprint, and I'm find I have the obituary section, I think I will put it back in the stack to be recycled.

The Rec Center at the
Old North School

When I was walking this morning, it occurred to me that I could write about the rec center at the old North School in Delaware. First, I will have to explain what the old North School is.

I started third grade at North School the year my family moved to Delaware. Two years later I went to East School. Old North School was a homey type of school that had an open center located with all the classrooms making a circle around the common area. Delaware had four elementary schools with one located in each quadrant of the city. They had been named North, South, East and West.

After 6th grade, all of the students from the four elementaries went to Frank B Willis School for grade 7 through 12. At that time, the population of Delaware city and county didn't hold a candle to what it is today. The rec center originated from the work of a group of seniors in their "Problems of Democracy" class back in 1945. The center was housed in several different locations before ending up at the old North School.

So, what about the rec center? By the time I had gotten to Willis, a new North School had been built several blocks from the old one. Thus, the old North School building became the rec center. It was a place for all the high school students to enjoy. The common area in the center was full of overstuffed furniture, small tables, and even had a phone. Plus, in that common area, we had a nice upright piano.

You were lucky if you were there at the same time as someone who could play it. Of course, we did a lot of singing of 50s' music. Who of us can ever forget singing "Cruising down the river on a Sunday afternoon" as well as "Slow boat to China?" When we entered by the south door we were met by Mr. and Mrs. Charles Moore who were the wonderful couple who ran the place. I think the admission was a nickel. They had a concession stand with pop, chips, popcorn, and candy bars for sale. Upon entering the common area, you had your choice of each of the classrooms to go to, depending on what you wanted to do. The old 4th grade room was for dancing. The other rooms had a ping pong table, a pool table (which the guy seemed to monopolize), checkers, table shuffleboard, card games, and places to hang out and catch up.

If you would like to see the old rec center building today, it's at 248 N. Washington St. and is now the Delaware City School administration and school board building. The last time I visited there, the beautiful skylight had been reopened in the common area. It had been closed for years to save on the cost of heating the school.

I want to add a little about the naming of the East and North schools. The East School was named Conger School for James C. Conger who was my 6th grade teacher, as well as the principal there. I remember having our hearing tested in that same 6th grade room. The school nurse blindfolded us, put a pocket watch up to our ear and then slowly walked away. We were to tell her when we could no longer hear the watch ticking. One of the boys got a lot of attention because he insisted he could still hear the ticking even after the nurse had left the room.

The new North School was named Smith School in honor of Mr. David R Smith, who was Superintendent of the Delaware City Schools. He had been in the army and had rank of Colonel.

When our Willis class had one of our reunions, we invited Mr. and Mrs. Moore to come as our guests. However, they sent their regrets. They said they remembered us and wanted to come, but their health wasn't good enough to make the trip. I was sorry that happened because they were a big part of our lives during all of those evenings we hung out at the rec center.

Writing about the old North School brought back an old memory of mine. If my memory serves me correctly, we, as students, were asked to bring milkweed pods to school. I had always thought the reason we were given is that they would be sent away to a place that made them into parachutes. But, since writing the above, I learned that the soft white fluffy insides of the milkweed pods were used to stuff the lining of the military jackets for warmth.

The rec center had often been mentioned by persons writing to The Gazette about all the good things they experienced while growing up in Delaware. It would be great if today's high school students had a similar place to go that is safe, chaperoned and fun. They may not be dancing to "Slow boat to China" but they could be dancing, just the same.

Are You Worrying
or Sleeping?

There is no doubt about it at some time in all our lives, we have had things to worry about. A couple of years ago, my daughter, Carolee, gave me a great piece of advice about not worrying. She said, "Mom, you have a lot to think about, but nothing to worry about." Those few words have helped me lessen my worries about things I can't do anything about.

I have been a worrier as far back as I can remember. When I was only 7, we were quarantined in with scarlet fever and I had to miss a lot of school. Having that big sign on the front of our house that said "Quarantined" was bad enough, but every day that I had to stay in bed, I worried about how much school I was missing. (Except when I was listening on the radio to "The Lone Ranger" or that other one, "The Shadow Knows," and of course, "The Great Gildersleeve.")

Now, I worry about George when he's out on the highway, driving his truck hauling a couple of horses to a horse show. Or anytime the roads are covered with snow and ice. So, what's the answer? Maybe we should try worrying beads. According to Webster's New World Dictionary, worrying beads are a string of smooth beads designed to be handled or stroked, as to relieve anxiety or nervousness. That sounds like a good idea. The dictionary goes on to give a name for a person who tends to worry especially over insignificant details. The name is "worrywart." Thinking of being called a worrywart is enough to make anyone want to quit worrying. I for one.

I think the key here is when it's about insignificant things. When you are not the worrier, it's easy to call another person a worrywart because what looks insignificant to one person may not be insignificant to another.

This is not an advice column by any means. Yet, I took it upon myself to go to the library and put the word worry in their computer. Up came a long list of names of books with worry in the title. I picked out three to list here.

Mind you, I haven't read them, but the titles looked interesting. First is "Breaking the worry habit forever!" by Elizabeth George. Second is "How your brain tricks you into expecting the worst and what you can do about it," by David Carbonell. Third is "Worrying cure--7 steps to stop worry from stopping you," by Robert Leahy. And, in addition, I ran onto a title that we have sung, back in the day, called "Don't worry, be happy." It's now a coloring book. It says you can color your way to a calm positive mood. Well, that might be worth trying.

Because of my previous job at the courthouse, I did a lot of worrying which was mostly in the middle of the night. I would sleep for about four hours and then be wide awake, worrying about how to get through the next day. To be in good health, you are supposed to sleep eight hours each night. For me, that never happened. If I got six hours of sleep a night, I was lucky.

So, in figuring the total amount of sleep I lost, it came to a minimum of 11,600 hours of lost sleep over those 16 years of working. There was a book I read, called "Sleep smarter" by Shawn Stevenson. I highly recommend it because it may help you sleep more and worry less.

He writes, "It's been shown that human beings get the most beneficial sleep during the hours of 10 p.m. and 2 a.m. and any sleep that you get in addition is a nice bonus. You are made anew by honoring your body and getting the sleep you require. You require sleep to be the greatest version of yourself, and no pill, potion, or tactic can change that."

He goes on to help the reader try to figure out why they aren't sleeping and what they can do about it. Worrying seems to be a good topic to write about, and in doing so, I find it's tied in with sleep. We may not be worrying about anything specific, but if we're not sleeping, we end up worrying about not getting enough sleep.

I need to end with reminding you of the words that have helped me. "You have a lot to think about, but nothing to worry about."

An Amazingly
Weird Experience

I had walked a long distance and the temperature was in the 80s and very humid. I knew I needed water, so I headed back to the hotel to get out of the heat and to get some water to drink. I made it back to our room and drank the water at room temperature. I also had an aspirin with it.

I knew that something was wrong with how I was feeling and decided to stay and rest while my two daughters, Cathy and Carolee, went out again. I thought I would be OK to sit and read, but that was not helping how I felt. I had a couple of pains in my chest and my head felt heavy, but nothing more than that. The exhaustion was taking over so I decided to lie down. I knew I didn't want the maid to come in to clean, so I put the "Please no surprises" sign on the doorknob outside. I laid down flat on my back and was aware that my legs felt like they weighed a ton.

I was aware that I was in some kind of trouble. In fact, the next thing I can remember is that I was seeing a lot of white, not a light, just all white and it seemed to be just from my neck up. I could see a division of walkways divided by a white rope. It was all white and that's when I decided I might be dying. I knew I had no control over what was happening, I have heard that a lot of people die in their sleep and this might be what it's like. There was no pain, no pain at all. My head just felt very, very heavy. During that time, I heard my name "Kay" said three times.

I knew no one was in my room, but I heard my name. I kept opening my eyes for a second to see if I was still in the room and I looked at the door to the room each time. Otherwise, I didn't move. I felt that it was all beyond my control. I didn't want it to appear that I had died, just that I was asleep when my daughters came back, so I moved my arm off my chest. I wondered about the implications of this happening now.

Was I ready? Yes, I guess I was. I didn't fight it. I just let nature take its course.

I was pretty much done at my office. I had done a lot of work to clean up the house and sort clothes and the only stuff left to do was more than I could do alone. So, I had really gotten myself ready for this happening. Then somehow, I decided that I could get up and try to walk.

My legs were no longer heavy. I wasn't sleepy. I felt rather refreshed and decided that it may have been an exit point that I didn't take. I was fine. When my daughters came back, we left for the rest of the day until after midnight that night.

The above words were written the day after I returned from a trip to Cleveland with my two daughters. We had gone to see two Cleveland Indians baseball games and stayed in the hotel that is within walking distance of the baseball stadium. We had gotten up early that morning and walked down a hill to get a good look at Lake Erie. It all began during my walk back up to the hotel.

The reason I wrote that we were out until after midnight, is that due to a rain delay, the game lasted that long. Since I had such an amazingly weird experience, as soon as I got home, I got a piece of paper and wrote as fast as I could to be sure to get it all written before I forgot any of it. Never at any time did I feel that it would have been a dream. Maybe it was a heat stroke.

All I know for sure is that I never had an experience like that before or since. And I remember that each part happening as if it were yesterday. This all happened on Saturday, August 29th, 2004. On that very week, Florida was suffering from the damage of another hurricane, which had the name of Charlie. The same as they are now suffering from Hurricane Matthew.

Because the hurricane had done some property damage to my daughter Cathy's home, her husband had to stay there to take care of it. Since they had the tickets for the baseball game, as well as their flight tickets and their hotel reservations, Cathy came home alone and we ended up spending the weekend with her seeing the Cleveland Indians. And what a weekend it was. You might say it was an amazingly weird experience that I will never forget.

Thoughts After the County Fair

To be writing about the Delaware County Fair when it's been over for a couple of weeks, may not make any sense. But I decided to do it anyway. Those of us who go to the fair just to see the races, or my favorite show, Phil Dirt and the Dozers, have no idea what all happens after the last show's history.

First, I think about the grounds people who have to clean up the mess that's left behind. For the biggest mess of all, the back stretch of the racetrack, wins a blue ribbon. One year we raced in the last race of the day, and by the time we left the paddock to take our stuff back to the barns, the walkway was covered with discarded beer cans and bottles, losing betting stubs, programs, food wrappers, and papers of all kinds. It was so bad that we had to walk on the track. We could do that since there were no more horses to race that late in the day.

I have always noticed that there are a lot of rusted old folding chairs tied to the chain link fences around the track from one year to the next. When the big race day arrives you may have noticed people carrying in their good chairs and sitting in them after they've taken down the old chairs that were being used to reserve their places at the fence. I've yet to see anyone putting them back up after the race.

I'm guessing they may bring the old ones back sometime after the fair is over.

When you are over on the barn side, it is rather difficult to see over the heads of all the other people standing around who want to see the races too. Because of the difficulty of seeing over others' heads, George brings two big buckets and a 10-foot, 2-by-12 board to the track the night before the big race. During the races, he turns the buckets upside down, about eight feet apart, and puts the board on top of the buckets.

By standing on the 10-foot board, at least eight people can easily see the horses on the track. Before he ever thought to bring a board, we just stood on the buckets. I took a picture of them standing on said buckets and entered it in the photography competition. I called it, "Watching the Jug on a Bucket" because there is a special race called the Old Oaken Bucket, that is only for trotters, with the Jug being for pacers. I thought my title with the picture was good enough to win a ribbon. Sorry, but no such luck.

What happens to all those beautiful flower arrangements? This year, by Tuesday, a lot had turned brown and died because of the heat, and/or lack of water. They must have been judged earlier because it was sad to see those blue, red, or white ribbons hanging on the vases of dead flowers.

Once I went to the fairgrounds the day after the fair was over, and it was sad to see the empty places where so much excitement had taken place just 24 hours earlier. If there was any leftover pie at the Buckeye Valley tent, I'm sure those hard-working BV students would have had no problem of disposing of it.

I see that I just called the BV building a tent. Old habits are hard to break. It was a tent back in the day before they got to build the present building. I am also reminded that there used to be at least three churches that put up food tents somewhere between the buildings and the track.

On the years it was bitter cold during fair week, the BV food building became the place to go. I have always heard the barn people tell how great their breakfasts are there. It sounds so good, it almost makes me want to get up before daylight and go there for bacon, scrambled eggs, and coffee.

Another thing that happens after the fair is over is when the children who have 4-H projects have sold their prized animals and have to go home without them. I understand a lot of tears have been shed by the 4-H kids when that happens.

A very long time ago, I was asked to buy a pig from the 4-H sale at the fair. Never having been in 4-H, I didn't know what on earth I was going to do with a pig, so I didn't buy one. Years later, I found out that I need not have worried because you don't have to take it home. It can be sold right then and there for market price. So, the total amount the person actually pays is a difference between the selling price and the market price. But, if I had bought it, I could close this article by saying that my little piggy went to the market.

Big, Beautiful $5 Bill
for 16 Hours Work

Most senior citizens can remember when a $5 bill was a lot of money. When I was six years old, I thought 80 cents was a lot of money. The first time I counted the money in my Piggy Bank, I had exactly 80 cents. They were all pennies except for a couple of nickels that found their way in there too. Eighty cents could buy 16 regular-sized candy bars back then.

The next time I had any money coming in was when I helped my older brother with his paper route on East Central Avenue in Delaware. He paid me 5 cents a week. All I had to do was deliver the newspapers to the houses on the side streets off East Central Avenue.

During that same time, I was asked by a neighbor if I could wash a lot of dishes for them. They said they would pay me five cents. That seemed good, so I went over. Never had I seen so many dirty dishes! And I was from a family with seven kids! Piles of dirty dishes were sitting everywhere. Not just in the kitchen, but in the living room, as well. There wasn't a spot that wasn't covered with dirty dishes, silverware, pans and skillets.

I have reason to believe the neighbor girl was being paid 10 cents to do the job and got me to do them for her for five cents. That's because I remember hearing laughing all the time I was washing.

When I was 14, I got a real job. It was every Saturday from 7:00 a.m. until 11:00 p.m. that night. I worked for a family with four children ranging in ages from 3 to 9. While both their parents were working outside on their farm, I was inside taking care of their kids. I fixed their breakfast when they got up, as well as their lunch and supper.

As an aside, I want to note that some people call the evening meal "dinner" and others call it "supper." I have an 8-year-old friend who uses the word "dupper," a combination of both words. She said she can't have it the other way, or the word would be sinner and that would not be good. I also mopped the kitchen floor and picked up the house. After the parents were finished in their fields, they got dressed up and went out to dinner and a movie and by were home by 11 p.m.

For my whole 16-hour day, I was always paid with one big beautiful $5 bill. That was the richest I have ever felt! With the going rate of babysitting back then being 35 cents an hour, they should have paid me $5.60, but I guess I was too blinded by that big old $5 bill to care about the extra 60 cents.

This leads to other babysitting jobs. The minister of our church asked me to sit with their three children on Sunday evenings while he and his wife went out to dinner. They always had the same thing for their Sunday night supper. It was tomato soup with popped corn on top. That ritual led me to believe that all ministers children had tomato soup with pork popcorn as well. I knew we never ate it at our house, so I thought it must be some religious thing.

I also babysat for an economics professor's family and was always paid with a stack of coins that came out exactly to the penny of what I had earned. To this day, I remember all those dimes, nickels and pennies as he handed them to me in a perfect stack, nickels on the bottom, pennies next and dimes on top.

By the time I was 15, I had a job for every day after school taking care of two children. I took care of the kids from after school until their parents got home from work. I also got their evening meal and I had it on the table before I left. There were always instructions as to what to cook, so I learned a lot about cooking. Often, they had friends over to eat supper with them. It wasn't too hard for me to cook enough for four more, but I was glad I got to go home before having to do all those dishes!

I am writing about a $5 bill because a friend told me that when she sees a young person in a restaurant with their parents, and they are very well behaved, and do not have a phone in their hand, she goes to their table and gives the young person a $5 bill.

They are always thrilled to have it when she tells them why they were chosen to get the money. Since hearing her story, I have been paying attention to how many young people have phones in their hands while eating out with others. This past Friday, my husband and I were eating out and couldn't help but notice as a middle-aged couple each had iPads and they were on them their entire meal without saying one world word to each other.

Back to my thoughts on a $5 bill. Even if it was a lot of money years ago, I think of the work I did for those 16 hours to earn $5. And now it's possible to have that much money given to you just by being polite to your own parents during a meal.

Answers in the
Back of the Book

———————

My favorite classes at Willis High School in the 50s, were all the math classes I took from Mr. Felts. I took algebra 1, 2 and 3, as well as plane geometry, solid geometry, and trigonometry. Whenever I watch Big Bang and see Sheldon writing on his big white board, it reminds me of Mr. Felts saying, "Kay, go to the board." Of course, what I was doing at the board in high school was, by no means, anything close to what was supposed to be going on in that sitcom. But, it brings back good memories to me.

For our homework in Mr. Felts class, the answers for all the math problems in the book, were in the back of the book. If you are working on your problems and didn't have the same answer as the one in the back of the book, you had to go back over all the steps to find where your mistake was, correct it, and go on to get the correct answer So, when you were done, you were really done. And you knew you were correct.

He said that's one of life lessons. Math teaches you how to think. The second thing to know is that our test and his classes were all open- book. He said that's because that's how life is. If you need to know something, you can go look it up. Of course, you have to know where to look. For instance, if you need to know how much air you need the tires for your car, you can open the front door and you will find the answer inside the door frame.

He had certain things that he liked to talk about, too. One was the law of averages. Since it was Halloween recently, I'll use the children coming for a trick or treat as an example of such a law. From the moment we turned on our porch light, children began to come to our door for candy. It was a steady stream of two or three children all the time from 6 until 7:30 p.m. By the time it was over, around 200 children had come to our door.

That was the law of averages at work. If it wasn't for said law, we could have all 200 kids trying to get on our porch at the very same time. A second example of said law, could be a potluck supper. When I have attended suppers where everyone brings anything they wish to fix, it always turns out to be a wonderful variety of food. Because of the law of averages, you won't find everyone bringing a pie. You get the idea.

In my younger days, I wanted to be a high school math teacher just like Mr. Felts. I like that he never graded our homework. He just marked off our names in his grade book when we turned in our paper. His theory was that if you didn't do your homework, you would not be able to pass his tests.

He also had a way of standing at the board and doing a lot of writing and without turning around, he would say things like "Jim, go spit out your gum." And still never turn around to see if Jim did. I also remember him talking about things like, "All squirrels are small animals, but not all small animals are squirrels." Often you will hear older people say, "I wish I knew then, what I know now."

But, when it comes to all my math education, I wish I knew now, what I knew then. Because, as I sit here today, I would be hard pressed to be able to pass any of his tests, even with knowing that the answers are in the back of the book or the test would be open book. But, I will credit his classes with furthering my thinking ability.

I had a chance to get to know his daughter. She told me that when her dad died, he had prearranged for the florist to deliver two bouquets of flowers to his home. They were to be there for them when they got home from the funeral. One for his wife and the other for his daughter. They were to thank each of them for all they had done for him.

I remember a quote that said, "If you can read this, Thank a Teacher." Some years ago, I decided to send him a note of thanks for being such a great teacher. By then he was 87 years old. He wrote back telling me how surprised and pleased he was to get my note, since it had been 23 years since he retired.

Since I always called him Mr. Felts, I was surprised to see that he signed the note as 'Ray Felts.' I never thought of him having a real first name. He was just that wonderful teacher who had always told us to live our life, knowing that all the answers to any and all of our problems are out there somewhere. You just had to know where to look.

Memories of a Cabin in the Woods

Everyone should be so lucky as to have their own cabin in the woods. Of course, you may have to build it yourself, like my husband, George, did. It all started when he was much younger and used to go hunting on the property that is now Recreation Unlimited.

When he became familiar with the lay of the land, he found a piece of property shaped like a triangle. The longer side of it was a creek (Alum Creek) with the other two sides meeting at a corner where two roads crossed making a natural border. It was three acres of land that had not been used for so long that it was just a mass of trees and vines that you could barely walk through.

George approached the owner and asked if he would sell those three acres to us and he did. That was in the 60s. After George spent a long time clearing out the wild vines, he could tell it was a perfect spot for building a cabin. Building a cabin on land with no electricity presents a problem.

You can't have electricity unless you have a building on the land, and you can't build on the land without electricity. So, he had to build the cabin, piece by piece, in what we call our 'town barn,' and take them out to the location and put them all together. To begin with, he built a giant table because the cabin had to be up on stilts.

This was because of the possibility of flooding. The giant table was 12 feet wide and 32 feet long and would serve as the floor of the cabin. The front door was given to us by the man who owned the drugstore in town and had just gotten a new one. It was two-thirds glass. The windows came from someone else who was also doing some remodeling.

We had another two doors that we called French doors that opened at the end of the living room area. We had a bedroom and a counter space we called the kitchen.

We bought an authentic ice box for our refrigeration. Eventually we got electricity in the form of a security light. And with a lot more work, the cabin took shape and we began staying out there on weekends. We even had an outhouse.

My favorite spot was the fire pit that was close to the cabin. We kept the fire burning most all the time we were ever there. At that time, we were MYF (Methodist youth fellowship) leaders. We had several parties for them out there. They could play volleyball, as well as miniature golf with those little plastic golf balls that have holes in them. We buried big open cafeteria-type cans for the nine holes, so as to resemble a real golf course.

One weekend the MYF kids stayed all night. The boys slept on the ground around the fire and the girls slept on the floor inside the cabin. One girl drew a very good picture of the cabin, including the bonfire. She captured the view looking at the walkway and steps leading up to the porch that had been added.

Some years later, during the winter when the cabin was all closed up, someone broke in and took a lot of what we had had in there. They left the door open thus allowing animals to get in and ruin what was left. After that happened, an acquaintance wanted to buy the cabin land. You might say they gave us an offer we couldn't refuse, so we sold it to them.

I remember the day we signed over the deed. When I got back to my office, I felt that an overwhelming loss had just taken place. The loss of being able to go out there and enjoy sitting around a big campfire, walking around in the woods, or having other people come out to enjoy what George had built. Or, just listening to the peace and quiet.

If you would drive out there today, there is nothing left to show that there was ever a cabin on that land. The wilderness has taken over again. And the cabin, security light, outhouse and fire pit are all gone. There was nothing left. Nothing but the beauty of the trees with the yellow leaves this time of the year, the pine tree on the corner and the water still running in the creek.

It's a little odd not to have thoughts of the cabin for years and years, and then just this past Saturday, have it pop into my mind to write about.

But even more unusual is that on the very next day as I walked into our family reunion at All Occasions, I saw my old home movies (now on DVD) being played on the dining room wall. And after just a few minutes of watching, I saw our cabin right in front of my eyes. It took my breath away to see it again after all these years.

The Estaves Family
Came from Cuba

Because of the recent headline news out of Cuba, I am reminded of what our small church did to bring a Cuban family to the United States in the late 1960s. At that time, there was a program that allowed churches to bring a number of Cuban families to America.

We had a retired lady at our church, whose name was Litta, who had already been in the VISTA program. She had served in Wynne, Arkansas, where she lived with the family and taught them, among other things, the necessity of using clean water. When she finished a year in that program, she took on the challenge of having our church bring a family from Cuba to live in our small village.

After the seemingly endless forms were filled out and approved, a Cuban family had permission to fly into Port Columbus. And Litta was there to pick them up. No one else we knew could have ever pulled off such a complicated feat.

She had no idea what the situation would be when they stepped off the plane. And before she knew it, they were here. They did not speak English and no one in our church spoke Spanish. We had rented a house for them to live in, and all the furnishings were in place, right down to the forks, knives and spoons. However, the day they arrived, the stove that heated the house, quit working. George remembers trying to fix it, while the new family of five wrapped themselves in blankets to keep warm.

Their last name was Estaves. The father brought his wife, two small sons, and his mother with him. Mr. Estaves had to have a job here, but under the conditions, the only work he could get was manual labor. In Cuba, he had been a doctor, but since he had no license to practice in the U.S., he had to find another type of work. Somehow, we managed to get them some help with the language barrier.

I remember there were people in the vicinity who came in the evenings to help them with their English. When our weather got warmer, you could have seen their two little boys running around outside with no clothes on. That's what they had been used to doing back in Cuba. However, that did not go over very well in their neighborhood here. It wasn't long before there were six in the family, when they had a new baby daughter.

One of the rules about their being able to leave Cuba, was that everything in their home had to be perfect working order. Not one light bulb could be burned out, or any piece of silverware be missing. I remember a discussion about the fact that they had to have keys for everything. It was one of their hardest problems to get the right keys for things that they weren't used to locking.

Also, the car had to be in perfect running order and clean from top to bottom. They had to have their home in perfect order because as soon as they left, someone else would be living there.

Getting and keeping everything in order caused some delays in the plans for their arrival. When they finally flew out of Cuba that day, they did not know if they were ever be able to return. Their time here was both challenging and rewarding.

They stayed here, in their rented house during 1968, 69 and 70, but we're very happy when they got to move to Miami, Florida, and live among other Cubans. Soon after getting to live in South Florida, Mr. Estaves got to become Doctor Estaves again, and his wife, Mrs. Estaves, got to become a doctor as well.

Years later, in 1985, I took a year of Spanish at Ohio Wesleyan University. One of the requirements for passing the course was to give a

15-minute speech in Spanish. Fifteen minutes was a very long time for me to have to speak in another language. I had to tell a story with structure and have it to be understood by the rest of the class, as well as the professor. I was lucky that I remembered so much about the Estaves family and could tell their story in a lot of short sentences. Our professor told us that by the time we finished her class, we would be fluent in Spanish. I managed to be fluent for that 15-minute speech, but that was about all.

Back on that cold day, 50 some years ago, when a lady named Litta worked so hard to make this move possible, it changed their lives forever. Now, I think how frightening it had to be for them to come here, not speaking the language, not getting to practice in their chosen profession, and having to leave everything behind in Cuba.

They sent letters back to us for a couple of years, letting us know how thankful they were for our giving them this wonderful chance to experience our freedom. But as usually happens, we lost track of them, but we'll never forget the experience of having them here.

I Talked to Santa Claus!

You know how I know there is a Santa Claus? It's because I saw him, and I got to talk to him.

In all my life, I have never gotten to talk to Santa Claus and tell him what I wanted for Christmas. You would think that at my age, it would have happened. But it hasn't. Why not? When I was in the second grade, my older siblings took me to see him. But, the crowd was so large, we just stood and looked, but never got near enough to talk to him

I've seen Santa in parades in town, but only saw him waving as he passed by.

But, just a week ago Saturday, while I was greeting people at our annual "Christmas in Ashley" event, I saw him. I was walking past the room he was in and noticed no children were there at that moment. Without thinking, I just walked in and found myself saying, "This is the first time I have ever come to see you, Santa." And do you know what he said? He said something about having been at our cabin in the woods.

He didn't really say he had read my article about our cabin, he just started talking about having been at that retreat at our cabin with the other junior high kids from our church when they stayed overnight. This had happened over 40 years ago.

He had been there all right, because he talked about cooking food in our bonfire. You know cooking with a hot dog on a stick or wrapping food in foil and putting it in the hot coals. He has a booming voice that really sounded like Santa when I've seen him on TV.

But, this time I was going to have my chance to tell him what I wanted for Christmas, but I blew it. In all my life, I never got to talk to Santa, and I was right there, but missed my chance again because other kids started coming in the room. I went back to my place to greet people who were coming into the sanctuary. All I got to do was to wish Santa a very Merry Christmas.

What Santa doesn't know is that he really gave me a nice gift by telling me all he remembered about being there that weekend so many years ago. He remembered what he had done to make a nice memory for him that lasted all these 40 some years. Thanks, Santa Claus, for the gift of letting me know that you still remember.

There were a lot of wonderful people who came in our church that night. One was a 10-year-old girl, who was the granddaughter of the lady serving hot chocolate and cookies. She and I discussed that all 10-year-olds should start keeping a journal.

I remember now about getting to see Santa when I was out Christmas shopping several years ago. When I go shopping alone, I always pack a peanut butter and jelly sandwich to take along, as well as a bottle of water. But this particular day when I got hungry, and was about to eat my sandwich, I found I had forgotten my bottle of water.

Not many people can eat a whole double peanut butter sandwich without having something to drink. So, I went in McDonald's and got a cup of coffee. I had parked my car facing out onto Central Avenue and while I was sitting there eating my sandwich and drinking my hot coffee, the cars on the street came to an abrupt stop right in front of my eyes. My eyes focus on the passenger side of the car directly in front of me, and there sat Santa Claus

He was a passenger in the car and was all decked out in his Christmas best. At that time, I wondered where Santa might be going and what he was doing. Seeing him in a car is not his usual mode of transportation. He may have been there for only a minute, but it was a nice minute.

Why am I writing about being so pleased to talk to Santa? It must be because it's never too late. I forgot that my brother-in-law, Jerry, played Santa back in the 60s.

He had the whole red suit, wig, beard, black belt, everything to play Santa. We were having a party at our house for all the guys and wives and kids of the people who George served with in the Army Reserve. I was holding our two-year-old daughter on my lap. When Santa came in the room, the only part you could see of him were his eyes.

And that was enough for Cathy to recognize him and loudly say, "Jerry." No one else in the room had any idea what that meant, and the party went on. But in a second, she knew it was her uncle, Jerry Conklin. That was one of those times we never forgot.

I would like to add a few of the famous lines written by Francis P Church, who was the editor of the New York Sun on September 21, 1897. He had been asked by an 8-year-old girl named Virginia, if there really was a Santa Claus. He printed his famous reply in his newspaper, entitled it: "Yes, Virginia, there is a Santa Claus."

The following are just three sentences I have chosen from his reply. Mr. Church wrote: "He exists as certainly as love and generosity and devotion exists. Thank God he lives, and he lives forever. One thousand years from now, Virginia, nay 10 times 10,000 years from now, he will continue to make glad the heart of childhood."

Thank you, Mr. Church, and I also want to say to everyone young or old, or young at heart, Merry Christmas! The above was written before I attended the Buckeye Valley musical Christmas concert for senior citizens on Friday. I had heard so much about how good it was, I didn't want to miss it this year. And it was as great as I had been told. The choirs sang and the band played, and we had a wonderful lunch that was served by the high school students.

What a delight it was to get to have some of the high school servers sitting at our table. They wanted to make sure we had everything we needed or wanted. Thanks to all the faculty and staff of BV for giving the senior citizens a warm introduction to this Christmas season.

A Christmas Gift
Found in a Barn

When you have a horse farm, the horses come and go all the time. You could have 15 horses that need a new home and because you can make room for them, you take them in. Or, you can have one person who needs to find a new home for just one horse. Who could say no to such a needy situation? Whether it's 15 or only one, there is always a story about how they came to need your barns. For the sake of a Christmas story, I will choose the one about the one horse needing a new home. The horse used to be a standard bred racehorse that had become a horse for riding. It came to us under a sad situation when its owner had to give it up and knew that George may be able to find it a good home.

That's what everyone wants when they have a horse to give away. They don't want to part with it and will do everything they can to find it a good home. It wasn't for us to keep. She wanted her horse, named Jazz, to be given to a young person, who would take the best care of it and love to ride it.

So, you begin the hunt. Let two or three people hear the news, and people come out of the woodwork to tell you why they may want it, or can't take it. Luckily this story is a Christmas story, so you can see where I'm going with it. George knew of someone who had friends of someone who wanted a horse just like the horse we had.

She wanted a big black horse. And, this one fit the bill. It was big and black.

So, the phone calls began. Would it work out to give this horse to the friend of a friend? Sure! But, is this horse ready to be ridden? So, that's when Sarah comes into the picture and 'test rides' it several times, and it's looking good. Then the phones calls start up again and finally the plan is made.

Since it's getting close to Christmas, the man who wants the horse for his 12-year-old daughter, comes into the picture. However, he doesn't have his barn ready for a horse to live in, as well as the fact that fences need to be built in order for the horse to ever go outside said barn.

Lots of discussion back and forth about how the horse would be perfect, but he wouldn't be able to have this barn ready by Christmas Day. Hmm, so close. Well, if you are reading this, and know George, you can see it coming that he will keep the horse at our farm until the necessary work is done on the barn, and also that the fences and gates are built as well. So, that's the plan. Sarah is still test riding it to make sure it can be ridden by a young rider.

The dad of the girl who was to get the horse for a Christmas present, gets busy on his barn and fences. The horse is happy to be where he is, but little does he know what is waiting for him down the road.

As Christmas Day dawned, a big sign is attached to the door of the stall where the big black horse is stabled at our barn. The sign has the name of the horse, Jazz, and the name of the girl who find out that she owns it, as soon as she gets to our farm. The excitement spreads to everyone who knows what's going on. I was very excited and I'm not even a horse person.

The new owner-to-be is supposed to come to the farm in the afternoon. That could be anywhere from 1 to 5 p.m., since we want the surprise to take place before dark. When you have a stable of horses, feeding time is the busiest time of the day. Somehow, feeding time came and went, but no signs of the girl or her dad and stepmother. But, sure enough, just in time, they were there. They came up the driveway and parked their truck very close to the front of the barn.

And just that quickly, the girl was out of the truck and into the barn and on in the stall to see the horse. And just that fast, I learned that she hadn't read the sign on the outside of the stall door. The sign said something like, "My name is Jazz, and I belong to Madelyn." It was a big sign and had color lettering and I may have even seen some bows and balloons. She was inside the stall, brushing and patting and hugging the horse and had no idea that it's her horse.

Her dad tried to get her to leave the stall to go out in the aisle and read the sign, but she just wanted to be near the horse. Not wanting to tell her the surprise, she was coaxed out into the aisle to read the words on the sign. And what a great surprise it was for her to read it. She was a little speechless and overwhelmed with the meaning of those nine little words.

It took only a few seconds for her to know that she was the new owner of that big black horse named Jazz. Then the logistics of what to do with it set in. It would have to stay at our farm until the barn was ready. She couldn't take her wonderful gift home with her that Christmas evening. Eventually the fences were built and the barn was ready, and she got to take the horse home.

That all happened two Christmases ago. Since then, the previous owner was told that Jazz had been adopted by a wonderful 12-year-old girl whose dream it was to have a big black horse.

And she is happy to know now that Jazz has a very nice home. Since then Jazz has won ribbons at horse shows, and, of course, Madelyn was the rider. It was the perfect Christmas gift found in a barn on Christmas Day.

Shopping Downtown,
Back in the Day

Back in the day means different years to different people. For me to be writing something about back in the day, I am choosing the late 1950s. I have lots of very good memories of shopping downtown Delaware.

The following story takes place in Delaware on Sandusky Street between Central Avenue and William Street and one block on West Winter. If you had been with me on a day I went shopping, we would probably start by going in one of the two 10-cent stores.

Yes, we had a McClellen's and a Woolworth on the east side of Sandusky Street, near where the Hamburger Inn is now located. They sold candy in bulk, so we could buy 1/2 of a scoop full of good chocolate, which would be weighed and sacked up to take with us, to snack on while shopping.

And then, by jaywalking across Sandusky Street, we would head to Uhlmans, to look at patterns. In fact, we could pick out a yard of some nice material for $1.00, a pattern for 25 cents and a spool of thread to match the material, for 10 cents. I could make a new skirt for $1.35. We could also try on hats on the third floor there, because everyone, back in the day, wore hats when they dressed up.

Leaving Uhlmans and walking to the corner of Sandusky and Winter, we could walk half a block south to the News Shop. The News Shop is now long gone, but in the day, it was great for finding greeting cards, newspapers and every magazine imaginable. If you didn't know the store sold cigars, all you had to do was inhale then you knew you were in the right place to buy one.

If you weren't so inclined, you could smoke it right there inside the store. At the News Shop we could also check to see if one of our new favorite 45s was in. If so, we would take it home to play it over and over until we had memorized every word. That was back when we could tell what the words were.

Out on the street again, we would have to go to Barger's Jewelry to see what was on sale. It was the place to buy nice wedding gifts and/or birthday presents. The first location of Barger's, that I knew of, was on the east side of Sandusky Street in one of the storefronts where PNC Bank is now.

In that area of storefronts with Barger's Jewelry, were an Omar's Bakery, a sheet music store, and the entrance to the Delaware Hotel, which took up the rest of that entire building. One other thing about that same southeast corner of Winter and Sandusky was the outside stairs to the basement office for the Western Union. I just searched telegrams and read that Western Union no longer offers telegrams.

Walking south on that block was also Wilson's CJ, of Course. They sold dressy dresses and very nice men's suits. If we went inside, I'm sure they would allow us to try on their fur coats.

By then, I'd be ready for lunch. And if you are too, I know just the place to go. If we go on south to the next corner, we would find the L&K Restaurant. They had a counter space with six booths in the back section. They were known for their toasted pecan rolls.

Once while eating there, I ordered a hamburger, a milkshake and a piece of pie. An elderly man sitting nearby said for me to eat that while I was still young because I wouldn't be able to eat that much when I got older. And he was right.

After lunch we need to be sure to go to Sell's up in the next block on the east side of Sandusky Street. They sold everything imaginable in paper and bottles of ink with the well, and school supplies. If we need a good stationary, that was the place to buy it. We still need a place like that today, because some of us want to write a real letter now and then. Especially if it's a thank you note.

And let's not forget about the Western Auto store owned by Mr. Sullivan. We could jaywalk over to it from Sell's. While working at my office, I once needed to buy three bolts to fix a desk, and I found just what I needed at his store. He sold them in bulk, so he let me buy just three, and the cost was only 30 cents. We should also swing down by Oller Appliances to see if they have any new self-defrosting refrigerators in stock yet.

Then heading north from the Delaware County Bank, was the Boston Store. I remember it's the only place I could find size 11. Also, a lady I had worked with, Ruth Scott, was there with me once and said she never was a size 9, even when she was born. When leaving that store, if we turn west at that corner, we'll see the sign over the Winter Street Drugstore. You couldn't miss it because it had a great big sign that was only one word—"DRUGS." I don't believe that would pass the rule for downtown Delaware signs these days.

Since we would be right beside Buns, we could go in their full-service bakery. Before their fire, Bun Hoffman had a whole bakery filled with all kinds of cakes, cookies, pies, and donuts. There were pictures of college athletes all over the walls of the bakery.

One was a picture of one of our high school teachers while playing football at Ohio Wesleyan University. And no, I don't mean Mr. Felts. After we got a chocolate cake to take home, and said "Hi" to Bun, himself, we could go look at the flowers at Gibson's Greenhouse, next door. Now, Gibson's Florist is in the regular building across Winter Street.

Before our downtown Delaware shopping day has come to an end, I have to pick up my dry cleaning at the New Method Cleaners owned by Mr. and Mrs. Milla. Recently, I found out why the dry cleaner had the name of New Method. It's because Mr. Milla found a new and better way to dry-clean clothes, so he called his store the New Method. After paying for my dry cleaning, I found that after shopping all day I still had change left from my $5 bill.

Maybe I should have called this article "Window Shopping in Downtown Delaware Back in the Day." Thanks for going on the trip with me, I had a great time. Let's do it again soon.

The Wrecking Ball
Hit Her House

Our friendship began before the wrecking ball hit her wonderful house. In fact, it began as soon as my office was moved from the old courthouse to the Hayes Building, a little north on Sandusky Street. Her name was Georgia.

She and her husband lived next door to the Hayes Building, when my office was moved there in the summer of 2002. Often, they were outside working in their yard and our friendship began when I walked past their house on my way to and from lunch every day.

We had short conversations about the weather but got to know each other better as the months passed. I told them about my having lived further north on that same street and how I liked the swing on their front porch because it was just like the one on our porch while I was in high school.

And as the days passed, I learned more about their family and why they liked living on Sandusky Street, so close to the downtown area. One reason being the convenience of walking to the US Store downtown. They also like getting to sit on their front porch to watch the All-Horse Parade go past every year. She said she often had friends over to watch the parades with them.

Before the wrecking ball hit her lovely home, I had to be off work for medical reasons, and before I got back, her husband had died. What a sadness to imagine her alone in that big house. After her husband died, our friendship grew when she would call and say, "Kay, we must have tea."

When she fixed tea, it was fit for royalty, with crystal glasses, China cups and linen tablecloth and napkins. Many times before the wrecking ball hit her lovely home, she and I discussed how every chair, picture, and lamp reminded her of the wonderful life she and her husband had in that house while their sons were growing up there.

When she called one day and urgently said, "Kay we must have tea," I knew something was terribly wrong, and I needed to go over as soon as I could. She told me her house was sitting right in the exact spot they were going to build a new courthouse, and her house would be demolished.

Soon after that, she invited my daughter and me to lunch, and we got to take a tour of all four floors of her home. I could never do justice to being able to convey how nice it was. It was three floors with a full basement which was filled with antiques and their family heirlooms.

I think she told me there were 27 chairs in the basement. I got the idea that these beautiful pieces of furniture had belonged to members of her extended family. The first and second floors were almost identical, with living rooms, dining rooms, kitchens, bedrooms, and closets. And the top floor, with the four dormers facing each direction, had a floor in the center that would rival any dance floor you have ever seen. And every room was furnished lovingly with antiques.

Nothing could be done to stop time, as the clocks ticked on, to the day the wrecking ball arrived. There were even pictures of her house in the Delaware Gazette as the walls were coming down. I had retired by then. And by then, she was living in a twin single in a very nice location, and i went there to see her.

When I asked her how she was getting along, she said, "I feel like I'm sitting in a nice motel room, waiting for my family to come and take me home." With that, my heart broke for her. It wasn't too long until she had some health issues and was having to have physical therapy. She was doing very well for being in her early 90s by then. She's still called often and said, "Kay, we must have tea," and I would go see her.

I have a ceramic sleigh she had given me for Christmas several years ago. I usually gave her something chocolate. The last day I got to spend with her, she seemed very well except when she had a little trouble getting up and down.

When I got the call this past September that she had died, I knew I had lost a good friend. She had lived to be 97. I went to her calling hours and met her two sons and daughters-in-law, who had meant so much to her, as well as her three grandchildren she had talked about so lovingly over the years.

To them I was a total stranger, but to me, they were the faces that went with all the stories I had heard about them during the past 14 years while having tea. I wanted to talk to them about her but there was no time. My only thought, as I left the funeral home, was that I would certainly miss answering my phone and hearing you say, "Kay, we must have tea."

We Spent All Day
on an Airboat

We've all heard the line, "Be careful what you ask for, you may get it."

Well, I didn't exactly ask for it, but when our daughter, Cathy, turned 40, she wanted us to go out for a day in an airboat with her. The day was January 8th, 2000. By that day, the Y2K scare was behind us, and we got to go see Cathy on her birthday.

She lived in central Florida near Lake Hatchineha. Going out in an airboat had always looked like a lot of fun. So, my husband and I agreed to go since it was her 40th birthday and that's how she wanted to spend it.

The day began very early. We were picked up by three guys, Eddie, Buddy and David, who owned three airboats. They took us out for breakfast, long before daylight. Their mode of transportation was a van that had carpeting all over all the walls and floor, so it seemed a little claustrophobic. This was the beginning of not really knowing what we were doing, but trusted that Cathy did. After all, she is 40 now, and has always been a good judge of situations.

It was still dark out when we got to the house, and all we could see was the light on in the garage. We went in through a kitchen door and immediately saw food stacked everywhere. Stacks of dishes of pancakes, sausage, bacon, eggs, rolls, toast, fruit, and anything else imaginable for a hungry guest.

We were led to the dining room with a table as big as the room itself, but managed to get the nine of us around it. By now, it was not just the three guys, but the host and hostess of the house, and Cathy, her husband, Butch, George and me.

From the picture window in that room, I could see the beauty of a dawn just about to break. What a beautiful sight.

Following breakfast, seven of us got back in the van, out to the dock, and watched as the airboats were put in the water. Cathy's husband and the hostess didn't go that trip because there was not enough room. It may have been getting light, but the fog was as thick as, yes, you guessed it, pea soup. Before getting on the boat, we had to put earplugs in our ears. Once there, the ear plugs expanded to keep out all the sound.

We also had to wear a ball cap and put on glasses to protect our eyes from the 50-mile-an-hour winds. After all, the three airboats each had an airplane motor that ran them. When you sit on an airboat, your back is directly against the frame holding the motor.

And, if you think we could talk during our trip, forget it. Often the sound waves were blown away before we could even get the words out. I got to sit in one airboat with Cathy because it had a special seat for two people. The others had room for only one more person than the driver. So, George was with Buddy, Cathy and I were with Eddie, and David took the man whose wife had just cooked our breakfast.

We didn't see civilization for the next eight hours. What we did see, besides eight hours of water, were wild animals, such as wild hogs and alligators. We went across the big lake and into marshland where the airboats flew over water that was as shallow as one inch.

And they could skip right over the dry land that showed itself once in a while. It just so happened that hunting season was in at that time. I guess that meant they could shoot birds because they did. We didn't, but the guys did. Just when I wondered what would be next, all three boats pulled up on a small piece of land and we all got out and posed for a picture.

I had to wear my ball cap backwards and since there was a shotgun in the boat, we posed with it and had our pictures taken. It was a cross between what little I had seen of Duck Dynasty and the Beverly Hillbillies. (No, that's not fair to the Beverly Hillbillies.)

Just when I thought we ought to be heading for shore soon, one of the other airboats ran out of gas. Being out in the middle of the place called, "Nowhere," is not where you want to be when you run out of gas. My thinking was that if one boat can run out of gas, what about the others? But, not to worry. I think that's what Cathy was trying to tell me over all the noise.

The boat that George was in, pulled the other boat all the way back to civilization. We followed and made it just fine. After quick trips to the restroom, which we hadn't seen all day, they loaded up the airboats at the dock.

By then the sun was going down and it was suppertime. We got back to the van and were taken back to the same house and went back in that same kitchen that had stacks of foods everywhere. This time there were stacks of chicken, dishes of corn and pasta, plates of biscuits, sweet tea and homemade chocolate chip cookies.

It was great. After all, we were safely on land, we had wonderful food, and Cathy loved every minute of her new adventure. And, no matter what the age, isn't that what all parents want to see?

She Looked Just
Like My Grandma

While out for breakfast in a tea room in Florida, a lady came through the kitchen door and over to our table. As soon as I saw her walking toward us, I was shocked. She looked just like my grandma.

The closer she got to us, the more she resembled my short, thin, white-haired grandma. She looked exactly like her.

She walked up to our table where our daughter, Cathy, my husband, George, and I were already seated. She walked over to Cathy, leaned in and put her arm on her shoulders and started talking quietly to her. The woman was talking to my daughter in a very informal manner. She seemed so much like my grandma, I was stunned.

Then, she walked over to George and did the same thing. Who is this woman who looks so much like my grandma? I just had to stare at her. When she finished talking to George, she came over to me and put her arm on my shoulder and started to say something, but I couldn't concentrate on what she was saying.

Her manner and presence were so much like my grandma's, I didn't hear what she was saying to me. My mind was somewhere else entirely. Then, when Cathy couldn't wait any longer for me to say something, she said, "Mom, she wants to take your order."

We were there for breakfast, so the only thoughts that came to me was what I always ordered at Cracker Barrel. That would be a fried egg sandwich with a slice of tomato and mayo, on sourdough toast. And a cup of decaf coffee. And as I finished my last word, she turned and walked back into the kitchen.

Immediately, I had to tell Cathy and George that she looks just like my grandma. My grandma died in 1961, so Cathy never knew her and George was new to our family back then. So, they couldn't confirm my thoughts. She was our waitress and had come out to take our orders. They didn't have any menus and she didn't write down what we ordered.

But, soon, here she came carrying a big tray of food. I didn't realize that at that time, she had gone back into the kitchen and cooked everything herself before bringing it all out to us. She served Cathy exactly what she had ordered, the same for George, and then set that exact same sandwich down in front of me, that I had managed to ask for. Each was entirely different from the other orders.

How did she do that? I had to say something to her about what I was thinking, so, I asked her what her name was. She said, "Mae." With that, I had to tell her that she looked just like my grandma and that my grandma's name was also "Mae."

Since Mae can be spelled two ways, either May or Mae, I asked her how she spelled it, and she said MAE. And you guessed it, my grandma spelled her name that way also. When I told her my story she said she would be pleased to be my grandma and that I could call her that.

And during our talk, she happily told us that on her next birthday she would be 75. Since it was our first time there, and with no menus, we had no idea what the cost would be. She told us that it's $7 for each breakfast, no matter what you order. So, we paid our bill and left.

We didn't get very far down the street when I said that we have to go back and take her picture because anyone who knew grandma won't believe this had happened. When we went back, she was very happy to go out on the porch of the tea room and pose with me for some pictures.

The tea room was in a large house that used to serve as a hotel back when passenger trains stopped on the tracks across the highway. Now, just the dining room was being used as a tea room. The kitchen was still the big kitchen and had pans and skillets hanging over the cooking area. And what used to be the living room, was a smoking room when customers were allowed to smoke inside.

We were told that we could go upstairs and look around to see how it had been a hotel at one time. They had one room with gift items to buy, and the other rooms were all empty. You could see how they could have been individual sleeping rooms. As for bathrooms, we are assuming there was one down at the end of the long hall.

After we got back to Ohio, I sent her copies of the pictures we had taken of her and me together. I sent a note along, asking her to write back and tell me about herself. Within a week, I got back a long letter telling me of the very hard life she had lived. The next year, while on vacation there, we went back to the tea room, and were told that she was in the hospital for tests, so we missed her.

I sent her a Christmas card this year and addressed it to Grandma Mae. We had been driving past that tea room for over 20 years and I always said that the next time we came down, I want to eat there. They don't serve every day, but when they do serve lunch, you have to eat whatever the one dish that they make for that day.

Hopefully, when we go back again this spring, we will get to see her, and I can again experience the feeling of being in the presence of my grandma. That would be nice.

TV Viewing,
from Then to Now

Since I am going to write something about TV, I will start from the first time I saw it. That unforgettable day was in 1947 when I went across North Sandusky Street into a little store.

The whole store was just one room that had been added on to a house. Ironically it was called "Morehouse's." There it was-- a TV set that was turned on. It had a very small screen and was sitting on the counter near the cash register. The picture was very snowy, and the sound had a lot of static, but I could tell that a woman was talking to some puppets. It was called "Kukla, Fran and Ollie."

What a miracle it was to see it with my own eyes! As soon as my siblings saw it, we wished we had a TV, too. We could tell when anyone on our street got a TV just by looking at the roof on their house to see if it had a TV antenna. Those homes were also buying TV dinners and eating off of TV trays, so as not to miss a minute of anything that was on.

Fortunately, soon we had our own antenna on our roof. We were living high. And anyone remembering back that far will remember the TV stations didn't come on the air until about 4 p.m. and signed off by either 11 p.m. or midnight.

Some people would be eating their supper in the kitchen and leave their TV running in the living room. That's because we were told it was hard on the TV tubes to be turning them on and off a lot. Speaking of those tubes, if the TV didn't work, all we had to do was to look inside from the back, and pick out the tube that wasn't lit up, pull it out, run down to Moore's store on South Sandusky Street, get a new tube that matched the number on the old one, bring it home and put it where it belonged, and voila, the TV was working again.

Today, if your TV doesn't work, you just buy a new one. That's because we are told it would cost more to fix it, than to buy a new one.

So, what else was on except Kukla, Fran and Ollie? Fifteen-minute segments of a Perry Como show come to mind. By 1948, Milton Berle, aka Uncle Milty, was on every Tuesday at 8 p.m. with his show put on by Texaco. He was live, as most all shows were back then. Wildly funny, for sure.

I don't like to be reminded, but late in the evenings, professional wrestling matches were on. The wrestlers had names such as Gorgeous George, Don Eagle and Kay Bell. I didn't like that type of program at all. I went to work one day and mentioned to Judge Henry Wolf that I didn't like that wrestler with the name of "Kay Bell." I lived to regret that I ever said that. Because Judge Wolf called me "Kay Bell" from that day on.

Other people who heard him call me by that name, started calling me that name, too. I don't miss not being called that name anymore, but I do miss the people who used to call me Kay Bell.

A popular show of the week, that began in 1952, was "Your Hit Parade." That's where the top 10 songs of each week were played every Saturday at either 8 or 9 p.m. I think the song, "This Old House" sung by Rosemary Clooney was #1 for at least 10 weeks in a row.

I don't have to write anything about how today's TV is different from when it first came out. It was invented years before we ever heard of it, but I read that when Milton Berle came on every week, the purchases of TV sets skyrocketed. Soon the soaps started up, and the TV news shows got more competitive as time went on.

There were only three choices of stations: ABC, NBC and CBS. (Recently, I read that the more choices you have of anything, the more bored you become. Could that be why TV remotes are so popular?)

Speaking of news, who could ever forget when Walter Cronkite took off his glasses, looked up at the clock and announced that President Kennedy had just died (and he gave the exact minute) on November 22, 1963? And that was the first time I heard the expression that "everyone knew where they were and what they were doing at that minute." I know I do.

To end on a much lighter note, I think that one of the best written half-hour comedies was "Frasier." I just found out that I can watch some old reruns of his show on my computer. I plan to do that very soon, since there's nothing on cable that I like.

Also, the series of Lucille Ball and Desi Arnez shows were very popular. Even now, in 2017, their series of TV shows is said to be on TV somewhere in the world every hour of every day. I don't think I'll ever forget when Lucy and Ethel were working in a candy factory and trying to keep up with the conveyor belt as it was speeding by.

Just think, because of reruns, there are people right now, somewhere in the world, laughing because of Lucille Ball. (Or in my case, Kelsey Grammer, aka Doctor Frasier Crane.)

A Special Guy
Named Clyde

T he first time we met Clyde was when he was in kindergarten and he walked past our house to go to school. His mom had asked me to keep an eye on him as he walked by, so as to know that he was getting there safely.

Over the years that followed, we got to know Clyde pretty well.

His schooling went from the classes at the Ashley school to classes in two Columbus schools, and ended with his graduation from Buckeye Valley High School in 1984. One of his favorite teachers at BV was Aldena Runyan. He has sung her praises ever since meeting her. She taught his special education classes and he progressed a lot under her leadership.

Another of his favorites was Thad Seely. When I think of Mr. Seely, I am reminded of how Clyde can imitate his voice. It's a riot when he gets started on things that Mr. Seely had said and then switches immediately over to Bill Clinton's voice. He has several other persons' voices he can imitate to a T, that are sure to make you laugh.

Sports have always been an important part of Clyde's life. Even though his coordination wasn't the best, he excelled in powerlifting. I don't know if he even knows how many gold medals he has won over the years while in Special Olympics.

Recently, since his eye surgery, I have learned that, with goggles on, he is taking tennis lessons. There is also a chance that he may get to go back to powerlifting next year. And then we can't forget that while in high school, he was the equipment manager of the BV football team for three years.

Clyde has a very supportive family. His mom, Gerry, has always been a wonderful mother to him for every one of his 50-some years. With speech lessons, doctors' appointments, and school events, she has always been there for him.

He had two very nice grandmothers in his life, too. I remember taking him up to Massillon, Ohio, to drop him off for a week's stay with his mom's mom and then going back up to bring him home. I think one of the nicest things his grandma said was when she told him he was her favorite grandchild. After all, he was a special kid.

His sister, Alice, has a heart of gold. Also, Clyde and his significant other, Becky, had a special commitment ceremony several years ago. We got to be there with all their friends and family to enjoy their happiness on that special day.

Clyde goes to "All Our Friends" in downtown Delaware and also has a part-time job at "Creative Foundations." He has a couple of very good providers who are there to take him places when necessary. Also, Clyde had a regular job at Kroger for 13 years. He sacked groceries and stocked shelves.

I'm sure he met a lot of new people while working there. He has attended church for most of his life. Since he has been staying with his mom during his recuperation from eye surgery, George and I took him to church with us a couple of times. While there, he met up with some people he had gone to school with, back in the day. He never forgets anyone.

One of his most recent friends is Doctor Papa, who did his eye surgery. I heard he refers to him as just "Pap." The surgery has resulted in Clyde being able to read a lot better than he had for a very long time.

If Clyde is your friend, he'll be your friend for life. Thanks, Clyde, for being our friend ever since your days back in kindergarten when you walked past our house on your way to school.

50 Mother's Days
with Mom

Whenever my siblings and I get together, we usually mention something about our mom. It's usually about the food she cooked, or clothes she washed, and hung outside to dry, no matter what the weather.

And the time she endured having only a pump in the kitchen to bring cold water from a well, into the house. And then having to heat all the water on a stove. Or how she could stretch the food budget to feed all of us, while all our growing was going on.

We all called her mom, and our children called her grandma, but her given name was Carolyn. Rarely did I ever hear anyone call her that.

Too bad, because it's such a lovely name. She hardly ever left the house because of a severe hearing loss that happened when she was a child.

There is a framed picture of her, with our dad and her seven grown children, on the wall in my dining room. The picture was taken at their 50th wedding anniversary party in 1974.

He was 74 and she was 71 and it was one of the best days in their lives. Almost all their children, grandchildren and other family and friends were there for the party. Our dad had been ill for the previous eight years and died just five months after that party.

As I look closer at the picture, I wonder what she might have been thinking as it was snapped. Since I see that she was holding daddy's hand, she may have been hoping he could make it through the day. Reason is that he had had a stroke and lost most of his short-term memory, so he was living in the past.

He could have been wondering where his children were. We were all there, it's just that now, we were all grown up. Mom may have been thinking about how fast the last 50 years had flown by.

She may have had a flashback of the times she had to change all our diapers, or sign all our grade cards, or fix all those meals with the food she had canned, or pick out our clothes from the Sears catalog, hoping they would fit, or when she saw to it that everyone had something to open on all those Christmas mornings.

Mom lived 13 more years after our dad died. Once I remember her saying that she missed him every day. She got along fine until she broke her hip when she was 79 years old. Most times people say that they fell and broke their hip.

However, the doctor told us that it's really that the hip breaks first and that causes the person to fall. She was always thin and weighed about 120 pounds. When she could no longer be left alone, she had to be moved to a nursing home. She spent her childhood living in her parents' big house until she got married. Then our dad moved us around to about 10 different houses.

But she liked that little town where she grew up, so much, that she tried to have a subscription to their weekly newspaper wherever she was living for the rest of her life. She didn't seem to mind at all that she would be going to a nursing home since she got to go back to the place of her childhood home, which was in Johnstown, Ohio.

It was a cold rainy April day in 1987, when all her children were with her at St. Ann's Hospital on the day she died. We began arriving at 6 a.m. and spent the whole day with her, preparing for the inevitable. She had the same nurse from morning until she died that evening.

One of the things we asked the nurse was how they knew when to call the family in. We were told it was when the blood pressure drops to a very low level. And then she added that our mother had just reached that low level. So, we stayed close.

The last thing she did was to try to tell us something, but she spoke in such a whisper that we couldn't understand. So, she lifted her hand and made a gesture like she was trying to tell us it didn't matter.

And at that same moment, she was gone. Just as quietly and peacefully as anyone can imagine. The nurses asked us to leave for a few minutes while they took out her breathing tube. When we got to go back to see her, they had a short ceremony. The chaplain said some comforting words and one of the nurses, very quietly, sang a beautiful song. I had not known of that kind of service being done before.

It took all of us to plan her funeral. She was buried next to our dad where the stone was already set. The rain had gone by then and there wasn't a cloud in the sky. I remember something I had read once about grief being when something ends before we are ready for it to end.

How true those words are. Every Mother's Day, for the past 30 years, since she died, I have thought a lot about my mom's life with our dad and her having seven kids to raise. She was 21 when she married, then went from 41 years of raising her family, right into eight years of taking care of our dad, and then to 13 years of being a widow. I never heard her complain once.

I want to write a couple of thoughts I have been having while proofing the story. First, I want to say again that her given name was Carolyn, and that I had 50 Mothers Days with her before she died at 83.

Roses, Lily of the Valley
and Honeysuckle

We all have different feelings about different flowers that have come into our lives at different times. One of my favorite flowers, lily of the valley, blooms around the first part of May.

There's a song that describes them as "White coral bells upon a slender stock..." I can remember when I picked my first lily of the valley. I was visiting a friend from the 4th grade, and her grandmother told me I could pick a bouquet from her yard, to give to my mother for Mother's Day.

She had hundreds in bloom around her house. She told me they had "spread." I had no idea what that meant, but I picked them anyway. It took both hands to hold them all. Then to top off the bouquet, she gave me a red tulip to put in the center of it.

It was beautiful and I headed for home, which was on the other side of the Olentangy River. Just before stepping on the bridge, a lady caught up with me and asked if she could buy those flowers from me to give to her mom on Mother's Day. I just said "no" without even asking what she would pay me for them.

Did I turn down a dime, or a quarter or more? All I thought about was that they were for my mom.

My next flower adventure came at a prom in high school. I had been invited to the prom and was pleased when a corsage was delivered to my home. But, when I saw the flower, I was embarrassed to even wear it. I thought it was ugly mostly because it was gray. Come to find out, it was an orchid. I had no idea it might have been rare and expensive. I had a lot to learn.

When walking into a funeral home, the scent of flowers fills the air. At the funeral of a family member, the flowers gave me something beautiful to focus on when I didn't know what to say to anyone. It was comforting to just sit and look at the beautiful colors of all the flowers.

After a service at the cemetery, it's always nice to see people carrying a flower with them as they go walking back to their cars. At the funeral home when my grandpa died, the only remembrance I have is that it looked to me like flowers were clear up to the ceiling.

I don't remember seeing my grandpa, just all those flowers covering the entire wall of the room. I was only 5 at the time.

Having a flower garden is wonderful, too. Years ago, a lady named Mrs. Barber, who had a flower garden, brought some to church every Sunday to put on the alter. From the first blossoms in the spring, right through the last flowers in bloom before it snowed, she was there with beautiful flowers, come rain or come shine.

We have a rose bush that's still alive, that came with our house when we bought it back in the 50s. It's a monthly rose that blooms from May to November. However, for several different winters, it looked like it was frozen out, but when I dug down to the roots, and babied it along, it lived. It has two buds on it as I typed this today.

While writing about roses, I remember once I found one rose in a bud vase sitting on my desk at OWU. It was on the morning after the graduation ceremony back in 1984. A student who had just graduated left it for me to find. It had a note with "Thanks" on it.

I am assuming it was because of my helping him a week or so before that. When he was rushing off to catch a bus to get to his golf match, he had to stop for an appointment with a professor in our department. He set his golf bag against the chair and went into the professor's office. While gone, two guys came in my office, picked up his golf bag and took it down the hall.

Although I was busy, I was aware of what they had done. When the student came out, he saw his clubs were gone. I knew he was desperate to catch his bus, so I showed him that his clubs had been taken to a classroom down the hall and put behind the door.

He was so grateful because it was not only an important match, but I remember it having something to do with being hired as a golf coach after graduation. He not only got to the match on time, but he was hired as a golf coach at the University of Alabama.

Now he is retired and just this month, in the OWU magazine, he was listed as being inducted into the 2016 class of Collegiate Golf Coaches Association of America Hall of Fame. Congratulations Mr. Spybey.

The scent of honeysuckle brings back all the best memories of my childhood. Honeysuckle grew on the trellises of the front porch of the first house we lived in when we moved to Delaware.

The scent of it always brings back all the good memories of my new life of living in that house on Union Street. It was 1945 and lots of good stuff was happening.

The war was over, my sister's husband would be soon home from the Pacific, we could walk to wonderful schools, there were lots of nice people in the neighborhood, my brother, Bob, got a bike for his paper route, and best of all, for the first time, I remember feeling safe.

A Glimpse of Life in the Children's Home

My memories of the Children's Home began when my family first moved two blocks south of the Home, on North Sandusky Street in Delaware. The Home was a huge white structure sitting at the edge of town, on top of a big hill just off U.S. Route 23.

My first knowledge of the situation was when I saw a lot of kids walking past our house on Saturday afternoons. Eventually, I learned it was because the owner of the Strand Theatre invited the "Home kids" to come to the movies every Saturday afternoon, for free.

The only thing I knew was, for some reason, these children weren't living with their own parents. And, I felt that whatever was going on, had to be hard on them. I remember they had their hair cut off very short. I was in the 7th grade and thought about the fact that if our parents couldn't take care of my siblings and me, we could end up there, too.

The first girl I got to know from the Home was in my junior high school homeroom at Willis School. I thought she was lucky in that her hair had not been cutoff short because she got to come to school with her hair in braids or curls.

Although I lived close to the Home, I knew nothing about what went on inside while she was living there. She moved away before the beginning of our senior year. I lost track of her until I saw her article in the Delaware Gazette about her organizing a reunion of the Children's Home kids, that was to be held in 2007. Her address wasn't given, so I called The Gazette and they let her know I wanted to contact her.

Later, she invited me to come to their reunion and that's where I got to see her. At that time, she wrote a book titled, "When Times Were Young." When I got a copy and read it, I learned a lot about how hard her life had been when her dad dropped her, and her six siblings, off at the home. She was only 10 years old and had to stay in the home for the next seven years.

She was taken there by her dad because her mother had been killed in an automobile accident, and he couldn't take care of all his seven young children, who ranged in age from 3 to 10 years.

She wrote in her book about there being no end of problems. One of the problems that bothered her a lot, was that she wasn't allowed to see her little brothers very often, because the boys were kept at one part of the home, and the girls, at another part. This applied to when they played outside, as well.

Another of the rules was that the parents of these children were only allowed to come to see them for two hours, once a month, on a certain Sunday afternoon.

Life was very hard in every way for her. When it came to clothes, she said that what few clothes she had all went to school every day because someone else was always wearing them. She also said that she was supposed to be paid for the work she had done in homes for people in town. However, when she left at the end of her junior year at Willis, to go back to live with her dad, there was no money saved for her, as it had been promised.

Another hard part was having to get out of bed every morning by 6 a.m. and get all their chores done before eating their breakfast of cereal and cocoa. Chores included dusting, mopping, washing, sweeping, cleaning everything. And then walking to school and getting there on time. It was one mile to Willis school.

After seven years of living at the home, she and her siblings moved back with their dad. Little did I know when I saw her at school, what all she had been through before getting there each day. Or, how much work she had to do after school.

She only got to have two new pairs of shoes for the entire seven years she was there. She wore a friend's FFA jacket for one whole winter because she didn't have a coat of her own. If any of the children wanted a drink of water, there were no drinking fountains. They had to get water from the bathroom sink, cup their hands, and drink the water they were able to hold in their hands.

I reread her book this past week and had to e-mail her to say how sorry I still am, that she and her siblings had been treated so badly. It was as if they committed a crime, and they were there to be punished, when the only reason they were at the home was to be taken care of, because their mother had been killed in an automobile accident.

Elizabeth
Called Today

_____

When I answered the phone, the voice I heard was familiar, but I couldn't place it until she said, "This is Elizabeth." (Her name is changed for this article.)

Just hearing her voice reminded me of a time earlier when we were sitting on the sofa in her home, late one afternoon, discussing where the horizon line was in the huge painting on her north wall. This painting looked like a multi-colored sky with the waves of an ocean.

At that time, the sunlight was coming in from her west window in an adjoining room. As the minutes passed, and the sun was going down, the colors in the painting seemed to change with it. This made the horizon line look like it could be on various other levels of the painting. A few months later, while at the doctor's office, I found myself sitting across from the artist who had done the painting. Since I had the opportunity, I told him about seeing one of his paintings and wondering where the horizon line really was, because it seemed to change as the lighting in the room changed. He remembered the painting, and said that other people had mentioned the same thing to him.

When Elizabeth asked about my older daughter, I told her that recently I had read an entry in an old journal about something she had said when she was 10. She said that since her three-month-old little sister was now laughing a lot, she was looking more like "a real human being."

It was good to hear Elizabeth's familiar voice with her slight accent. I thought of the day we had lunch at a deli in downtown Delaware. We sat on skinny bar stools and drank hot tea. I was mesmerized by the refinished old hardwood floors that now shined to a high gloss. This was the same floor I had walked on as a teen, when the Boston Store had occupied the same space on the northwest corner of Winter and Sandusky streets. During lunch, she and I discussed her recent trip to see her mother. And, how just two inches more of space of leg room on a plane, makes all the difference in your comfort on a long trip.

I was also reminded of her inviting me to a party at her home that November after the local election returns had come in. Back then, overhead projectors flashed the returns on the wall of the hallway on the first floor of the old courthouse. When I walked up North Franklin Street on my way to her house, I noticed that many of those nice homes had their porch lights on. The neighborhood looked like a great ad for Realtors to use when selling houses on that street. When I got to the party, it was evident that I may have been the only registered Republican in her house full of guests.

As I think of it now, I am reminded of a retirement party we had both attended for my sister at the university. When I saw her, I noticed that we were dressed alike. We both had multi-colored, horizontal-striped cardigan sweaters, with black skirts.

As we stood talking, I noticed a peaceful-looking woman, standing off to my left, who seemed to be waiting to speak to me. She introduced herself as the woman who called me a couple of months earlier in the year, to try to convince me that having chemotherapy wouldn't be so bad. She had been having chemo treatments herself, at that time. When she heard about my surgery, she called three or four times to try to lessen my worrying about the impending treatments I was facing.

As it turned out, I didn't have to have any treatments at all! Miracles do happen!

The phone call I am writing about, came from my friend, Elizabeth, back in 2005. I have been retired for less than three weeks, when she invited me to her home to meet with some friends who get together to discuss their writings. The instructions were to write something to bring with me when I came for lunch.

This article is called, "Elizabeth called today," because most of what I have written here, was originally what I wrote and took to her home that cold winter day. All of the women there also had written short articles with interesting storylines. One was about her grandchildren, another about something going on in the world of politics, and a third was about a flood.

My attending this little get together was one of the first steps on the ladder that has led me to be writing the article that I'm writing for the Delaware Gazette today. Mostly, because after I finished reading what I had written, one of the women in the group told me that I have "a whole shopping bag of ideas, so you need to get writing."

You just never know how one phone call can make a big difference in your life.

What I want to say here and now to Elizabeth is, "Thanks for calling."

It Takes a Barn to Make a Farm

When driving down country roads, do you ever pay attention to the barns at different farms? Some farms have three or four barns, while others may have only one.

There are five different buildings at our farm. Three are for horses, one for storage, and one is an indoor-riding arena. Several years ago, we realized that the three horse barns needed to be painted. So, our daughters, my husband and I set out to paint, not only the barns, but all the fences and gates as well.

We got together all the ladders, brushes, putty knives and sunglasses, that were needed to do the job. By the time we finished we had used a total of 68 gallons of paint to cover everything. It took us the whole three months from August through October to do the job. Time wise, it worked out very well, because as we changed the calendar to November, the weather changed to bitter cold.

When your barns are an important part of your life you pay more attention to other barns. It seems that some barns are in good shape, while others are about to fall down.

When some farm families passed their farm down from generation to generation, often the year it was originally built had been painted on the front barn. We've seen some as far back as the late 1800s.

The next thing you may notice is how well their barns are kept up. You won't find broken windows or roofs blowing in the wind at these farms. They may be used as housing for horses, cows or sheep.

On the other hand, you might see long, low buildings with a lot of exhaust fans running. They will be housing pigs, chickens, turkeys or ducks. When pigs in these pig farms die, and have to be buried, the pig farmer uses horse manure and sawdust to help the animal decompose. So, a pig farmer will haul away manure from a horse farm for this purpose. It's a win-win situation.

A lot of barns that once housed animals are now used for weddings, and other celebrations where a lot of people need a big space together. There is a big barn in Stratford being remodeled for this very purpose. Or, you can find a beautiful brand new barn on old U.S. 23 North at All Occasions. It has just recently been completed for weddings.

Barns that are still good, but no longer used, are being torn down and the framing timbers are used for remodeling older homes, lodges, sports clubs and ski resorts. You will find that older barns were built with wooden pegs which were used at the corners to hold the framing together. You won't find these wooden pegs used anymore because of being too time consuming. Now, nails serve that purpose.

If you want to see a lot of work going on in barns, you need to go to any livestock farm where work goes on seven days a week. These barns are filled with livestock that have to be fed, stalls that have to be cleaned, and buckets that have to be filled with clean water. As for cow barns, the cows have to be milked twice a day, every day of the week. At some stables, the owners of the horses come on a daily basis to take care of their own horses, usually to get them ready for horse shows.

If you want to see a very interesting cow barn that has been converted into a very nice church, drive north on U.S. 42 out of Delaware. While living with his family, my husband milked a lot of cows in what is now the basement of that church. The upstairs part, that was the hay mow, is now the sanctuary.

I've been told that since some horses, and other livestock, do not like to cross a bridge, a roof was put over the bridge to make the animals think they were going into a barn. Of course, I'm referring to covered bridges. There is a new covered bridge on Whetstone River Road in Marion County. You may enjoy going to see it, and while there, get out of your car and walk across it. It's beautiful.

Barns are a very important part of any farm. If you didn't have any barns, could you still call it a farm? The house would be just a house sitting out in the middle of a lot of land.

When I see an old barn barely able to stand against the wind, I often wonder what it looked like when it was newly built. Why did the farmer fail to repair the vital parts that held it all together? I'm told that no matter how bad a shape a barn has become, it can still provide a good home for owls. They are needed to keep the mice and rat populations down.

So, you may want to think of that the next time you are out riding on the country roads. It takes a barn to make a farm, whether it's only one or several more.

Forgetting Faces
and Names?

How many times have you seen someone who looked familiar, but you couldn't remember their name or where you knew them from?

I have had it happen many times lately and assume it is caused by the aging process. You know the feeling, there you are, face to face with a face that you know you have seen before, and should know, but nothing connects to give you a clue as to who it is.

Years ago, I was in line at the old US Store, standing behind two ladies who were acknowledging each other. They each referred to the other as "Dear." On my way back to work, it dawned on me that the reason they called each other "Dear" could have been because they couldn't remember each other's name. I laughed it off as being a long way down the road before that would ever happen to me. But it wasn't very long at all.

Another time I was standing near a woman in the bank, who kept looking at me and I could tell that she wanted me to wait a minute before I could walk away so she could say something. Since I didn't know her, I considered going right on out the door. But, she walked over to me and all I could think of was that I didn't know her at all. What was she going to say? She didn't call me by name, she just said, "How's your brother?" (I have two brothers, so which one was she wondering about?)

Stupidly, I said he's fine. (Since they both were fine, so far so good.) Then she said, "I haven't seen him since school." That had to have been 40 years ago. Then she said something about an upcoming class reunion and she hoped to see him there. I was trying to think which year each of my brothers had graduated. My mind went blank on that thought, and I knew I was in too deep, so I just gave up. When she said she had a crush on him in school, I asked which brother she was talking about and she was more than glad to tell me his name. Her final question was, "What does he look like now?" That stopped me in my tracks, and I heard myself say, "He looks a lot like me." She really didn't know me, she just wanted to talk about my brother.

Sometimes the most important thing about a person you can't place is not their name at all. You just need to know where you know them from. Their name won't matter because they will just want to talk about the place you have in common. I have learned to go through a list of places in my head when this has happened. Recently when I was faced with the said problem, I asked myself if I could have known her from school, or from any places of my employment, or an old neighbor? Nothing fit. I was just ready to admit that I didn't remember her, but I held back another moment and she said the magic words: "Are you still being a "pen pal" this year?" With that clue, I remembered where I knew her from.

I've read that it's a compliment if you ask someone their name, rather than going away without knowing. When you look at it that way, it helps. I'll just chalk it up to having too many other faces in my head and I can't pick out the right one fast enough. It's a proven fact that as we age, the synapses in our brain become slower and slower to connect. Not a problem. I'm not in a hurry. I'm retired and my life is my own. I'm realizing that when we can't find their name in the speed of a flying bullet, we can just wait patiently and hope to get a clue. Recently something like that happened at a church bazaar. A woman walked in and sat down beside me and started to talk. I knew I knew her, but how? I could tell she knew me well from what she was saying. Right then and there I should have said, 'I can't remember your name.' But I didn't, we even had our picture taken together and I couldn't think of who she was. But, it finally came to me.

To save you the frustration of what I went through that day, my advice is that if you see someone that you can't remember their name, you have two choices. One is to right away, confess that you know their face, but can't remember their name. Then the second choice, which may work, would be just to call them "Dear."

She Wanted to Ride
a Real Horse

Katie is the name of our neighbor girl who lives near our farm. She will soon be 12 years old, but we have known her since she was four. That's when we learned that all she wanted for her 5th birthday was to ride a real horse.

The only horse she had gotten to ride up until then was the plastic horse at the store that will move if you put a penny in the slot. When I was told that's what she wanted to do, I told her dad that I could make that happen. This was because we had a horse she could ride at our farm, and I would come to get her on her 5th birthday.

So, we decided on a time, and I went to their house to pick her up. When she came out, her sister, brother, dad and mother came, too. We all walked over to the horse barn and that's when her wish came true. That day was the first of many days and years to follow, when she came over to be near the horses.

During one of the times she was over, her mother told me that she also likes to read and write letters. So, I told her that if she dropped the note off to me at the barn, I would drop a note off for her at her home. That's when I found out that she could read and write exceptionally well for a 5-year-old. Thus, a friendship began, with the notes going back and forth. It wasn't very long until she started coming to the farm by herself. Then she started coming to our house and reading books to us. She liked to stay for supper, too. When she did, I needed to cook "Katie food" which were certain things that she liked and we liked as well.

By the time she turned 7, she was coming to ride, inside the arena, several times a week in the mornings before she went to school. Some of these early morning rides were very cold but it didn't seem to bother her a bit. I guess the horse kept her warm.

There is a lot of riding that goes on in the cold of winter, so the kids ride inside the arena. The riders aren't as cold as their parents, so George built a viewing room with a heater, where they can sit and watch their kids ride. George put up a trail ride which means he put up cones to ride between, a bridge to ride over, some long poles to also ride between, as well as a mailbox to open and close. She always wanted to stay after riding to brush and clean up after the horse.

When we took her to the Standardbred Pleasure Horse Organization (SPHO) awards banquet with us, she got to see the prizes being awarded to other kids and she decided that she wanted to be a part of the winning prizes, too.

When Katie was 8, we had a horse named "Just like Sonny." It belonged to a 10-year-old girl named Charlotte. In 2013, Charlotte went off to college, and left Sonny at the barn for Katie to ride. By then she was learning to Post and Canter. That was an exciting time. Katie also liked to give tours of the farm and explain what was going on there.

Also, when she was 8, she rode by herself in the 12-and-under classes at the SPHO show. She also showed in the fun shows at Cashman's farm. Eventually she won in a class for 18 and under. At every SPHO show and fun show that Katie has been in, she has always won at least one blue ribbon, as well as having many second and third places.

Katie has continued to ride ever since that day she turned 5. With her parents having to go to work before Katie had to go to school, in the kindergarten to 4th grades, Katie came to our house every morning and I walked her over to the school. She also came after school until her parents got home from work. And sometimes she even stayed for supper.

In her 5th and 6th grades, she leaves on an early bus in the morning and then after school she comes to the barn to help do all the feeding of the horses. This is a job that teaches her a lot of responsibility.

For all last seven years, she has been getting to enjoy the real horses that she longed for as a small child. She had her picture on the cover of "Youth Beats" magazine in 2014. This is a horse magazine for children.

There was also a story about her and George in the "Hoof Beats" magazine for horsemen, that same year. By now, she probably has at least 100 ribbons in her room, as well as a lot of trophies, too.

She has certainly come a long way from that little girl that I picked up that first day. That's where her story started and who knows where it will go from here.

Back to the One
Room Schoolhouse

I n 1957 when I first met my husband, George, he wanted to show me the one-room schoolhouse he had attended in the second and third grades. He remembered right where it was, and drove right to it. It seemed to be sitting out in the middle of nowhere. It was just a small, unlocked brick building, filled with pieces of old farm machinery and bales of hay.

It was just one large room with about five windows in it. He is always pleased to relive some of his memories from there. There is one story that has stuck in my mind ever since then. It was that each Monday morning, the teacher gave each student one small paper cup that was shaped like a cone. And that one paper cup had to last them all week. They used it for drinking the water that they had to pump, by hand, out of the well.

Then a couple of years ago, he met up with Harry, who had been one of his old classmates from that one-room school. They hadn't seen each other since their 4th grade together. The next time the subject of the one-room schoolhouse came up, we decided to try to find Harry's phone number and call him to meet him for lunch. It worked out, and we met last week.

I got to go along and listen to them talk about all their memories. And as usually happens, the more they talked, the more memories each of them could recall. A lot of what they liked to talk about were the discipline problems that happened in class. And the punishment of being sent to the coal shed. Harry told us that his mother often wondered why he often came home with a lot of coal dust all over his clothes. And they hadn't forgotten about how cold it was out there in the winter months, either.

If they had done something really bad, they got paddled. Both guys laughed over the memory because their teacher had used a plastic belt that didn't hurt a bit. My one question that day was, "How were the students sitting so as to separate one class from the other?" Their answer was that they sat in a row. Since I didn't know quite how to picture that dividing them very well, I had to ask them to explain.

And they did, by saying they were one right in front of the other from front to back. I am still thinking that it wouldn't it have been better to have each class sitting in their own circle? But I'm sure that their one and only teacher knew what she was doing.

When all the classes are in one room, you learn a lot of different things that way. For instance, when one class sang, the others could all sing along. Or when one class practiced for a play, they all saw it going on. When George was in the second grade, there was no one in the third, So, when he moved up to the third grade, there was no one in the fourth.

The students came to school on a bus, as well as the teacher, who rode the bus with them. These one-room-school houses were built several miles apart. When the parents came for a PTA meeting in the evening, the children came, too, and played on the only thing on the playground, which was one merry-go-round. When the meetings were over, everyone got to see a movie inside the school. We can't forget that they had two outhouses, one for girls and one for boys.

If you had to use the outhouse, you raised your hand and pointed your finger toward the outhouse, without speaking a word. It was especially fun to get to know each other's siblings and the other classes, too. The one teacher did everything. She was not only the teacher for grades one through eight, she was the custodian, disciplinarian, nurse, principal, music teacher, drama coach, and more.

She had to be in school the entire 180 days just as everyone does now. They also talked about having to fix the fire in the coal stove after getting to school each morning. So, you can imagine how cold it would be for most of the morning until that one room got warmed up. If you were especially well behaved all week, then on Fridays you were rewarded by getting more minutes added on to your time at the last recess of the week.

The students either brought their lunch, or their parents brought it to them each day at lunchtime. One more story was about some unknown person sawing off the pump handle. I guess it wasn't sawed off completely, since they could still get some drinking water. As far as they know, it's still a mystery as to who did it. Whenever they spoke of their teacher, they had no idea if she was married or not, but she was definitely called Mrs. McClain.

Before George and I met up with Harry for lunch last week, we drove all over the outskirts of Marion trying to find their old schoolhouse. After all, 60 years had passed since the last time we were there. Just as we were ready to give up, we found it. We saw a brick building with a lot of windows off in the distance.

As we got closer, we could see that it had been turned into a very nice home. And the closer we got, the nicer it looked. We pulled up in the driveway, went up to the door and knocked. No answer. As we were about to drive away, I noticed their mailbox with their address on it. So, I copied it, and when I got home I sent a letter to them. I just addressed it to the resident of that address.

I was bold enough to tell them that we would like to come back to see inside, if they would allow it. Yesterday I got an e-mail telling us it would be fine.

Their letter mentioned that they would like to hear George and Harry's memories as much as we wanted to see how the old one room school looks today. Who knew? Who would believe that two young boys in the third grade would ever come back to see their one room schoolhouse, 70 years later?

My Lifetime Fear
of Dogs

I'm guessing that everyone has a fear of something. My mother feared snakes so much that she couldn't stand to even see one on TV. My fear came from my dad telling me to stay away from dogs because they would bite me.

He probably only said it a few times, but it stuck with me all my life. And so my biggest fear has always been that I will be bitten by a dog. My latest memory of being afraid of a dog was when a big dog followed me down the street when I was out walking. He wanted to walk right at my heels.

There was nothing I could do but hope you would just go away. I just kept walking and he kept following. No one else was on the street. Since no one was home at my house, I didn't want the dog to run in my house when I opened the door. So, I went to the neighbor's house and knocked on her door, but no answer.

The dog followed me down her porch steps and out to the street where I went to another neighbor's house and knocked on her door, but no answer there, either. I knew the people across the street were home, so I went over there, with the dog still at my heels.

I asked the neighbor if he would please get the dog away from me. So, he came out, took a hold of it, and let it inside his house. When I was safely home, I realized that the dog was still inside the house across the street. The next thing that happened was when I saw the man come outside with the dog, put it in his car, and leave.

Since I've never seen that dog again, I have often wondered what happened to it.

At this point, I need to address the fact that not only am I afraid of dogs, but I'm not really comfortable around any animals. I did a lot of babysitting with children in my teens, but never in a house that had a dog. That was always my first question when I was asked to be someone's babysitter. The only thing that ever came close was when I was a substitute sitter for a family I didn't know.

The kids asked me to reach up on the top shelf of their bookcase and get a book down for them. When I did, a dead mouse fell right on me. I can't tell you how hard those kids laughed at the stunt they had pulled on their new sitter. I was glad I never had to substitute there, again.

Another happening was when I was at a meeting in a friend's home. I was just sitting there, enjoying the topic of the evening, when her dog came into the room and jumped right on me. I have often heard that if you are afraid of an animal, they can sense it. While all the other people in the room were laughing at that happening, I told myself that I was never coming back to that house again. And I didn't.

While campaigning door to door, dogs can present a big problem. If I heard a dog barking after I had knocked on someone's door, I just put my literature on the porch and left.

If the door was opened by the resident, it was a waste of time, because more time was spent by the owner trying to control her dog, than was spent conversing with me.

Recently, I have come to know a perfect dog. It barely barks and does not jump on people. She is quiet and just looks around to watch what's going on. Her name is Flo. If I had been around such a nice dog in my childhood, maybe today I wouldn't be sitting here writing about by fear.

Once when I told an acquaintance that I was afraid of dogs, he said he felt sorry for me. Terribly sorry that I had been made to fear such a wonderful thing as a pet dog to spend time with and love. When I hear of social agencies that want to take dogs to nursing homes so elderly people can enjoy them, my thought is, "Please don't ever do that to me when I become incapacitated."

I've read some very good books about dogs. "Marley and Me" by John Grogan, for one. And I can't forget Lassie being one of my favorite TV shows back in the day. I'm happy for people who love their dog. I have read of dogs that have saved their owner's lives. Also, dogs that have made it known that the owner should follow them somewhere to find someone in distress.

I've heard it often said that a dog is man's best friend. Well, it's a good thing I'm not a man. When someone told me about her dog sleeping in her bed with her, I just wanted to cringe.

At this time of my life, I can't ever imagine getting over my fear of dogs. Recently, someone told me that he got over his terrible fear of dogs by the time he turned 9. Of course, I had to ask how that happened. He said it was because he found a safe place to be where the dog wouldn't jump on him.

It was on his bed. And when he knew he had a safe place to go, he got used to being around the dog and realized it wasn't going to hurt him. I think my dad thought he was protecting me from being bitten, but those few words of warning turned out to be a lifetime of fear.

Remembering My First
Real Job After High School

W hen I realized that this article will be published on August 23, it brought back a lot of memories of how important that date is in my life.

The reason is that August 23 was the first day of my first real job, when I was just out of high school. I graduated in June, but had no future insight. My family had moved to a farm in the country, so I went there to live right after my graduation ceremony. During the rest of June, all of July and the first week in August, I had nothing to do. I was living in the country and had no transportation, no money, no future, only that I knew I had to get a job. That August, my dad asked someone who worked at Grief Brothers, if they had any jobs open there. She said I should come in for an interview and that she would make an appointment for me to do so. She was even so kind as to take me to work with her that morning and bring me home after she got off work that night.

While waiting those eight hours while she worked, I spent time at the old Delaware library, and then walked down Sandusky Street to do some window shopping. That's when I luckily ran into Connie Jones, a friend from school, who asked me to go on a weekend trip with her, and her family, to North Tonawanda, New York, to see Niagara Falls. I was thrilled. When we got back to Delaware, her dad told me about a new job opening at the recorder's office in the courthouse. To make a long story short, I had three interviews and got hired. My first day of work was Monday, August 23, 1954. That day was a pivotal day in my life. I went from no hopes of any future to walking right into my future.

Moving forward to May 1988, is when I both graduated from Ohio Wesleyan University and ran for the office of county recorder, in the same week. I won the primary election on May 3 and graduated from OWU on May 8, 1988. Since I had no opposition in the general election, I began as recorder on January 2, 1989. To this day, I still think of the difference from what it was like during my first year as recorder, and then my last year, when I retired at the end of 2004.

Because of the growth of the population of Delaware County during those particular 16 years, there was an ever-increasing number of deeds and mortgages that came into the recorder's office every day. As an example, what used to be a 10-acre piece of vacant land, was subdivided into 44 building lots. So, where there was only one deed before, there became 44 deeds and 44 mortgages and other miscellaneous documents to be filed.

In the very first year I was in office, we took in $215,726 in fees for recording the real estate documents. And, we had five employees. In the last year of working, before I retired in 2004, we took in over $3,236,240 in fees. And, we had eight employees. If you look again at the difference in the amount of money our office took in during those two years, you will see a $3,000,000 increase in the total fees from my first year in office in 1989 to my last in 2004. All the money came directly from filing fees of deeds, mortgages, subdivision plats, and other miscellaneous documents. This increase of revenue is definitely a rock-solid example of tremendous growth of Delaware County during those 16 years.

And since I like math so well, I kept track of the profits the recorder's office made during my 16 years in office. With the total fees coming in during my tenure being over $17,644,928, we ended those 16 years with a total profit to the county of over $5 million! Also, we reached the mark of recording more documents during my tenure as recorder than having recorded in the previous 180 years! It was suggested to me at that time, that I should have that statistic printed in The Gazette, but I was too busy to get it done. But, here it is, finally, in this year of 2017.

Many times I've heard that no one makes it on their own. I knew I needed all the help I could get. So, I want to thank each and every person who worked in the recorder's office while I was recorder. We started out with having to get a computer system installed and up and running the first day of 1990, and had to deal with all the updates and changes from then on. We also went through having walls torn down as our office expanded by two more rooms, and then in May 2002, we had moved all our four rooms of books of recorded documents, across Sandusky Street to the newly completed Hayes Building. It was sad for me to have to leave that wonderful old courthouse behind.

I appreciate every one of the employees for showing up and doing a job that allowed for the real estate records to be complete, and in the best order possible, for all the landowners of Delaware County. Thank you!

Special Bond: Horses, Kids and 4-H

Ever since the first little kids came to our farm and asked to ride, I have been aware that there is a special bond between children and their horses. It's amazing how unafraid many can be, even the first time they get close to a horse. We were told about a little girl, and her brother, whose parents had taken them to see a real horse. The little girl reached out to the horse and wanted to pet it, while her brother, a little older, went in the opposite direction, not wanting to get near it. That girl has ended up coming to ride at our farm since she turned 10. She's in college now, and her name is Sarah.

Most of the children who have come to our farm to ride have been girls. One little girl, Kailey, got on a horse, patted it, and even walked under it when she was only about 3 years old. She did not have a bit of fear of that huge animal standing in the middle of the aisle at our barn. I was there when she won her first ribbon in a horse show at Hilliard Fairgrounds. The amazing part was that after she was all finished with her horse, and had hung up the ribbon she had won, she wanted to walk around and look inside all the other stalls that had show horses in them. I watched this little, then five-year-old, as she studied each and every one of the horses. I don't know what she was thinking, but her manner made me think of the way you see judges act when they are judging 4-H exhibits.

Soon, I will be leaving to go to the barn to see some new children I haven't met. They are having some kind of a "ride out." I decided I should do a walk through to see what's going on that's new to me. The kids and their horses who come to ride are brought there by their parents. If George doesn't get there early enough, the driveway will be full, leaving no room for him to park. I thought I could eliminate that problem by getting a sign that says, "Reserved for George." It never did get put up.

On hot days, it surprises me that the inside of the barn is cooler than almost anywhere else. Several years ago, a woman had a big birthday party for her old Standardbred horse at our barn. She brought a big arch made with colorful balloons for the makeshift horse stall for that day, lots of food, and a decorated cake for the party for her 35-year-old horse. I thought I would just drop by, but when I got there, it was the coolest place I had been all day. So, I stayed and listened to all the horse enthusiasts standing around and telling their horse stories about the oldest horse each of them had ever known. The birthday horse's nickname was "Grandma."

After writing the above, I went over to see all the kids who showed up to ride. They were aged from 8 to 17 years. These kids are members of 4-H, and their leader, Naomi, is a licensed instructor for both 4-H and riding. The work that is going on now is in preparation for this year's Delaware County Fair. Naomi's children, Sidney and Trent, were there with their older sister, Cora, who was a lot of help for them. Besides being a very good rider of horses, Cora can ride a pogo stick that we have at the barn, without using your hands to balance herself. We think it comes from her riding bareback a lot, and that gives her the muscles to be able to control the pogo stick that way.

There were a total of 11 children who showed up to ride. One, who had only been there to ride by herself before, came this time and got to ride with the big pack of ten others. Her name is Alex. As they all finished, and came leading their horses through the barn, I asked each one if they were having a good time. One hundred percent answered with a big smile "Yes!" What a thrill to see such enthusiasm! It's always a great sight to see the smiles on the faces of the riders when they have succeeded in getting the horse to perform correctly in any of the classes where they are shown. And, also when they win a ribbon, no matter what color it is.

I don't want to leave out a couple of teens named Mattie and Tristen, who are also in 4-H and taking lessons in preparation for showing at the Delaware County Fair. Some children who were there are considered "ship-ins" because they don't keep their horses at our farm, but have to bring them from home for every lesson. When our younger daughter was in 4-H, she had to take her horse to every meeting. When George had to hitch the horse trailer to his truck, and load it and unload the horse for the meeting, then have the lesson, and then load the horse again, haul it back home and unhitch the trailer after unloading her horse. I used to think how much easier it would have been if she was showing a chicken.

Cleaning Out
Our Town Barn

L ong time ago, we bought a big old brick building in the village, because we had gotten a boat, and needed a place to store it. Since it was on a side street within one block of downtown, we eventually started calling it our "Town Barn." Originally, the building was built for a church. After it was no longer used by the church, the building was used as a place to pluck chickens, as well as selling eggs and cream there, too. History has it that two fellows invented the "Chicken Plucker" in that very building. It was later being used for storage, so we bought it for a place to store our boat.

Back in those days, when we were a lot younger, we thought it would be a lot of fun to learn to water ski. So, we took the boat over to the Delaware Dam area. The water wasn't very cold in the summer, so with a lot of practice, I could get in the water, ski around to my heart's content, drop the line, get back in the boat, and never get my hair wet. After several years of enjoying skiing, we bought our farm. With all the work to be done at the farm, there was no longer time for skiing, so we sold the boat. With the boat no longer taking up space in the town barn, more and more stuff accumulated to take its place. We let a couple of people use it for their yard sale. However, when the sale was over, they left the stuff there they didn't sell and they never did come back to get it. So, after a lot more years of accumulating more stuff nobody wanted, we knew it was time to clean it out.

Where do you begin to clean out a barn that's full of things that are of no value to you any longer? This was a long time before we ever saw the

TV show "American Pickers." A lot of this old stuff was never originally ours in the first place. A lot of people we knew just wanted some place to put things they wanted to get rid of. For instance, big old, overstuffed chairs, as well as old broken-down bikes that needed a lot of repair. Also, a lot of broken windows that had a few good panes of glass left. And, a lot more stuff that comes under the heading of "too numerous to mention."

The only thing that interested me was my mother's buffet. To anyone else, it was just the average everyday buffet with two big drawers in the center, with doors that open in the front at each end. But, this particular buffet had been in every dining room of every house I had ever lived in during my growing up years. We can't remember how it ended up in our town barn, but there it was, in need of a lot of work to fix it up.

I don't know where we got the idea to give everything away, but that's what happened. I made a big sign with just one word on it, "FREE," and put it out front. George moved a lot of the interesting stuff outside, got a lawn chair, and took up residence in front of the town barn to see what would happen.

Immediately, people stopped to see what was going on. After all, the sign said "free." The first person to stop was a guy who was glad to find that we had a lot of chairs he could fix up, since he did reupholstering. When we gave him all seven of them, he was one happy guy. Another man wanted all the panes of glass because his wife wanted him to build a greenhouse in their backyard. Another was a kid named Jamie, who wanted all the broken bikes.

The giveaway was held on a Saturday and Sunday, several summers ago. Spending all weekend over there felt like we were on some weird type of vacation. Everyone was happy to get what they wanted and we were happy to get rid of it. As evening came on the second day, we were almost completely cleaned out, except for the buffet. A young man showed up and said he would like to have it and would refinish it to look just like new. I was undecided about letting it go, but he convinced me that I should let him have it, because when he was finished, he would take a picture of it and bring it back for me to see. Well, if that same young man is out there, reading this article, I am still waiting to have you bring me that picture of mom's buffet, as promised. It would do my heart good to see it in its original beauty again.

Soon after our big giveaway, a neighbor said he wanted to buy the town barn, so we sold it to him. We still talk a lot about the days when we were very young and the type of life we lived back then, including our summers of skiing at Delaware Dam. Now when I walk past the town barn, I see the bricks are beginning to disintegrate. I remember the problems we had with kids throwing rocks and breaking the windows. (That's where all the broken windows came from.) I haven't ever been inside it again, but something tells me it might need another cleaning out in the near future. I don't remember what we did with the "FREE" sign, but maybe it's still in the barn. It would come in handy if the new owner wants to use it.

If I Didn't
Have Vertigo

I f I didn't have vertigo, I would be going to the races today at the Delaware County Fairgrounds. Every year, Aunt Mary invites us to sit with her in her box at the races sometime during the week of the Delaware County Fair, home of the "Little Brown Jug." If I didn't have vertigo, I would be out the door in about an hour to pick her up and go have lunch at the Buckeye Valley Building. I will miss having one of their fish sandwiches with the two or three little packets of tartar sauce that make them taste so good. What is it about eating outside that makes everything taste so much better? And, I will miss seeing and hearing one of the high school bands as they walk past the tables, toward the midway. It's always great to get to be near a live band while it's marching past!

I have had vertigo for about 17 days now. I remember reading once that having vertigo is like hanging on to the floor because you are afraid you will fall. Yes, that's right, the word is floor. In case you have not experienced vertigo, this is the definition from my Webster's New World dictionary: A condition in which one has the feeling of whirling or of having the surroundings whirling about one, so that one tends to lose one's balance; Dizziness.

The very first time I had vertigo, I had a prescription filled for it at the old Revco store on the east side of North Sandusky Street. That medication was the first I tried, and after just one pill, I was not dizzy anymore. That's because my whole body turned to stone and I couldn't move at all! The medication for it has improved over many years since.

Back to what I would be doing today, if I didn't have vertigo. I would get up to sit in the shade, up in the grandstand, and read the racing program with the interesting names of over 100 horses that will be out on the track to race today. Such crazy names as "Getonmybikenride," "Golden Gottawyn," and "Icingon De Cupcake." I would plan to take a walk around the track because you never know who you might run into. At this time in our lives, we aren't as familiar with many horsemen as we used to be. We still miss getting to see Bob Davenport, and Doc and Frankie Todd. We also miss a couple of the retired drivers who were out on the track a lot, too. They are LeRoy Stults and Billy Walters.

Getting to sit in the box seats near the finish line is always like old home week. If you have been going to the races for 20 or more years, you will have seen the same families and/or friends, sitting in their same places. I used to always see the Henry Wolf family up there, as well as knowing the ushers who faithfully turned up to show people to their seats. When I managed to get together with some of my classmates from Willis recently, the guys were talking about their old days of skipping school to get to usher at the fair. And, of course, we always see the two guys use their rakes to smooth over the tracks at the finish line before each race.

Some of those tracks are made by the horses as they cross the finish line, while others are made by the people who run down from the grandstand to get in the win pictures. Instead of getting blue ribbons, racehorses will win either a blanket or a trophy. Or, they could win both, if they had the fastest time.

An owner, who's a friend of ours named "Freddy," won both a blanket and trophy last year at the Delaware Fair. Since I know he is racing again today, I will be interested to see if he wins again. Happiness is getting to be in somebody's win picture, whether you are the owner, the trainer, the driver, the groom, or friend of the owner.

I have been in the race of my own today. I want to get this article finished. If I didn't have vertigo, I wouldn't have to stop, here and now, to go lie down. That's because "MyDizzyVertigo" is winning.

Two Poems
for Today

———————————

Back in the 1990s, I wrote several poems to give to my siblings as Christmas gifts. The poems were about my memories of our childhood together. It seems that because of the difference in our ages, we all have different memories of growing up in those different houses. The first one is about going to visit our grandma on Sunday afternoons. She was a widow and lived alone in her own home.

When we got to grandma's, she was always sitting in her living room, and that's where she and our dad talked the whole time we were there. Because of our mom's hearing loss, she mostly just sat and listened as best she could. As an adult now, I often wonder what they had been talking about all those long afternoons.

The first poem is called, "While grandma talked to our dad."

Going to grandma's on Sunday, was almost what Sundays meant.
So, usually after our dinner, we got in the car and went.

All the way there we usually argued, about who got a window seat.
Or if the window was down too far, or who didn't have room for
their feet.

When we got there, we had to be quiet, while grandma talked to
our dad. We fidgeted, fretted, sighed and paced, but never really got
mad.

Sometimes we walked downtown. In Croton that's no big deal. A block of stores and a railroad track, and cousins with little appeal.

Grandma was a little lady, with white curls and very tanned skin. She always wore a housedress, and had pierced ears with no earrings in.

I wish I knew what they were talking about. Not knowing makes me sad. I guess I should have listened, while our grandma talked to our dad.

My second poem is about my favorite meal of mom's, apple dumplings. Usually for suppers and Sunday afternoon dinners, we had a "meat and potatoes" kind of meal. And we always, always, always, had some type of dessert. We had either pie, cake, cookies, ice cream, or at least a graham cracker covered with chocolate icing. The last thing I purchased at the Nectar in downtown Delaware before it closed, was the same thing, a graham cracker covered with chocolate icing, which cost $1 apiece.

My favorite meal in the summer was when the only thing she fixed were apple dumplings. These were pieces of peeled apples covered with cinnamon and sugar, wrapped in pie crust and baked. They were about the size of a softball. We poured cold milk over them and ate them while they were still hot. My best memories were when we could have as many as we wanted. And sit and eat them wherever we wanted.

My second poem is called "Apples Wonder-Full."

Every summer and fall when we were kids, mom made us a special treat, she called them apple dumplings and we ate all we could eat.

We also had other special foods, like suet pudding and quince pie. They were treats other kids never heard of, and their mothers couldn't buy.

We didn't have to set the table, we just grabbed the bowl and spoon.
We ate that gooey chewy crust, whether for supper or at noon.

My favorite spot at one of our homes, was outside on the back porch
floor. It was cool out there and not too far, to run back and get some
more.

There should have been a different name to call a dish so great.
Apples Wonder-Full was my choice, because we ate and ate and ate.

To make them as good as mom's, is a goal we'll never win. I wish we
could all go back, and have some more of hers again.

A Tale of Two Desks,
Built with Love

As I moved my hand across the top of my desk just now, I was again aware of what a beautiful desk it is. It was made so well, that I have to look closely to see the line between the individual boards that make up the top. And, I am reminded that my son-in-law clamped and glued each of these boards together to build this desk. If it wasn't for the different grain in each board, I wouldn't be able to tell where one board begins and the other ends.

It was a retirement gift from our daughter, Cathy, and her husband, Butch, whose real name was Raymond. This handmade, hardwood cherry desk started as a hardwood cherry tree growing somewhere in this area of Ohio. Until now, I didn't know there is a difference between what is called the hardwood cherry tree, and the regular cherry trees that produced the cherries we eat. A hardwood cherry is known for the beauty of its grain, thus is used when building very nice furniture.

This particular tree was cut down and sawed into boards by Clear Run Lumber Company, which is just east of here. They also dried and planed it, on one side, so it would be ready to begin construction. While Cathy and Butch were visiting here in the summer of 2004, Butch bought enough board feet for two desks. He took those boards to their home in Florida, drew up the plans himself, and built the first desk for Cathy, and the second desk for me. I didn't know Butch was making this desk for me until January 2005, right after I had retired. What a nice surprise it was!

When he told us that my desk was finished and ready to be picked up, George and I drove our truck to Florida to bring it home. It is so beautiful! It has all the parts for a computer to take up residence: the slide out shelf where the keyboard sits, as well all four drawers that are 32 inches in length. It was built in three different pieces: the beautiful large top, which is 34 inches by 60 inches, and then the two separate filing cabinet-type drawers that are the right size to hold the top at the exact level necessary for me to use while sitting here. The drawers have beautiful handles with the matching handle for the door.

It's hard for me to imagine all the work it took to build this desk, and all its perfection. However, inside the upper right-hand drawer is an album of pictures Cathy had taken of every step as Butch was building it in his shop. The dates on the picture show that it took three months for him to build it. Cathy took 60 pictures of the entire progression from the first board sitting in the shop to the finished product. She then put them in a 5-by-7-inch album that is to always stay in one of the drawers in the desk.

It's interesting to know that this hardwood cherry tree that grew right here in central Ohio, is ending up staying in central Ohio. I have spent nearly every day for the past 13 years sitting at my desk: writing, emailing, or looking up stuff. It's the nicest piece of furniture I have in the house. Did you know that if you take a bar of soap and rub it along the tops of the sides of open drawers, they will slide in and out more easily? I didn't, but I do now! Cathy put a bar of pink Camay soap in one of the drawers for me to use, and it's still there.

This article isn't like my others, that are about horses and kids, nor is it about old Delaware. It is just about two desks, mine and Cathy's. We took another load of hardwood cherry boards with us when we went to Florida to pick up this desk. Those cherry boards were purchased in Ohio because you can buy that type of wood more inexpensively here, than what it would cost in Florida. Those boards were supposed to be used, by Butch, to build new cupboards for their kitchen.

Sadly, the new cupboards never got built because Butch became very ill and died 11 years ago this month. Although Cathy doesn't have new cherry kitchen cupboards, she took all the doors off of the top row of the old cupboards, and the kitchen looks very nice that way.

That load of cherry wood we took down in 2005, is stored in her shop, up near the rafters. Who knows what it will eventually be used for? What I do know, is that thanks to Butch, it will never be for anything as special as the two identical desks he built: the one that was for Cathy, and the one that was for me.

Bubba and Bevis,
The Gentle Giants

B ubba and Bevis were the names of the two draft horses George got in the spring of 2005. George had retired from racing harness horses and had always wanted to have a team of draft horses.

There is a place in Amish country called Mount Hope, where they have horse auctions. The first horse George got there, he named Bubba. He was 18 hands high, black and weighed over 2000 lbs. They are Percherons, which is a breed of draft horses that originally came from France.

George grew up having a team of them back in 1948 when he was 10 years old, and hadn't been around any since. His interest was renewed because of seeing them out in a field at a friend's farm on State Route 42. Now that he had one Percheron, he needed another one to make a team.

So back to Mount Hope he went, and found another big black 2000-pound Percheron, and named him Bevis. Next, with his team, he needed two sets of harnesses. He found just what he needed from a friend who sold them to him for a decent price. George's dad showed him that putting that much harness on those two big horses is almost a two-man job. Now, he had everything needed to pull something, but nothing to pull.

Well, if you can believe this, a guy down the road just so happened to want to sell a covered wagon. And it wasn't long until we were making a place for it in our barn. It was every bit like the covered wagons you see in the old western movies. They can seat at least 10 people. So when we put everything together, we went out on the streets of our village to get them used to the territory.

I am not comfortable in some horse situations, but I did get in the covered wagon. Everything was fine, until we came to the railroad tracks. That's when Bubba and Bevis decided to go up the tracks instead of crossing them. When I saw what was happening, I jumped off the covered wagon as fast as I could and headed for home.

Eventually, with more training, they did very well on the streets. A lot of people came out of their houses to watch, and some even jumped on the wagon. This is about the time when George's dad got to drive the team. He hadn't driven any Percherons since 1948 and enjoyed being back at the reins.

That September, George entered them in the All-Horse Parade in Delaware. However, so many people wanted to ride with us in the parade, that the covered wagon couldn't hold them all.

So, George converted his hay wagon to a homemade covered wagon and we took at least 16 people with us. Because of the inclines on North Sandusky Street, he knew he would have to have a brake to be able to help control the speed of the wagon. So, he invented a break that he could use manually, and it worked.

The parade route is three miles long, so we had time to allow two girls from our farm, Sarah and Charlotte, to drive during some of the trip. Anytime someone would want to have the experience of driving a team of horses, George would let them hold the reins and drive. They would also get the experience of stopping and turning corners. We always decorated the wagon with red, white and blue streamers, and an American flag.

In order to haul the two "big boys" as we called them, we had to convert his four-horse trailer to be a two-horse trailer to get them both inside. As a team, their weight was exactly 4120 pounds, and since they have very calm dispositions, they are often referred to as the "gentle giants."

Bubba showed in horse shows with George driving, using a big-wheeled Amish road cart. He did well enough to win a blue ribbon at every show he was in. The other horse, Bevis, was shown at horse shows and riding classes by the girls at the farm, because he could walk, trot and canter. It was a big thrill for them to show a draft horse in a fun show.

After several years of being in the All-Horse Parades, Bevis died. About a year later, Bubba got down in the stall and couldn't get up, due to old age. He had to be put to sleep by the vet. He was laying inside a stall in such a way as to completely block the doorway. So, to get him out, George had to remove the entire front of the stall, board by board.

During these years since Bubba and Bevis died, George has often talked about getting another team of Percherons. But, he always says, "My wife and daughters don't want me to, because they think I'm getting too old to be wrestling with 2000-pound horses." And his wife and daughters are absolutely right.

The Phone Call
No One Wants to Get

<hr>

I t all started when I answered the phone early in the evening on a spring day several years ago. After I said "Hello," I heard a man's voice ask to speak with my husband. I assumed it was someone calling about needing something to do with the farm. (This was before we had our own cell phones.) He wasn't at home at the time, so I asked if I could take a message.

Then the man said, "Are you Kay Conklin?" Well, that got my attention, so I said, "Yes." The next sentence came as quite a shock. He said, "This is the Clark County Coroner's office." If he said anymore at that moment, I don't remember, because I immediately knew there was no reason the Clark County Coroner's office should be calling my house. I knew exactly where both my daughters and husband were at that moment, so it had to be the wrong number.

Then the man said, "We are trying to find the phone number of the mother of Richard Conklin." I was still positive that he had the wrong number, because at that moment, I didn't think I knew any Richard Conklin.

Then the man said, "There has been a traffic accident. We need to notify the victim's mother." Now, it was an even stronger feeling that I hoped he had the wrong number, because he just used the words "accident and victim."

Then the man said something about a motorcycle. Other words were said, but the only one that registered was the word, "motorcycle." Then I finally realized that he could be talking about our nephew, Rick, because he rides a motorcycle. In fact, he has a shop and repairs them as a business.

I think the man again said, "I am calling to find Richard Conklin's mother's phone number." At that moment, I said, "You have to leave your number and I will find out what it is, and call you right back." With that, I hung up and tried to put the pieces together. I know that coroners notify families in case of a death. And he needed to find the phone number for the mother of a guy named Richard.

And, it could be Rick because he was always a single guy, meaning his next of kin would be his mother. Rick's dad had died when Rick was a child. Noting the time, I realized that Rick may have been on his motorcycle going home for supper.

Other phone calls were made, and soon the Clark County Coroner's office was given the phone number of Rick's mom, who was living out of state. The calm, peaceful life that we have been living before the phone call, was over. Richard, always known as Rick, was our nephew, and had been a part of our lives for all the 37 years he had lived. Next came trips to the funeral home in Springfield. There were calling hours that lasted for hours.

Then, after the funeral the next day, there was a procession up and down the streets of Springfield that consisted of many biker friends leading the way for the rest of us friends and family.

By that fall, there was a case in the courts concerning the drunk driver. We had to go to the Clark County Courthouse where the case was filed. The report was that he had been struck by a drunk driver and had died at the scene. Would the driver have to go to prison?

Wasn't the law such that if you were drinking and driving, and caused the death of someone, it was mandatory that you go to prison for eight years? In Rick's case, the drunk driver was a frail, 79-year-old gentleman, who had been to an anniversary party that afternoon and had a couple too many drinks.

The judge was told by members of Rick's family, that they felt that Rick would not have wanted the driver to have to serve eight years in prison. The driver was given five-years' probation. This also meant house arrest for 90 days, a lifetime loss of his driver's license, paying restitution, as well as his own lawyer fees. But, no prison time.

The driver was driving directly into the bright late afternoon sun on a two-lane highway, as he headed west. Rick was coming from the west in the other lane. At the corner, as the driver was turning left onto a side road, Rick was on his motorcycle at the same spot on the highway. Rick was hit and died at the scene. It was a very sad situation all around for everyone involved.

And every so often, still, when I go to answer the phone, I am reminded about what happened to our nephew, Rick.

The Trials of
Being in Court

T his article covers my being on jury duty, as well as also being a defendant in a civil suit, observing in traffic court, and being a witness for a woman in a case that never should have gone to court. The lesson I learned in each, is that being involved in a real court case is nothing like what you see on TV.

Only once did I ever have to serve on jury duty. Serving on a jury, years ago, was an event I have never forgotten. My experience had to do with a young man who was on trial for selling drugs.

I was asked a lot of questions by the court before I was chosen to be on the jury. During the trial, a lot of defense witnesses seemed to be friends of the defendant, who testified that he wouldn't have sold anyone any drugs at all. At the end of all the testimony, we were given some instructions and sent to the jury room to vote on whether we thought he was innocent or guilty as charged.

As soon as we walked in the jury room, immediately one of the jurors very loudly said, "We all know he is guilty, so let's vote that way and get outta here." Wow, that was a shock.

Thank goodness there was someone in the room who finally said, "Wait a minute! I have to sleep nights and I need to be sure he is guilty before I vote that way."

A lot of us were relieved at that moment, and so the process began. We were so split in our decisions, that we had to ask the judge to answer some questions pertaining to the findings. It's not easy to remember all the ins and outs of the discussion, so I will just move on to the fact that we ended up with him being found guilty.

It was then that we learned the guilty verdict would mean spending time in prison. With the law written as it was, that's the way it had to go. I cannot describe it any better, than to say I was so upset over the whole experience, I didn't want anyone on the witness stand to ever recognize me anywhere. So, the very next day, I got my hair cut off very short.

I have also been in a situation when a jury was to decide something that was a part of my life. The point that I want to make is that when I took the stand to testify, the attorney for the plaintiff wanted to make me look bad in the eyes of the jurors.

So, the attorney tried to make a big deal out of the fact that I didn't know the difference between a combine and a hay baler. Or was it a corn picker? Well, I didn't know either one, but who cares? I'm not a farmer. That having failed, he tried to make it look like I didn't own my own home.

He said that I lived in some apartment somewhere. And I told him that I did not live in any apartment, I owned my own house. Then he said that there were no record of my owning any property, thus meaning I was wrong.

That's when I explained to the jury that I bought my house before I got married, so it was purchased in my maiden name, so it wasn't in the name I had then.

He still didn't want to be wrong, so he started asking other questions as to how much my mortgage payments were. Having a mortgage was just more proof that I really did own my house. So, the case proceeded from there. I had the whole experience of waiting the time that it took the jury to deliberate and have them come back in the courtroom and hand the judge their verdict.

We won the case, so it all turned out well. Of course, we had a wonderful lawyer at that time and I have always said she deserved a star. After that situation in court, I had a survivorship deed made out so as to have our property in both our names, and that included my name being changed to my married name that I have now.

While in high school, our Problems of Democracy class had to spend a couple hours at City Hall, where the municipal court used to be, while persons who got traffic tickets came in to plead their case.

One case I have never forgotten was when the judge yelled as he bawled out a woman for running a red light. I sat there listening and was scared to pieces and right then I knew I would never speed anywhere at any time.

And that "scared straight" experience worked, because I have never gotten a traffic ticket. It took me a long time to get over the fear I had of that judge. Years later, I got to know him and found that he was a very nice person, but I never forgot how afraid I was of him while I was still in high school.

Once, I was asked to be a character witness in another court case of a woman I had known for several years It was a minor case and should have never gone to court in the first place. Also, in that case, the prosecutor tried to make me look bad so as to discredit anything I've said in favor of the defendant. Thank goodness, the defense was found not guilty, so all turned out well.

You never know when you may have to appear in court. But if you do, may you have good representation, be able to speak in your own defense, and with jury duty, know you are doing your civic duty.

Courthouses Old and
New in Delaware County

---

66 "New courthouse now open" was the November 7, 2017-headline in the Delaware Gazette. To my knowledge, talking about a new courthouse for Delaware County started back as early as the year 2000. Office holders got serious about the need to have a whole new courthouse, because of the enormous growth spurt going on in the county. I remember the forming of the "2020 Committee." Back then, they projected that by the year 2020 it would be necessary to have a much larger courthouse with an additional judge or two.

I see the cost of the new one was $39.2 million. In the first discussions of the costs, it was to have been $50 million. In the year 2000, that was an unheard of amount of money to spend, especially since the new Rutherford B Hayes building was just being built. It's good to see that the new courthouse was built for around $10 million less!

In August 1954, I walked in the front door of the old courthouse for the first time. I had just been hired as a new, additional employee in the recorder's office. Back then, almost every county office was housed in that one building. The recorder's office, along with the treasurers, the auditors, the probate court, the clerk of courts, and the common police court, were all housed on the first two floors. That's when there were windows that opened in every office. These tall windows had screens to put in, to allow for fresh air to come through.

They needed the fresh air because there were a lot of people smoking in the courthouse then. Almost every desk and countertop had space for ashtrays for the convenience of smokers. The recorder at that time smoked a cigar all day, every day.

There were also windows in the basement offices that housed the Board of Education, the Board of Elections, the engineer's office, and the commissioners, who had one room down there where they met every Monday. You could always tell which one belonged to the commissioners, because there was always a spittoon sitting outside their hall door.

The old courthouse never had a parking garage, nor did they have any handicap or limited parking. The only reserved spot was beside the back door. It was for the recorder at that time, who had polio and was confined to a wheelchair. There wasn't an elevator in the building until he was elected and one had to be built.

That is also when anyone who wanted to come inside, could walk right up the front steps and right in the front door. The permanent locking of the front door of the old courthouse became necessary. The last day it was open, Ed Flahive and his wife, Jean, came into my office and said that they wanted to be the last ones to go out through the door. So, at 4:30, they left the building, and it was forever locked behind them.

The decision to lock the front door was because of an increase in domestic violence cases that were being heard in the courtroom up on the 2nd floor. And county employees and the public had to be protected from the persons who may have wanted to bring a gun or knife into the courtroom. From then on, everyone had to walk around the courthouse to the back door and go through a metal detector that was installed at the basement level.

A lot of changes have taken place in the area just north of the corner of Central Avenue and North Sandusky Street. It's good to know that the old courthouse will stand, and be housed by offices. A lot of homes had to be torn down on Franklin, Union and Sandusky streets. The first houses torn down were facing North Franklin Street. This made room for a parking lot for the old courthouse.

That was followed by the homes that were replaced by the Hayes building. These were homes facing both Sandusky and on both sides of Union Street. Then came the Elks and the Leffler house being torn down to make room for this new courthouse. Just last week, the offices of the Probation Department moved out of the double house on Court Street, and also out of the smaller house on Sandusky Street. They are now, also housed in the new courthouse. The parking garage that is built into the new courthouse will be used only by the employees of said building.

As I write this, I am reminded of my first day working in the old courthouse. I was only 17 years old, and fortunate to get to go to work in the Recorder's office as a deputy recorder for 12 years, which eventually led to my being elected to be the recorder in 1989. If my memory serves me correctly, on my first day employed by the county, Major Sampson was the auditor, Claude Williamson was the treasurer, Judge Barrett was the probate judge, Mr. Elliott was the engineer, Don James was recorder, Judge Whitney (not Duncan) was the common pleas judge, and the clerk of courts was soon to be Ruth Scott. The sheriff was Harley Wornstaff with both his home and his office being behind the courthouse in the old jail. I am also aware, and sorry to say, I believe I may be the only person still living who was working that day in the old courthouse in 1954.

My Pen Pal,
the Duffy Girl

A new experience in my life started one evening when I was at our library and noticed a very small slip of paper taped to the check-out desk. It wasn't much larger than a post-it note.

It was asking for anyone who would like to be a pen pal to 5th graders, to please sign up. I thought it would be an enjoyable thing to do since I had just retired. I called the number listed on the paper and before I knew it, I received the letter from my very first pen pal. We gave her the nickname of the "Duffy girl."

We were not allowed to know their last name or address and they weren't allowed to know ours either. The pen pal letters were sent back and forth by way of the volunteers at the Senior Citizens Center, who read every one of them to see that they met all the requirements. When you sign up, you have to promise that you will attend the orientation as well as a party at the end of the school year. That is when you finally meet your pen pal in person. I signed up for the whole experience and enjoyed every part of it.

I always looked forward to reading the letters from my pen pal. They were written on real stationary, and she had decorated the pages with pictures and stickers. This pen pal letter-writing situation lasted from February to May of her 5th grade.

Then, in May, all participants were to meet at the Buckeye Valley West school cafeteria. When I arrived at the cafeteria that day, it was filled with both men and women senior citizens, who were as excited to be there as I was. We were about to meet our special pen pal. One lady said it was like adopting a child from another country and waiting to see them come off a plane for the first time. The students were brought in the cafeteria by their teacher, and all stood in a line across the front of the room.

They sang several songs while we looked them over, trying to guess which one would claim us as their pen pal. The teacher, Mrs. Rose, called off their names one at a time. Mine was one of the very last. When her name was called, I stood up so she could find me in the crowd. And there she was, a very pretty girl with a big smile and green fingernails.

Since we already knew so much about each other, it was easy to break the ice. Each pal had four things to do. They took us on a tour of their school, read us a story they had chosen, played a game and had refreshments. And we all came together again for a group picture before the bus came to take them home.

I was very impressed at how pleasant it was to be a part of the tour and get to see all the amazingly good artwork on the walls. She read a story to me that was called, "Mrs. Bindergarten goes to Kindergarten." She read so well, I thought she would make a great elementary school teacher someday. We played checkers, using Hershey kisses for the checkers.

Before I knew it, it was time for refreshments in the cafeteria, and have a group picture taken. Just as the picture was snapped, the buses were outside to take the students home. The event was over. As I watched her go, I was wondering if I would ever hear from her again.

The only way I would know is if I received the real letter that she had written and sent to me that had her full name and address on it. That meant her parents had given her their permission for us to continue to be pen pals. I didn't have to wait long, because that next week when George brought in the mail, he said, "You have a letter from the Duffy girl." And I opened it and read it out loud before I even finished my lunch.

We wrote lots of letters back and forth. In our letters, we made plans for George and me to go to a couple of her softball games to see her pitch, and then for her parents to bring her out to the farm, so she could ride a horse. While there, we cut up a cold watermelon. Her dad said, "There is nothing better than getting to be outside in perfect weather eating watermelon while standing around in a horse barn."

Since they liked horses so well, they rode on our wagon for the All-Horse Parade that following September. I think her dad even drove the team of Percherons. And I noticed that no one had more fun than her parents had because they knew more people on the parade route than we did.

It was such a wonderful experience for me to be a pen pal, I signed up for six more pen pals in the years that followed. I didn't see the Duffy girl again until a couple of years later when I attended a band concert at the high school and she came out the door at the same time we did. And there she was, all grown up, wearing high heels and all. I think she might be graduating this year.

I'm wondering if she will choose to be an elementary school teacher. Or, had she said something about wanting to join the FBI? But this I know for sure, whatever she chooses to do in life, she will be right up there with the best of them. And I will always remember her as being my first pen pal, and that we will always refer to her as the Duffy girl.

Happens Only
in a Small Town

"Only in a small town" is a phrase I have found myself using often in the years I have lived in Ashley, Ohio. It all started years ago when I was listening to the car radio on my way home from work. The song being played was a very beautiful piece of Christmas music.

I wanted to find out who was performing, so I sat in my car and listened until the song ended. It was just 5 p.m. when the announcer said it was the "Trans-Siberian Orchestra" and the title had the word canon in it. Since it wasn't totally dark yet, I decided to walk over to the library and ask if anyone there had ever heard of it. Luckily, one of the librarians said she had it on a CD at her house. And, if I wanted to walk home with her right then, she would loan it to me.

So, no sooner had she said those words, we were on our way to her house to get it. I was back home by 6 p.m. and was listening to it again. So, in just one hour's time, I had heard it, found someone who had it, borrowed it, and was playing it in my own home. That's when I said to myself, "Only in a small town."

Another time when I was used that phrase is when I was talking to a friend who lived around the corner. She was thinking of selling her house. We ended up discussing the good points of living in a small town. Her house was just down the driveway from the elementary school.

She had enjoyed having her children get to walk to school during their elementary years. Since the levy recently passed (by two votes), there will be a new elementary school there by 2018. Then, we got talking about other conveniences in a small town.

For instance, there is a swimming pool, tennis courts and a shelter house within walking distance. Add to that, we have a wonderful public library within two blocks of both our homes.

Later, I started thinking of other places I could walk to from my house. On my daily walks, I pass the post office, two pizza places, three churches and my sister's house. And we have a Dollar General which has come in handy for a lot of necessary items while running a household.

If we need a tire fixed, or a motorcycle tuned up, you can leave them at either of the shops and walk back home. We are pleased to have our own EMS station at the western edge of the village. And I don't want to forget the playground at the school that also has a softball diamond for summer league games.

My favorite thing to do when I am out walking on a bitter cold windy day, is to stop in at the laundromat. For a quarter, I can put my coat, scarf and gloves in one of the dryers. I do that to warm them up so they will warm me up for the last part of my walk back home.

If you have cause to want to talk to our mayor, his office is just around the corner of that same block. While there, you might run into our village policeman who's on duty. And by the 15th of each month, you can walk there to pay your water bill. And, we have a new fire station located at the northern edge of our town.

When I see the long rows and rows of houses in some subdivisions, I wonder how kids can go anywhere without being driven in a car. Or, with all the condos that look just alike, how would they be able to find a friend's house if they aren't positive of the house number? And it's very convenient to have a store within walking distance when you need a quart of milk, or a loaf of bread.

One of the subdivisions in Delaware, up near the fairgrounds, is a 10-acre piece of land that years ago was subdivided into 44 building lots. That

10 acres includes all the streets, as well.

Another place that is within walking distance of my home is the Villa. It is a government-subsidized apartment complex for senior citizens. At the moment, plans are being made to build new apartments on that same land. There are times a visiting nurse comes to check residents blood pressure as well as offering flu shots. We also have a newly opened restaurant in town, as well as a drive-through, and a place to get ice cream cones on hot summer days.

A couple of Easters ago, when I walked past our church, I saw an artificial bunny rabbit sitting in front of the door. He looked familiar because I had seen lots of them placed all around our library. So, I stopped at the library and told the librarian that one of her bunnies got loose and was down sitting on the front step of the church, if she wanted to rescue him.

That's just another example of things that can happen in a small town.

The Magic of Christmas Never Ends

———

66 **T**he magic of Christmas never ends and its greatest gift is family and friends."

This sentence was on a Christmas card, and it pulls together our thoughts about the holiday that is coming back into our lives in just a matter of days now. To put it another way, I read this first somewhere, too: "Christmas is special. It's filled with good cheer. That's why its memories last year after year."

The good memories we have about Christmases do last year after year after year. Sometimes when you are experiencing an event, it becomes more meaningful as time passes. Usually you are not aware when you are doing something that it will become a special memory later on. In other words, you just never know when you're making a memory.

Who knew that when my mom turned on the Christmas lights of our Christmas tree when I was in the second grade, that the memory of seeing that tree light up, would still hold a spot somewhere deep inside my brain these many years later? Think about some of your Christmas memories. Do Christmas songs play a part in your wonderful memories? Soon after our church choir sang "Mary did you know?," written by Mark Lowry, it went on to become one of the best new Christmas songs.

I'm sure you are aware that a lot of our favorite Christmas songs have been around since before color TV. I was told about a young man named Tim, with early onset Alzheimer's, being taken to church and was able to recite every word of every prayer that he had ever recited earlier in his life.

Or, another man who knew every word of the songs he had sung before Alzheimer's set in.

Doctor Douglas Scharre of the OSU Medical Center published this statement in the "Columbus Monthly" in 2010: "Music is linked to old memories, which are stored multiple times deep in the brain, in parts not affected by the Alzheimer's. Familiar music brings joy and tranquility."

While we are on the topic of music at church, we should all let the organists/pianists know how much we appreciate all the practicing they do to prepare the beautiful music that we take for granted while sitting and enjoying the wonderful familiar music that makes Christmas feel so good.

Attending Christmas Eve services is a special time for everyone. Especially when many churches have everyone holding lighted candles during the singing of the closing hymn, "Silent Night." If you haven't attended such a service lately, plan on attending this year.

The anticipation is the best part of celebration. Whether all the things you hope for, come true or not, it's fun to think about. While growing up in a house with six siblings there was always a lot of gifts under the tree. Most gifts were inexpensive things we bought, or something we made. In our younger years, we each bought one thing for each of the other members of our family. I don't remember anything I ever received, but what I still treasure are the moments while we were all together opening them. A wonderful quote I read in the "Real Simple" magazine last year was about a group of professional people who had asked some 4-to-8-year olds, what does the word love mean? One of the boys replied: "Love is what's in the room with you at Christmas, if you stop opening presents and listen."

In the few days remaining before Christmas Eve and Christmas Day, there will be a lot of rushing around going on. Before I get busy, I want to add another few words that I read in an old Charlie Brown comic strip. It was a picture of the characters standing outside around a decorated tree. And one of them said, "It's not what's under the Christmas tree that matters it's who's around it." So, let's all take a lesson from Charlie Brown and be thankful for the people in our lives who are family and friends who are going to be around us this Christmas.

Merry Christmas! Enjoy the magic of Christmas that never ends.

Mystery That Seems
Impossible to Solve

It all happened this first week in January, when I just finished supper dishes and walked into the living room. As soon as I got past the doorway, I noticed a picture on the shelf by George's chair. I thought it was just a picture in a folded-up newspaper. Immediately I said, "George, the guy in that picture looks like your brother, Jerry."

And by then, I was close enough to pick it up. It wasn't a newspaper, it was just a picture of his brother, Jerry. Neither of us knew how it could have gotten there. It was one of those small 2-by-3 inch, black and white, individually posed school pictures. It had the words, "School Days 57-58" on it. It had been taken when he was a freshman in high school at Elm Valley (now known as Buckeye Valley).

If you ever had seen him then, you would have noticed that one of his eyes was different from the other. That's because not long before that picture was taken, he had lost his right eye. It happened when he had been making some Christmas decorations in their basement. He found a can of artificial snow, but he couldn't get it to spray. So, he put it next to the big old coal furnace, thinking it would work if he warmed it up. However, when he picked up the can, it was too hot to hold, so he dropped it. When it hit the floor, it exploded and came back up and hit him in the face. This terrible accident caused him to lose his right eye.

How could it have happened that this old picture appeared on the shelf by George's chair, without us knowing it? But, there it was, in complete sight!

After we kept saying the same thing over and over, we realized that we had a mystery on our hands. Because of the bitter cold, snow, and ice, I haven't left the house, nor had anyone else come in the house, for several days. When we ask our daughter about it, she had no idea how it could have gotten in our house, either.

You already know from the title of this article that we still haven't solved the mystery as to how it got there. After writing the above paragraphs, I got the idea I should look through my old photo albums to see if we have one exactly like it. And sure enough, I found another one just like the one that appeared on the shelf. But, the one we found on the shelf, has "Jerry Conklin, 9th, Elm Valley" written in his own handwriting on the back. However, the one I found in an old album has nothing at all written on the back. The plot thickens!

Jerry didn't have an easy life. As a preschooler, he was severely electrocuted when he touched a live electric line that had been knocked down. Then as a freshman in high school, he lost his right eye. And then in 1975, when he was only 33 years old, he died of cancer. That was when the cancer research was trying to see if cancer cells would die if they were exposed to the outside air. Therefore, while he was a patient at a Columbus hospital, they tested it out on him by opening wounds on the upper part of his arm. That procedure caused him more pain and suffering, but didn't cure anything!

Jerry was married and had a son, Rick, and a daughter, Connie. (Rick was our nephew who was killed in the motorcycle accident I've written about in a previous article.) Jerry always played Santa Claus for the village, and was a member of the Masons and Eastern Stars. He was also a volunteer fireman, and was the youngest of George's three brothers.

Often, when anyone first saw his artificial eye, they would say, "It looks good!" Then he would say to them, "It doesn't look at all." He was a sweetheart.

Over the years we've all had things disappear from our homes. If they are never found, we can just chalk it up to the fact that they must have been accidentally thrown out with the trash. However, when something appears in our homes, without knowing where it came from, or how it got here, that's another story.

What Was School like 60 Years Ago at Elm Valley?

When our phone rang right after lunch, it was the lady from Buckeye Valley East Elementary school, who had asked George to come to speak to the third graders. We thought it was tomorrow. Turns out it is today, and it was time for him to be there. So, we grabbed our coats and jumped in the car to drive the one block to the school and ran to the office. We got passes, and the secretary led us up to the third floor where all the third graders were waiting.

When we stepped inside, we saw about 70 students sitting on the floor and wondering what was going to happen next. The reason George was there was to tell about some of the memories of what his school was like when he was a student there, back in the 50s. The teachers wanted their students to have some idea of what the differences were in the past 60 years of the school, because it is about to be torn down.

George started out telling the students how the school was run when he had gone there from 1953 to 1957 in grades 9 through 12. He graduated from there 60 years ago. It was called Elm Valley back then.

The entire top floor of the building was the high school, with the lower floors for grades K through 8. The cafeteria was in another building, which is gone now. The gym had chairs instead of bleachers. They had both boys' and girls' locker rooms. The boys' locker room was where the high school ballplayers dressed for their football and basketball games. The girls' locker room was for the visiting team to use.

Only the boys played sports. There were no girls' sports, except for getting to play volleyball in gym class. A lot of banquets were held in the gym. Sports banquets, Future Farmers of America banquets, and lamb banquets, to name a few. The gym was used for dances following special home games. Once a year, they had a "Sadie Hawkins" dance. That's when the girls asked the boys to go to the dance. The gym was also used for the high school graduation ceremonies. Sometimes the boys had basketball practice in the little gym, that is now the cafeteria. Once a high school football game was played in six inches of snow. They couldn't tell where the lines were, but they played anyway.

They had FFA classes for boys and home economics classes for the girls. The whole school always knew when the girls were baking cookies. He also told the students that when he was in the 3rd grade, he had attended a one-room schoolhouse.

After that much history was given, the students got to ask questions, and there was never a time some of the students didn't have their hands in the air.

Three different students asked George if he knew certain people they named. And when George knew all of them, each one very proudly said, "He's my grandpa!" The names mentioned were Dart, Lavender and Crist. One student remembered lamb banquets being mentioned and wanted to know if they really ate lamb. From the response, I don't think any of the students like the idea of eating lamb.

They asked about the showers in the locker room, and he said it consisted of just four shower heads. And then a boy asked if the showers had curtains. When George said they didn't, the students seemed to be a little embarrassed by that answer.

Another boy asked him what he did for fun when he was a kid. He said that since he had always lived on a farm and had three brothers, they played basketball in the haymow, as well as baseball out in the fields. Then he told how much fun it was when the FFA had a pest hunt each year.

Elm Valley was in competition with other high schools as to which one could kill the most pests. Mice, rats, and unwanted birds come under the heading of pests. Since it was a competition, they cut the tails off the dead mice and rats and took them to school to be counted. The school with the most tails of dead pests won. With that discussion, the students all looked quite surprised as well as a little puzzled.

One student asked if he had a telephone. He said they were lucky if they had a wall phone, and he demonstrated what a wall phone was like. Also, they did not have a TV yet when he was in the third grade. And when asked if they had electricity, he explained that his home did, but not every kid was that lucky.

When they asked about having buses, he said he rode a school bus every day during his years in school. When asked how he sharpened his pencils, he looked around the room and when he found a regular pencil sharpener on the wall, he pointed out that he sharpened his pencils just like they still do today. Maybe they thought he had to sharpen them with a knife.

They were interested if his one-room schoolhouse had restrooms. He told them they had outhouses. One boy asked if they were like a Port-a-Potty. He explained that they were separate wooden structures, and you didn't want to have to stay out there very long, especially in the winter.

By then, George realized that time was running out, so he said that from then on, he would only take questions from ones who had not been called on. At that time, one of the boys asked what happened if a kid misbehaved. George said they would get paddled by the teacher of the class. And, he added that not only did they get paddled, but when they were in high school, they had to go to the school shop to get a board and make their own paddle to be used. And when being paddled, they had to lean over a table and get three whacks. I saw lots of unhappy looks after they heard that. Then he added that the girls always seemed to be well behaved, and he didn't know of any girl ever getting paddled. The girls looked a little happier after that statement. Just as time was running out, George was asked how old he was. He told them he will be 80 next month. That's when I heard the word "old" being passed around.

All too soon, time was up and the class all cheered. We laughed all the way home about how fun it was to spend an hour of our lives in the school down the street with 70 wonderful third graders. And we want to thank the teacher, Robin Clay, for asking George to come over to speak at Buckeye Valley East before it's torn down. For my husband, George, it's still his old Elm Valley High School, which is filled with his good memories of the 1950s where he spent his high school years. And, just so you know, no, he never got paddled.

Coming up with Ideas to
Write About Can Be Difficult

T he split second I hit the "send" key to send my article to the
Delaware Gazette, it's gone! Then comes the realization that I am
in the position of starting all over again to write another article.
That's when I wonder if there really is another subject I could write about
that would be considered decent for publication. Once I thought about
using the title of "Persons, Places or Things."

I've already written about the person, Dr. Judith Held, who kept
after the symptoms of my pain until she got me to the right place and
probably saved my life. I've also written about the place called the Brown
Jug Restaurant and everyone who used to eat there and who I still miss.
And, I have written about the thing that was our cabin that George built
in the woods. And, just this second, I realized that they are all gone! The
Brown Jug building still sits empty, Dr. Held is retired, and the cabin was
completely destroyed by intruders and animals.

The most recent thought I had has to do with seeing two containers
of pepper, sitting close to each other on my kitchen counter. One pepper
container was recently purchased. It was sitting close to the previous one
I had purchased at least eight months ago. I noticed that the top of the
lid of the newer one came right to the bottom of the lid of the older one.
Separated, they look like the very same size. But, I see that the newer
can has three ounces, while the older can had four ounces. What I was
wondering was if I had paid the same price for each of them. I don't
have the receipt for the older one, so I don't know. I would never have

noticed that one was smaller than the other had they not been sitting side by side.

I would like to also mention something about our boxes of green decaffeinated tea. The box used to be packed very tightly with tea bags. But, the latest boxes I have been buying have about a fourth less bags in the same size box. Am I still paying the same price as I was when I was getting a fourth more tea bags?

These two situations remind me of a couple of old "Andy Rooney" shows that were on CBS at the end of "60 Minutes" every Sunday evening. Once he held up a roll of toilet paper and showed that the number of sections in the newly purchased one was a lot less than the previous one he had purchased. And each was the same price. In a later program, he pointed out that he found that a pound of coffee is no longer a whole pound. The newer can was a little smaller. I am assuming that this is being done to keep the price down, but you are getting less for what you buy at that price.

This is probably happening a lot and I need to pay more attention. I should also include the price of different sizes of bags of potatoes. Whether you buy five pounds or eight pounds, they are the exact same price. I used to think that it was better to take the eight-pound bag, but after several times of doing so, I noticed that the ones at the bottom of the bigger bag were spoiled. Am I not using them up fast enough, or is it the smaller bag full of newer potatoes? I'm not sure which, but from now on, I think I will settle for the five-pound bags.

Just one more thing I would like to mention that I have been noticing lately. I see that the slices of bread are getting smaller. The sandwiches you order in a restaurant look the same, but with smaller slices, so you get a smaller sandwich for the same price as when we had larger slices of bread. But, to shine a positive light here, when you buy a dozen eggs there are still 12 eggs in the container, and when you buy a gallon of milk, it still shows it's a whole gallon.

All of the above ramblings have occurred to me while trying to think of something to write about for my next article.

Another subject I could write about just occurred to me. About 30 years ago, I got the chance to ask a published author of children's literature how she went about writing all her books. We met up at my husband's high school class reunion. I have never forgotten what she told me. She said that first, you start by writing everything you can think of pertaining to your subject, on pieces of paper. Then, when you read it over, you know you need to tear up at least half of it, or even more. Then, keeping your good part, you get more pieces of paper, write out more of your subject, read that over, and end up tearing up some of what is on those pieces of paper, also. And on and on that way until you are totally satisfied with everything you have left. Thus, you have your own book! I have never forgotten those instructions and have incorporated them into my method of writing.

For myself, writing is like a big puzzle. First, I throw all my words on the computer screen that pertain to the topic I have chosen. Then I start taking out unnecessary sentences, rearranging what is left, and fixing mistakes. I keep doing that until I have all the good parts in the right places where they belong. Then, when I proof it for the last time, and I feel good about all the parts, I know I have finished my article.

Hopefully, one of these days soon, I will come up with a topic that would be good enough for my next article. I hope so, anyway.

Our Dads Were Brothers,
I'm Glad to Have Known Him

If your parents had siblings and the siblings had children, you are fortunate to have cousins in your life. One of my cousins was Doyt Grandstaff. Since our dads were brothers, and they had two other brothers, all four families got together at least once a year for Thanksgiving at each other's homes. The earliest Thanksgiving I can remember having with Doyt was when we got to sit on the stair steps to eat our meal. That's because, with so many people, there weren't enough chairs. But, our cousin, Doyt, wasn't sitting on the stairs, he was in a wheelchair. Over the years that followed, I learned a lot about him, and I admired him greatly.

When Doyt was in high school, he played football, basketball, and ran track. But that all ended when he had a terrible accident that caused him to be paralyzed from his neck down. It happened on the last day of summer vacation after football practice was over, and he and some other guys on the team had gone to the Glengary pool in Westerville for a swim. He had just pushed off from the side of the pool into the water and ended up severely damaging his spinal cord. This happened on August 31, 1943. He wasn't expected to live more than two months, but he lived for 46 more years. This all happened long before there were any of the handicapped facilities we have now. At that time, there were no large rehab centers to take care of persons in his conditions, except in California and New York City. But, there was a place in Cincinnati that oversaw his care while his devoted mother took care of him.

Two years after the accident, Doyt was able to graduate from high school. Because he was a country boy at heart, he then took some agricultural correspondence studies through Ohio University. He learned about soil improvement conservation. He ended up purchasing three different neglected farms, improving each one, and selling them at a profit. Later, because he enjoyed teaching a Bible class for adults in his church, he chose to pursue a teaching career. He entered Otterbein College and began the long process of taking enough classes to be certified to teach learning disabled children. During that time is when he was listed in "Who's Who in American Colleges and Universities." One memory of mine is from his very first day as a student at Otterbein. When the person who was helping him go down the steps in his wheelchair lost control of it, down they went, wheelchair and all.

Eventually, he was certified to teach elementary children who had learning disabilities. An article I kept from an old Columbus newspaper shows him with a child sitting in his chair with him as he was taking her down the hall to tutor her in his little office. He once told me that he always tried to teach a lesson that hadn't come up yet in the regular classroom, so that when it did come up, the child would already know something about it and would do well. In fact, Doyt was chosen to receive the honor of being "Teacher of the Year" for several times during his years in Westerville elementary schools. He was much loved by the students and the faculty.

Shortly after starting his teaching career, he married Charlotte, who was the youth director of Minerva Park Church of Christ. This was where he also served as an elder and a youth sponsor. I always thought that since his wife, Charlotte, was a registered nurse, she must have met him while he was in the hospital and was swept off her feet when she saw him. I also thought his voice was just like the actor Henry Fonda's. But I was wrong about how they met. Charlotte told me they had met at church and were good friends for 12 years before their marriage.

Having a wonderful voice, he did a lot of speaking in churches. Once I heard him speak at the Church of Christ in Croton, Ohio. He talked about eternity. He gave an example of how long eternity would be. He said that if you pick up one grain of sand from the beach on the ocean, take it with you and cross the ocean, and deposit it on the beach on the other side, and then come back and get another grain of sand, and take it to the other side of the ocean, and keep that up until you add every grain of sand from this side of the ocean on the other, that would give you an idea of how long eternity would be.

While I was working in the education department at Ohio Wesleyan University, Doyt came there to speak to the education majors. It was videotaped by the department. Years later, I remembered about that tape and asked the department if I could copy it as a gift for Charlotte. But, sorry to say, it wasn't to be found. It would have been priceless, because there he sat, a certified teacher who was a quadriplegic, speaking to the future teachers who would be teaching students with similar handicaps, as well as those with learning disabilities. When they left that afternoon to go to their handicapped parking place, they found a parking ticket on the windshield of the van. He was ticketed in spite of the fact that his van had the usual handicapped license plates, as well as being evident that it had a chairlift. His wife brought the ticket back to my office, and I saw that it got to the right department.

Just six months before time for his retirement from teaching, as he was getting ready for school one morning, he told Charlotte about feeling pain in his jaw. Then he asked, "What does it feel like to have a heart attack?" Those were his last words. The EM S took him to the hospital, and he was put on a ventilator, but, in spite of that, he died just 12 hours later. It is now been almost 30 years since his death, but anyone who knew him will always remember the impact he had on their lives and the lives of their students.

Chance Meeting Leads to Interesting Story

Y ou never know who you may meet when you are walking down Sandusky Street in Delaware, Ohio.

My story begins when I often saw the same older gentleman walking north on Sandusky Street while I was walking south. This was back in the day when I was still working and was going downtown for lunch. He looked a little familiar, but I could not ever place him. We always spoke in passing. Then one summer day, before I retired, we each ended up waiting for the traffic light to change on the corner of William and Sandusky. It just stayed on red while the cars kept zooming past us. After standing there much longer than usual, I said to him, "I don't think this light is ever going to change!" He agreed, and then I decided to ask him something I had been wondering about: "Are you one of the art professors from Ohio Wesleyan that I never met when I was working there?" And his answer came right back, "No, but I am one of the art professors from Ohio State that you never met."

What did he say? Did I hear right? Is he really an art professor? Just that very second the light changed, and we walked into the busy street and parted ways. As time went on and we ran into each other again, he assured me that before his retirement he really had been an art professor at Ohio State.

Now, I have to insert a few sentences to make the story make sense. Every so often, The Gazette used to publish a whole page of poems. I think it was called, "The Poets' Corner."

It was my favorite page to read. I especially liked the poems of Ruth King. Once, I even wrote her a fan letter. With no address given, I sent it to The Gazette and they got it to her.

Now, back to the art professor. By the fourth or fifth time of passing on Sandusky Street, he told me his name was Bob King. By coincidence, one evening as I was walking in the front door of Grady Hospital and there he was, walking out the same door. He stopped me and said that he had just come from visiting his wife, who was up on the second floor. And, he called her Ruth.

Putting two and two together, I asked, "Is Ruth King, the woman who writes poetry, your wife?" He said that she was, and that she had always been happy that I had sent her that fan letter.

Really? He asked me to go up and meet her, so I did. A nurse showed me her room and when I told her my name, she insisted that I recite my favorite one of her poems for the nurse.

Wow, that caught me off guard. Luckily, I had memorized one, and I will insert it here.

"Pessimist and optimist seemed to be two different breeds of man.
Pessimists say, it can't get worse.
Optimists say, of course it can!"

Ruth King told me her story of how she became interested in poetry. In a class she had taken, the professor always gave the students a topic to write a poem about. One was to be about "The Willies." She asked if I knew what the willies meant? I said it was slang for something that had to do with feeling nervous about something. But she chose her own meaning and wrote about two guys whose first names were each Willie, and they were trapeze artists. Good idea.

She also told me that her husband, Bob, paints a picture for her every morning and has it at her place at the breakfast table when she gets up. Because Bob was so pleased that I had sent a fan letter to Ruth, and that I had gone to see her in the hospital, he gave me a set of four of his bird paintings. Each was different and very lovely. I framed them and kept them on my shelf in my office.

It wasn't long before I read that Bob King had died. I went to his funeral and got to talk with Ruth again. It was at the Liberty Presbyterian Church in the original smaller white frame building, not in the new one that looks like a barn. I certainly enjoyed meeting such an interesting couple. They had spent their later years still writing poems and painting pictures.

I think about the fact that I never would have met them had I not been in the right place, at the right time, and that traffic light on Sandusky Street had stayed stuck on red so very long ago.

Bird Nest Provides Opportunity to See Nature at Work

The first day I realized that something was going on outside our upstairs bathroom window, I never dreamt of the experience I was in for.

We found a bird's nest being built onto the outside of the screening on the window. Robins had built a decent-sized nest on the very edge of the ledge. How the nest was attached took some study. It must be a type of spit glue Mother Nature has provided to make it possible to attach the whole nest to such a small part of the screening.

We can look down into the nest, which is just a few inches from the inside of the window. Days went by and they kept working on it frantically. Being the outdoors person that my husband is, he assured me that the nest was attached well enough to survive the spot they had chosen. When the weather got warmer, I took out the window so as to be able to see the nest a lot better. But, when George got home, he put it back in, so as not to affect the life that was about to take place in that nest. He told me that soon, the mother robin will be laying her eggs, and we will get to see them. Them? How many are there going to be? His guess was three, and he was absolutely correct. Several days later, we counted them individually as they filled the bottom of the nest. Three beautiful "robin's egg-blue" eggs!

Then came a week of waiting for the eggs to hatch, as the mother and father robins took turns sitting on the nest. When I saw the very first hint of a robin, it looked like a fuzzy fluff. At the next look, I could make out the beaks as they each opened when their mother bird came with something that looked like a worm hanging from her beak. This kept up for several days, and then George asked me if I could make out the wings that were just then becoming visible. Wings? How could those little balls of fuzzy fluff be starting to grow wings already?

Once the babies were hatched, there was a constant brigade, by both their mother and father, of bringing food for the triplets. Being so high up on the second-floor level, there is no fear of predators. When I got to watch them for any period of time, the babies seemed to eat and then their heads would fall down, as if they had fallen asleep. Eating and sleeping, eating and sleeping, and growing very fast now. I have thought about naming them. The only triplets I ever known were a set I babysat when I was in high school. They had the names of "Fluffo, Crisco, and Spry." Perfect, since these robins were each just a ball of fluff.

At supper one night, George told me that the babies would be in the nest until they are the size of their mother. I don't think there's enough room in that nest for all three of them to become that large. But, he told me that Mother Nature has a way of working that out. I'm looking forward to seeing that happen.

I am reminded of something our older daughter said about two months after our younger daughter was born. At that time, our younger daughter was doing a lot of laughing. That caused our older daughter to say, "Now, she is just like a human being!" So, I will say the same for these baby robins, since they are so quickly taking on the shape of an adult robin.

(If you would like to see a seven-minute segment of film called "Angel Baby Robins," put that title in your computer and search for something that was published in 2016. It is a great piece of film that was almost exactly what I've been watching over the past several weeks.)

I know the day is coming very soon now, when our baby robins will fly off and be gone. Since we just had Mother's Day, I think there is a parallel story for any mother having babies and seeing them grow up so fast, and be gone so soon. As I sit here typing this article, I am very happy to still be getting to watch Fluffo, Crisco, and Spry starting to flap their wings, while still in their nest. But, as always, time is flying, and soon they will be gone. I hope we are lucky enough to get to see their first flight when they take off into the big world beyond our bathroom window.

As the day progressed, I kept watching the baby birds as they sat in their nest and seemed to be just looking off into the eastern sky. I hadn't noticed them being fed recently. But, just before dark, as I was looking at them, in one split second, all three of them flew out of the nest in three different directions! They didn't really fly, because they didn't know how to fly yet. They more or less just glided to the ground.

"OH NO!" I kept saying out loud, "OH NO!" That's not supposed to be happening! I ran downstairs and told George they had flown away, and he said they needed another week of maturing before they could ever make it on their own, so they were gone! When I got outside, the parent birds were screeching their heads off, flying frantically around up in the trees looking for their babies. Two had ended up in our neighbor's yard, hopping around. One of them got to the street and hopped across to the other side. Its mother was on the electric line watching and following. I couldn't watch any longer, because it was dark by then. I'd hope this morning they would all be back in their nest, but, I'm sorry to have to say, I found it totally empty.

Swings, Slides, Sandboxes, and Putt-Putt Golf

W hat a refreshing sight it was to look outside my dining-room window and be surprised to see a child's swing hanging from our new next door neighbor's tree!

Since the first time I saw it, they have added a sliding board, a table, and playhouse. It reminded me of when our daughters were very young, and we had our backyard filled with things for them to play on. We had two swing sets, a big sandbox, a tire swing hanging in the big cherry tree, and a baby pool. Lots of cousins, as well as neighborhood kids, often came to play out there. We enjoyed watching our old home movies that were taken over many of their growing-up years.

I wonder whatever happened to all those things they played on? There was also a child-sized picnic table George built that had a lot of use. All my siblings and I sat or stood around it to pose for a picture once. Of course, it was in the day before color film. And, whatever happened to the two swing sets? Since they were both given to us, we probably passed them on to the next little kids we knew of.

For a period of time, we had a large trampoline out there, too. The problems came when we were gone from home for a whole day. When we got back, there were signs that a lot of kids had been there, when they weren't supposed to be. They left hats, pop cans, candy wrappers, and papers.

So, because of that, it was gotten rid of.

If you ever saw our old home movies we had "back in the day," you would see when we made-up some tricks, so when the film was run backwards, it would be fun to watch. One was when one of my brothers rode a bike into the yard, jumped off, and let the bike roll away until it eventually fell over on its own. Then when running the film backwards, you would see the bike set itself up, go backwards to pick him up, and then continue out of the picture. Or the time when he drank a whole glass of something that looked like a milkshake. When that piece of film was run backwards, you could imagine how gross that looked!

One of our daughters once told us that all she wanted for Christmas was a sliding board. So, George got our first swing set, slide and all, and set it up inside the patio for the winter. Of course, that meant taking it all apart and putting it back together twice during that year.

When we bought our house, there were four delicious apple trees across the back of the property. As they got older, one of them fell over on our garden, thus that garden never made it. The other three eventually died. But not before being wonderful trees for all the kids to climb. We also had a sandbox that sat in the shade of the old cherry tree. One year, James came to stay for the better part of the summer, and he made a "pretend garden" out of the sandbox. (You might remember James, because he was the boy with the "pretend horse" that I wrote about in a previous article.)

One of the fun things to do for both adults and kids was the "holey ball" putt-putt golf course. George buried tin cans to use for holes and used little white plastic holey balls to hit with his golf clubs. Our next door neighbor and his guy friends played there often. We were told that one of the friends suggested to his grandfather that he fix one like it, at his farm. We heard that when the grandfather did, it turned into a real golf course, right here in Delaware County. We have often wondered if that is true or not.

Now you can understand why, when I saw that new baby swing out my window, it brought back so many wonderful memories of all the good times we had when lots of kids were here playing in our backyard with the swings, sliding board, and also climbing in the apple trees.

This Frustrating Thing
Called My Computer

The past couple of weeks have had some big ups and downs for me. The ups included going to Delaware and having lunch at Bun's, and the downs were all wrapped up in just one thing-- my computer.

When it doesn't work, I am frustrated because I know nothing about how to fix it. Maybe if I were an elementary school student, or even younger, I could fix it like they seem to be able to do.

They just hit a few keys and it's up and running again! You may be thinking that I should have taken some computer classes while in school. Well, I did, but no one would ever believe it. My problem is that the only thing I remember about those classes is that I learned how to program a cash register for a major grocery store. I learned nothing about fixing one.

The first time a computer and I were alone in the same room together was two weeks before I left my job at Ohio Wesleyan. That's when one was delivered to my office and put on a table to the right of my desk. That happened the last week before Christmas in 1988. When it was unpacked, it looked to me like it was ready to be turned on. But, no one said anything about it, so I continued on with my work, using my "Correcting Selectric" typewriter. I loved that typewriter! I bragged that I could type as fast as I could talk, or was it that I could type and talk at the same time? Well, one of those anyway.

And for the next many days to come, the computer just sat there with that "hear no evil, see no evil, speak no evil" look about it. I thought someone from somewhere would appear and say something about it, but no one ever did. I'm sure it was because we were in the very busy time with closing out the semester. So, it just sat there collecting dust for the rest of my days at that job.

When the new year of 1989 began, I was off and running, beginning my new job at the courthouse. The days of having a computerized office had not yet begun. In fact, it didn't begin for another whole year. It was on the very first day of 1990 when my world changed and I was a part of that paperless office everyone used to talk about. We were off and running with a brand new computer system. But the paperless part didn't take place in our office for a very long time. We had paper everywhere! That's because, at the beginning of using our computers, we didn't trust them enough to believe that they would really do the job correctly. So, we made paper copies of everything before we let the original documents go out of the office.

At the end of 2004, after 16 years of having all the help I needed with my computer problems, I retired. This meant that I was home alone, at my new desk, with my new computer, but no live person to come and fix it at the necessary times. I ended up with a love/hate relationship with my home desktop computer. I loved it when it was working, but hated it when it wasn't.

Dealing with a support system over the phone leaves much to be desired for me. My phone calls lasted as much as two hours. Oh, for the good old days back when I had my "Correcting Selectric" typewriter to use! I remember a whole generation of working people when everything was done on a typewriter. We didn't have such things as "updates" that came along far too often. You were able to go from job to job and not have to learn a whole new system when all we had were typewriters. Those were the days!

Knowing that I have such a love/hate relationship with this computer, you may wonder how it is that I am typing this article. Right now I am loving it, but one more time of it's not working, whether it won't backspace, or if the correcting procedure is fouled up, or heaven forbid, it won't even turn on, it's going to be toast!

Celebrating Mom on
Your Birthday

Happy Giving Birth Day were the first four words I saw when I turned on my computer this morning. That's because today is our younger daughter's birthday, and I was just about to send happy birthday wishes to her. But, she surprised me with those four words! What a great thing for any child, no matter what age, to be saying to their mother on their own birthday! It changed my whole day. I decided it was a holiday for me to enjoy. Rather than sweep the floor, I just let the sweeper sit. Rather than cleaning off my desk of excess paperwork, I decided it could wait until tomorrow.

I'm very glad I baked cupcakes yesterday as well as doing two loads of laundry, so I don't have any of that to do today. When fixing lunch, it took on a whole new feeling of enjoyment. Lately, I have been having food that we had never eaten before, so I continued to try something else in hopes it would be good. For example, making a cranberry pie with a canned of whole berries, and spreading it over a crust of broken Graham crackers, covering it with whipped cream, and sprinkle it with some crushed walnuts. I'll call it my "three-minute pie."

I think there should be some way to spread the word of wishing every mother a "Happy Giving Birth Day." It's a wonder the greeting card companies haven't made a new category of cards they could sell every day of the year. If they already have, I haven't seen or heard of any. They wouldn't ever have to change their display for them, because somewhere, every day of every year, there is a mother giving birth. And you know I don't mean the same mother!

I decided to put on my most comfortable summer clothes. I'm not much for watching daytime TV, so I kept it off all day. I have a new CD of only piano music, so I put it on to enjoy an afternoon of music that's from my past. Of the 32 songs listed, I know some of the words of most of all of them. It's nice to have those words running through my brain at this time of my life. Songs like "Unforgettable," "Fly me to the Moon," and Tommy Dorsey's "Boogie-Woogie." Another part of my anniversary day of giving birth was to take a nap. It certainly isn't the first time I've taken a nap in the middle of the day, but today I didn't have that usual feeling that I should be doing something more productive.

So, because of our younger daughter sending me those four words, my day turned into a special one. We will be joining her for supper, and luckily, I had already baked cupcakes to take along. It's been a great day so far, and it's only 3:30 p.m. Every mother should have the same day off as that of her child's birthday. All paying jobs have days off at some time or another. This means that in January, when it's our older daughter's birthday, I will be all set to enjoy another "Happy Giving Birth Day."

For years at a time, there are many mothers who never get so much as one day off. I once read a quote about mothers and their children: "For the mother, every day their child is under five years of age is back breaking, and every day after that, is heartbreaking." I don't believe every day is heartbreaking, but the potential for having something hurt your child will leave the same hurt for their mother. Another quote I read is: "A mother is only as happy as her unhappiest child." That says a lot, and all mothers know it to be true. It's part of being a mother.

Too bad my siblings and I didn't ever think of wishing our mother a "Happy Giving Birth Day" during her lifetime. She would have been happy. I'm sure. After all, seven kids would have meant she could have had seven days off each of her 61 years she was a mother. That's a whole week! I don't think she would have known what to do with herself after always being very busy every minute of every day. So, let's get the ball rolling and declare a new holiday. It won't ever be on any calendar, it will be up to each one of us to see that our own mothers are having a "Happy Giving Birth Day."

Reliving the
Good Old Days

This article consists of one-liners about subjects that were a part of living in Delaware County back in "The Good Old Days." There is no particular order.

1. Bun, himself, greeted everyone at the front door of Bun's Restaurant with menu in-hand. A favorite was the vegetable plate with all veggies and coffee, for 90 cents.

2. The city swimming pool was at the Delaware County Fairgrounds on Pennsylvania Avenue. Before being allowed in the pool, you had to walk through bleach to sterilize your feet.

3. All students in the Delaware City School system attended grades 7-12. They were all housed in one building. It was named for a man, Frank B. Willis.

4. The Brown Jug Restaurant, that has been closed for too long now, was originally located in the middle of the block over on Sandusky Street. That was before the days of Red and Ed.

5. There was a shoe store on Sandusky Street north of Winter Street that had an X-ray machine to use to test to see if your shoes fit properly. Not knowing better, we X-rayed them for fun.

6. In the 1950s, Ohio Wesleyan freshmen had to wear a red beanie to classes. If guys were caught without it on, they were dunked in Sulphur Springs. No dunking the women students though.

7. In 1952, when Dwight Eisenhower was campaigning for president and his train stopped at the crossing on East Central Avenue, an OWU student tossed his red beanie up for him to wear.

8. When living on Union Street, the iceman delivered ice for our ice box. As all kids did, we went out, climbed up to the back of his truck and got slivers of ice to eat. Great on hot days!

9. TV did not come on the air until 4 p.m., and then went off the air by 11 p.m. or midnight. Most all shows were live, even hour-long comedies, musicals and dramatics.

10. Doctor Lauer made house calls back in 1945. I don't remember what illnesses we had, but he came with his doctor's bag in hand and took care of us.

11. When I heard that Woody Hayes was fired from coaching football at Ohio State, I was trying on dresses in the dressing room of Uhlmans. The football world has never been the same since.

12. While having dinner at the Branding Iron on Old Route 23, Stubby Bowen, wearing his red jacket, sat down at our table. I asked him if he worked there, and he said, "I own the place."

13. There was a rec center at old North School, and for five cents an evening, all high school students had a chaperoned place to play games, dance, shoot pool, or just hang out.

14. For nearly 40 years, the Delaware County Courthouse closed all offices at noon Monday through Thursday during fair week. Now they only close at noon on Thursday for the Little Brown Jug races.

15. When the newspaper listed students on the honor and merit roles for each of the high schools, it used to take only a couple of paragraphs. Now, it takes a whole page.

16. When our nephew had a sporting event held at Olentangy Local Schools, all students from grades K through 12 were located in one single building, on the south side of Shanahan Road.

17. Delaware County Library used to be in the Carnegie Building. But now, the library is where an Albers store used to be.

18. People ate a lot of meat and rented meat lockers for storage of enough meat for a year. In the 1950s, you could buy 3 pounds of freshly ground beef for $1.00.

19. Bun's Restaurant had an upstairs banquet room in the original building that burned down. All high school seniors enjoyed a sit-down breakfast up there on their graduation day.

20. Sandusky Street divides the east from the west sides of town according to addresses, but the Olentangy River is the great divider of the east side from the west side.

21. A year ago, I was told by an east side business owner that if you were a girl raised in the east side, "you had to be tough." I was raised there for two years, so I guess that counts.

22. When you go in the bank building at the corner of North Sandusky and West Winter streets, there is an elevator to take you upstairs. There used to be an elevator operator on duty at all times.

23. When my sister's husband called home during World War II, he had to call the lady across the street, because most families didn't have even one phone back then.

The above 23 lines could be considered the "Good Old Days" for any senior citizen. I could go on and on about the changes in the city of Delaware and Delaware County, because the changes never stop. If you don't believe it, just pick up the Delaware Gazette and read the front pages. New subdivisions, more crime and more kinds of crime, new industry, lists of property transfers as well as birth and deaths are happening every day. And just imagine, these times now will someday be the "Good Old Days" of the future.

An Exercise
in Writing

T his is the first time I've considered beginning an article by writing "Dear Reader." It is because it will be something different from anything I've ever written before.

I found a book titled, "Writing Down the Bones" by Natalie Goldberg (1986). She suggests setting a timer to a certain amount of time, and with no preconceived idea of what to write, just sit down and begin writing when the timer goes off, and don't stop for any reason until the timer goes off again, letting you know the time is up.

My reason for using this idea is to encourage each of you to try it. You can set the time for any amount of minutes you want, and follow some of the requirements in her book. They include: keeping your hands moving, not crossing anything out, and not worrying about spelling or punctuation. So, my timer is set and here it goes...

Come along for the ride and see where it takes us.

"Since I have no idea what to write, I think I will begin writing about the clock on the wall in my dining room. It reminds me now of the clock that was on the wall at the courthouse when I first started working there back in the 1950s. It was there to greet me when I went in in the morning at 8:30 a.m., and told me when it was 4:30 p.m. and time to go home. It also told me when to go to lunch and when I should be back. At 4:30, it told me to stop. So, I stopped. Everything stopped. Everything.

Seeing that I typed that everything stopped, I am reminded of what my daughter, Cathy, told me when she was told by the doctor that there would be no more cancer treatments for her husband, Butch, and she had to call the hospice right away. And when she did, everything stopped. He didn't go back out to his shop, she no longer went to work because the hospice people were coming. A young woman came, Paige, I think. The hospice people brought a hospital bed into their home, and he only lived one more whole night. Paige told Kathy that Butch would be passing very soon. She showed her that he was changing color. He died at 4 a.m., so it was then November 1st.

All the time Butch was in bed, their dog, Omar, laid on the floor beside him. The minute Butch stopped breathing, Omar stood up. And stayed right there without moving."

Well... Well... My time is up. During the typing of the above paragraph, I was very nervous about what was coming to my mind and was not sure where it was going. It's rather hard to type when you're blinking back the tears in your eyes. It was a big decision as to whether or not I should use this for my article this week. So, I called Cathy and asked her for her permission to write about Butch's passing. When I read it to her, she said it would be fine.

I would like to write a little more about that long November 1st. After Cathy called us at about 6 a.m., we got a flight out of Columbus to Orlando, and after renting a car, we got to Cathy's house and we're driving up the driveway, to be with her, just as the sun was setting. I was glad we got there before dark. Some lady friends brought food to Cathy's house, and the neighbors came over for a bit, and there were more phone calls that had to be made. In review of what I have written, I see that I went from writing about the clock here at home, to the clock at work, and to knowing that 4:30 meant stop. When I wrote, "Everything stopped," I was reminded of Cathy's words to me after we arrived. Her words of "everything stopped" have stuck in my head ever since our son-in-law Butch, died on that long November 1st in 2006.

Since I began this article with "Dear Reader," I will close with my best wishes to each of you.

Hearing Voices
from Another Room

J ust as I woke up, I could hear their voices coming from out in the other room. They were a little muffled, because the door was shut, making it pitch dark.

What were they talking about? I could tell there were only two of them up this early. I didn't know what time it was because I didn't have a flashlight to see my watch.

The one window in the room had drapes over it, so no help there. The room was a place to store a lot of things, as well as having a chair that opened up into a bed for me to sleep in. Soon, I thought I smelled toast, or was something burning? I didn't want to get up and check. I just wanted to lie there, be comfortable and warm, and listen to them talking to each other. That's what I did when I was a kid. I was having a flashback about how it felt listening to them in the mornings. I remember not wanting to get out of bed, mostly because it was usually cold.

I liked listening to what they talked about as well as wondering if I would ever be as grown up as they were. How many years have passed since I last had this experience? It had to be a lot because I was only in the first and second grades when they were in high school. I knew these two voices as well as I know the back of my hand. It's because they were my two older sisters. And along with my two younger sisters, who weren't up yet, all five of us were together for a weekend at our oldest sister Ginny's house.

Other than their morning conversations that I could hear from my room, I don't have many memories of the older ones because we never played together. But, in the last several years, we have made up for that, because we have been playing cards whenever we can all get together. Growing up, there were always a lot of differences between us. One example is that they were wearing lipstick when I had just started going to elementary school.

Now as I listen to them, I wonder if they ever listened to me. Did they wonder how I was doing in school? I don't recall back then ever having any "one-on-one" conversations with either one of them. Would they still make fun of me because my hair was always such a mess? As a kid, someone nicknamed me "Mopsy" and I feel like it still fits. I always knew I didn't fit into their world. After all, I was just a kid.

The above words were written as one of my writing exercises. It wasn't timed. I wrote in longhand, without stopping, and completely filled two pages of notebook paper. It was interesting to read what came out on those pages. You might want to try it yourself sometime. I never thought I was a problem to any of my siblings. I always tried to be as independent as possible. Because I'm the middle child of seven, (we have two brothers) I have read a lot about the middle child being different from the other children in a family. One study found that no one ever pays much attention to a middle child. That was a surprise! But as I look back, there was some truth to it. I knew what my jobs were around the house, so I did them without being told. I had to do the dishes, help clean the house, keep my clothes in good order, keep an eye on the younger ones in the house, and be in bed by 9 p.m. It's a wonder they didn't call me "Bossy" instead of "Mopsy."

But, sorry to say, spending weekends at Ginny's is a thing of the past. She died two years ago this very day that I'm writing this. I wonder what she thought of me when I was a kid? I wonder if I had been a problem to her during that period of time? We were all living in the same house. If no one was paying any attention to me, maybe that's why I was always reading a book, or spending time at friends' houses.

I started writing this both as an exercise in filling two notebook pages without stopping, as well writing a few words about Ginny. I'm glad that, as adults, my sisters and I were able to play all those card games, which are usually held on each of our birthdays. In fact, on her last birthday, two years ago when she 91, we went up to her house and played two card games, one in the morning, and one in the afternoon. That was when I wrote her a song to the tune of Jingle Bells beginning with the words: "Playing cards, playing cards, playing cards today…."

In her last days, as she was growing thinner and thinner, she started looking a lot like our mom. She always had the job of being everyone's big sister. It doesn't seem like very long ago, when I was just a kid, who was wishing I could be as grown up as she was. In fact, right now, it seems like it was yesterday.

Hearing Loss Is
an Invisible Disability

For a long time, I have been thinking of writing about my hearing aids, but I didn't want to admit that I have hearing loss. Recently, I read a book titled "Shouting Won't Help", by Katherine Bouton (2013), and learned that I am one of 48 million people in America who has hearing loss.

I don't remember the exact day and time when I first realized I had a hearing problem. But, I do remember about 15 years ago, being in the back seat of a car and trying to have a conversation with someone in the front seat, and them saying to me, "You need a hearing aid!" At that time, having that said to me felt like an insult. But eventually, after having more signs of being hard of hearing, I made an appointment to have my hearing tested, and sure enough, I had a serious hearing loss. Therefore, I got my first hearing aids about 12 years ago.

I was fortunate that they lasted for 12 years. I had taken very good care not to lose them or drop them in water. But, recently, even with my 12-year-old hearing aids in, I could not hear anyone speaking at a normal level, especially ones that I could not see their face, in order to read their lips. And by then, I had long been using the closed caption on the TV to understand what was being said.

So, I went back to the same place where I got my first hearing aids. I had more tests, and a diagnosis of a need for stronger, updated aids. This was when I found out that in the past year, I had lost an additional 50 percent of my hearing in one ear, and a smaller amount in the other.

Therefore, I had to get a new set of hearing aids to help with my current loss. And while there for an appointment, I picked up the book from a table in their waiting room, that I referred to above, and decided to read it to learn more about my invisible disability.

The following is an assortment of facts I learned from Bouton's book:

Many of us are responsible for our own hearing loss> It's the noise we subject ourselves to day after day.

People who are raised where there is very little noise can still have perfect hearing when they are over 100 years of age.

The lighter your skin color, the higher your risk of hearing loss. Melanin exists in the inner ear. So, the darker your skin, the more pigment in your inner ear.

Ears are most vulnerable to damage when a child is young, or in their teen years at rock concerts, or when playing a lot of video games.

It's better to hear nothing than it is to hear too much.

What is music to my ears may be just noise to yours. You probably would not enjoy a sporting event in complete silence.

Restaurants should cut down on the level of noise in the background, because it would be better for comfortable conversations.

Hearing loss is an invisible disability. No cane, no crutches.

If you are speaking to a hearing-impaired person, and they don't understand, rephrase what you have already said.

If you are faking it, people might think you are arrogant, remote, absent-minded, distracted, or just plain stupid.

Usually you can't remember the name of a new person you have just met, because you are so busy trying to figure out what has been said.

The greater the hearing loss, the higher the likelihood of dementia, which is deeply distressing to the hearing-impaired person.

It is unthinkable to make fun of people with severe vision problems, obesity jokes are tasteless, but still, the hearing loss seems to be fair game.

Even the best devices are a poor substitute for nature's creation.

Stress makes your hearing loss a lot worse.

Depression leads to withdrawal, as does the fact that not being able to hear makes you uncomfortable in social situations.

Pretending to have normal hearing, day after day, is exhausting.

People who lose their hearing are afraid to be open about it because they fear the prejudice, as well as seeming much older.

Hearing-impaired people can't hear anyone with a beard or mustache because they can't read their lips.

Be sure to look at the person with a hearing loss when you talk to them, to be sure of having their full attention.

Hearing problems outnumber vision problems by tens of millions.

Two-thirds of Americans, age 70 and over, are hearing impaired.

Only one in five who need hearing aids actually ever get them.

"Deaf" is the term for people who have no hearing. "Hard of hearing" is a politically correct term for people who have a hearing loss.

If you desire more information about things like tinnitus or vertigo, as well as a lot of more on hearing loss, check out the book, "Shouting Won't Help--Why I, and 50 Million other Americans, Can't Hear You" written by Katherine Bouton.

The reason for writing this article is in hopes of taking some of the stigma away for being a person who feels they have to hide their invisible disability of being "hard of hearing."

Angels Come in All
Sizes and Shapes

This is a true story of something that took place about 20 years ago.

I was in my little mouse-house of an office at the old courthouse, working through the day's usual amount of recordings. In just a few seconds of time, everything I was worrying about changed from being rather small, to being something very large. One of the women from the back office came in my little mouse-house of an office and said something about there being a big mistake in the computer work. Big mistake. And that I had to come back and look at it right away.

So, after a big sigh, I followed her back to her desk. She proceeded to explain something that meant there would be tons of work that would have to be done over. You have to realize that we barely had time to do all the work of the day, without having to do over any of our work from past days. As I stood near her desk, I was aware of the other people in the room looking and listening to all that was transpiring between the two of us.

There was no doubt about it, this was an impossible situation. I remember the sickening feeling that I had as I stood there. I couldn't even think of the next step to take. Knowing that all eyes were on me, I knew I had to act.

Just as I felt my blood pressure was as high as it could possibly go, one of the women from the front office stepped in my line of vision and said that there was a woman at the front desk who insisted on speaking to me at that very minute. I don't remember what possessed me to leave to go see her, but I did.

When I got to the front office, there stood a very short, stout lady with curly gray hair, who was wearing a cotton house dress. She had a smile on her face and asked to speak to me in private. So, we went into my little mouse-house of an office, and I told her to sit in the rocker, while I sat sideways at my desk. First, she asked to take my hand, and while holding it, she said something that I will have to paraphrase here. "There is nothing you have to worry about. What you are going through right now will be taken care of immediately. You have nothing to worry about at all." What did she say?

How could she have known that I had a very serious problem in the back room? There was just no way she could have known. And as I said those words to her, she just added that everything would be fine. As I stared into her aged eyes, I found myself saying, "You are an Angel, aren't you!"

She just smiled. Out of the corner of my eye, I could see the small wooden Angel that I'd always kept sitting on my shelf in my office. So, I got up and put it in her hand as a gift for her words to me. I had just said the words of thanks to her, and she got up and walked out of the office. And with a feeling of confidence, I walked to the back room. When I got to the place where they were still all waiting to see what was going to happen next, we called the computer company and told them what had gone wrong. They said that they could fix it on their end, and not to worry about it at all!

Walking back to my little mouse-house of an office, it felt like my feet weren't touching the floor. Was she an Angel? I never knew of anything like that happening before. The very next day, when I returned to my office from lunch, I found a small block of wood sitting on my desk. It had six angels painted on it, and also these words were printed on it, "Angels come in all sizes."

The above experience all happened about 20 years ago. I remember it as though it was yesterday. I had never seen that short smiling lady before or since. Was she an Angel? If so, she had taken a potentially impossible problem and fixed it, as her mission on earth. I have always kept that piece of wood with the little angels on it, in the living room of my home. And I continue to wonder about that miracle that walked into my life that day.

We have now come to a season in our lives when we see a lot of angels, whether on Christmas cards, in church, or in store windows. Do you think you may have ever seen an Angel? If not, just think about the words on that block of wood, "Angels come in all sizes."

Two Floods and
A Wedding

D o you ever get it urge to jump in your car and go someplace on a moment's notice? Well, that happened last year when our daughter and son-in-law were having supper with us, and we were discussing floods in Ohio, mostly ones in Delaware County.

One flood took place in 1913, and another in 1959. And it just so happened that George knew of a presentation being given on that subject within the half hour. So, within a matter of minutes, we were in our son-in-law's car heading for the Barn in Stratford to hear said presentation. It was to be given by Mr. Brent Carson, who knows more about the history of Delaware County than anyone else we know.

We arrived just in time to sit down in the available chairs and hear about the very subject we had just been discussing. First, he spoke about the flood of 1913. I found some good statistics about it in the 100th Anniversary Delaware Area Chamber booklet: "Eighteen lives are lost and 500 people lost all or part of their possessions in the 1913 flood. Twenty-three homes were washed away or destroyed-- 34 more ruined, 40 bridges washed away, 60 businesses suffered sizable loss and $1.5 million estimated total damage. The Delaware Garment Company, formerly the Delaware Underwear Company, had to spread 20,000 yards of cloth and 500 dozen gowns on Ohio Wesleyan's campus to dry. A score of horses gradually climbed the steps of the Delaware Ice Company plant to avoid the rapidly rising waters.

Mr. Carson had a lot of interesting things to say, but because of our leaving in such a flash, I forgot to take something along to use to take notes. But, I do remember what he asked about the 1959 flood. Sometime in the middle of his talk, he asked if anyone in the audience knew what day in January the flood hit here in Ohio. I knew when it was, but I hesitated to speak. But when no one else said anything, I put my hand up and said, "It happened on Sunday, January 25, 1959."

Surprised, he asked how I knew that was the correct date. So, I said, "That's the day I got married." I could have added that it was a very warm day for January, and there was so much water everywhere in Ohio that my oldest sister, living in Paulding County, couldn't go anywhere that day, unless she wore boots and wanted to walk through the fields to a distant neighbor's house.

Also, another sister, who lived in Marion, had to take Route 23 from Marion to Delaware, then take Route 42 north to Ashley, to get to the wedding. When the wedding was over, George and I left to go on our honeymoon. As we drove away, we realized that about 10 tin cans had been tied to our bumper. I haven't seen that custom observed for a very long time.

We headed to Sunbury and then on east to Zanesville. From there, we went south to Marietta because that was where the only bridge was opened across the Ohio River. At that point, the water headed West and would eventually run into the Mississippi River. So with that happening, we were able to proceed south to Orlando, Florida, where we spent our honeymoon. Back in 1959, there were only two-lane highways all the way to Orlando. The interstates came much later.

Another quote from the same edition of the Delaware Area Chamber booklet about the 1959 flood was: "A flood in January of the Delaware Run is the worst since 1913, with stores on Sandusky and West Williams streets flooded. Many families evacuated their homes along the run and in the north section of the city about 27 businesses suffered major damage." Ever since then, people have talked about the water that ran in the back door of Benton's Furniture Store, through the whole store, and out the front door to go on across South Sandusky Street to the Delaware Run that runs along the Ohio Wesleyan campus.

What a mess that must have been! But the Delaware Dam was doing a good job of holding the water back from flooding Columbus. There's no doubt that the 1913 flood was many times worse than the flood of 1959, so, if you are interested in seeing some pictures of either flood, the Delaware County District Library has a collection of photographs of each one.

Who knew when we were planning our wedding that we would choose the same day as one of the two biggest floods this area had ever seen? As a matter of fact, it's almost impossible for George and me to believe that we will be celebrating our 60th wedding anniversary this coming January 25th. We have a lot of good memories of that important day, but one thing we can't remember is whatever happened to all those tin cans?

Offer We
Couldn't Refuse

I t's not every day someone comes up to you and says, "We want you to buy our house." But, back in 1958, those exact words were said to George and me by a lady at church, she then added something like: "Now that you are engaged to be married, you will be needing a place to live. We need the money you would give us for our house, so we can finish the new house we are building. And, we will be leaving some of our furniture in the house for you to use until you can get your own."

She was right about the fact that George and I were engaged, and when we got married, we would need a place to live. But, buy their house? Before we got married? Use their furniture for a while? It seemed a little odd. But, I knew the woman, and we trusted her completely. She also added that they would need for us to pay them for it by the middle of next month, which would be November, while our wedding wasn't going to take place until two months later in January of 1959.

When I went back to work the next day, a person from Sunbury Savings and Loan came in the office to file their real estate documents. I jokingly said to him that George and I had a chance to buy a house, and we weren't even married yet. I expected him to laugh, or say something like, "Are you crazy?" But, instead, he said, "I'm sure we could help you with that. Come to our office Saturday morning, and we'll see if we can work out a way to help you get that house. We may be able to loan you the money." The money? How much money are we talking about? I need to remind you that this was back in 1958.

That year the prices for land and houses, as well as people's salaries were nothing like today. The price for the house was $7000. It was on a quarter-of-an-acre lot and had three bedrooms, one bath, living room, dining room, kitchen, utility room and a front porch. There was a one-car garage in the side yard, and it also had four apple trees, one large pine tree, and three big elm trees spread over the rest of the property.

With nothing to lose, we decided to check out said company, and after discussing the terms, we thought it just might work out. But, there was one situation that had to be addressed. It just so happens that I had just turned 22 and George was still 20. In order to sign a mortgage, a person has to be at least 21 years of age. And so, with that piece of information, we assumed the transaction wouldn't be going through. However, they suggested that as an unmarried woman, we could put the house in my name alone. And that way, I, alone, would be the only one to have to sign the mortgage.

Back in the 1950s, you never heard much about a single 22-year-old woman buying a house and taking out a mortgage by herself. But, soon after that morning, on November 15, 1958, Sunbury Savings and Loan and I owned a house, and the deed and mortgage were in my name alone.

The first 10 years of living in our house passed quickly and we had a "mortgage burning" party, since the mortgage was then paid off. During those years, George built another room onto the house, as well as a double car garage and a screened-in patio. He also tore out half of the kitchen wall to make a counter for the benefit of having more sitting space to eat. Being near an elementary school, it was a good place to be raising our two daughters.

Like us, day by day now, our house is getting older. It needs a facelift, as well as some fresh paint. The hinges are creaking and the floorboards are squeaky. It makes me think of that Number One song from Your Hit Parade days in the 50s called, "This Old House." It is aging just as we are at this time of our lives. And, to bring us up to date on the purchase from so long ago, we now have a survivorship deed made out so that our home is now in both of our names. And, this one house has been our only home for every day of our entire 60 years of marriage.

More County
History, Please

The older I get, the more I am interested in "old" Delaware County. I am fortunate to have a copy of the Delaware Area Chamber of Commerce booklet, dated 1907-2007, and have enjoyed leafing through the pages and having a lot of good memories come back to me. Most of the dates and costs of items in this article are taken from said booklet. Maybe you, too, would be interested in how things used to be, when it comes to what, when, where, and why of old Delaware County.

When I was eight years old, our dad moved our family to Delaware. As we drove through town, on our way to find the house we were moving into, we passed the Strand Theatre. It was a welcoming sight! Some of the facts I just learned about the Strand were that it opened in 1914 at the same place, 28 East Winter Street, as it is today. It was considered an opera house at first, and then two years later, became a theatre. Interesting to think about the prices back then being 15 cents for main floor seats and ten cents for balcony.

Ever since we discovered the one-room schoolhouse of George's past, we have been interested in anything we can find out about them. I would have never guessed that in 1915, there were 111 one-room schoolhouses still operating in Delaware County. The last two closed in 1938. And, that same year, Delaware County had 2,263 farms in operation by their own-ers. It's always interesting to be reminded that back in 1921, gasoline was costing all of 29 cents a gallon.

Then in 1923, Delaware began drawing water from the Olentangy River and started building a water tower in the city park along Park Avenue. What a difference that made in the running of a household! So, Delaware city had its first water filter and treatment plant when it opened the 250,000-gallon Park Avenue water tower. Happy are the homemakers who then got to have running water in their kitchens and bathrooms!

In 1926, Delaware city had something we don't have now. It had street cars! What would it be like to have them on the main streets of downtown today? Something I had forgotten was that Frank B. Willis died while waiting to make a presidential campaign speech in Ohio Wesleyan's Gray Chapel in 1928. Having spent six years in Willis Junior High and High School, I must have said his name a thousand times during all these past years.

In 1935, the Hamburger Inn opened a 12-seat restaurant at the same place it is today. Glenn Hudson Sr. bought it, and the prices were 12 cents for a hamburger, 5 cents for a sweet roll, and 5 cents for a cup of coffee. Later, it became the size it is today with 34 seats.

All the years of knowing about the Little Brown Jug, I never knew that the very first Jug race in 1946 was won by Ensign Hanover and was driven by Delaware's own Wayne "Curly" Smart. Or, that the race was named for a famous pacer, and the first race had a purse of $35,000. Right after the first Brown Jug race, the Brown Jug Restaurant was established on North Sandusky Street in the old Deposit Bank building. Then in 1970, the restaurant moved to 13 West Williams Street, where it was very well known for over for the next 30 years.

Some newer residents may not realize that we used to have a drive-in theater called the Kingman, just south of town. It opened in 1948 at the US Route 23 in Cheshire Road location. It was opened by a former manager of the Strand Theatre, along with two owners of the Central Restaurant. At the same time as the Kingman's opening came the first television set in the city of Delaware at the home of Robert Scott on West

Williams Street. In just three short years, most everyone I knew had a television in their homes.

Near that same time, the L&K restaurant opened as well as the Delaware County Bank and Trust Company. So many places came into existence at the beginning of the 1950s, just when I was growing up and becoming aware of them.

This article has taken us from the very early existence in Delaware city of the Strand Theatre in 1914, up until the L & K coming in 1950. As I sit here typing the above history of Delaware County, I am amazed at how recent so many things happened that were a part of my life.

One of my main means of entertainment was going to double features at the Strand. And of course, I grew up going to the Delaware County Fair, as well as having toasted pecan rolls at the L & K after a basketball game at Willis. And, I had lots of lunches at the Brown Jug Restaurant for many years of my life. My mom, dad, and siblings benefited from having running water in all three of the different houses we lived in while growing up in Delaware city. And I do remember the opening of the Delaware County Bank on the corner of North Sandusky and West Winter streets.

I have written enough about old Delaware County history for this article. In my next article, I will pick up with memories from 1950 and forward. This is the first time I've written about something that takes two different articles to complete, and I've enjoyed every minute of it.

Remembering
"Old Delaware County"

In this article, I will be picking up where I left off in my previous article of two weeks ago. I had written about some of the happenings in Delaware County from the early 1900s up until the year of 1950. For this article, I have again used the "Delaware Area Chamber of Commerce booklet, 100 Years of Business 1907 to 2007" for the statistics I have quoted.

I remember the very minute it became 1950! I was 13, and it was New Year's Eve. By then, there were only four of my siblings and me still living at home with our parents. When everyone else had gone to bed, I stayed awake to see the excitement that was sure to take place when midnight came. I don't know why I expected to have something great happen, but I thought it would. I knew everyone was asleep. But, when midnight hit, nothing happened! Not one bit of noise or any shining lights, as I had assumed would happen. Not at our house or any other house I could see on the street outside. What a letdown it was for me! Here it was a new decade, a half-century mark, 1950 had begun, but not a sound or a light anywhere to be heard or seen! So, I went to bed.

A few changes started taking place in the world of having fun, when a new roller-skating rink, Skaters Haven, was built between Delaware and Worthington. It fit right in with an article written in 1952, by The Gazette staff of Virginia Cruikshank and "Red" Reed: "Delaware County whether it likes it or not is designed to be a Central Ohio playground… with the Columbus Zoo, zoo park, O'Shaughnessy Dam, and the Scioto Reservoir. Little did they know what the future held for Delaware County!

Another event that happened was when a City Municipal Court was established in Delaware. Henry Wolf was elected Delaware's first Municipal Court judge. During that first year for him on the bench, in fall of 1953, our senior class from Willis High School sat in on his court for half a day. The case I remember most was of a woman who had run a red light. By the time he got finished letting her know, in no uncertain terms, the awful things she had done, I knew, then and there, that I would never, in my whole life, ever, run a red light! And I haven't.

One of the next good things that happened was the A&W Drive-in opening on South Sandusky Street. It was the first time to have a carhop take our order and deliver it to our car. I remember them having "baby root beers" that were either free, or at cost of 5 cents.

In 1955, the face of Delaware city began to take on its new look. Land was being subdivided in rows of houses being built in a place called "Delaware Meadows." It was the city's first multi-street housing development. It was truly the first of many new subdivisions to be added to the plat books at the courthouse.

Then in 1961, the People's Store opened on West William Street and soon moved to North Sandusky Street. That store had the best sales of anywhere I had ever been. Thanks to the Kaufman owners, when they cut prices, they were really cutting the original correct price that had been, not some made-up price to make it look like a sale. Next things that opened were the Playhouse on the Green, Delaware Bowling Lanes, and the Pizza Villa. The Pizza Villa became a popular hangout for teens in Delaware. They had pictures on the walls of every teen who had ever worked there. And we can't forget that's also when the Branding Iron Restaurant opened on Stratford Road with Stubby Bowen as the owner.

In 1965, PPG came to Delaware and set up as the first occupant of the new Delaware Industrial Park.

Then in 1967, "a total of 13,160 soldiers from Delaware County were pressed into service for the Vietnam War with six casualties. The Cold War period between Korea and Vietnam saw the service of 660 citizens from the county." This is a direct quote from the Chamber of Commerce booklet.

Moving on to 1971, on a bitter cold night, William Street Methodist Church had a fire that caused a total loss of the sanctuary of the church. A firewall saved the education unit. Such a terrible hot fire on such a cold night that caused $450,000 in damages!

In 1974, the Delco Water Treatment Facilities were dedicated to provide water distribution to rural areas. And while writing about water, the Mingo Park Swimming Pool was open to the public by 1975.

Skipping over the 1980s, the most interesting part of watching Delaware grow has to do with the population of Delaware County, and how much it grew over a period of just 10 years. From 1990 to 2000 was the major part of the 16 years I was in office as the Delaware County Recorder. During those 10 years alone, Delaware County population went from 67,482 in 1990 to 111,714 in 2000. That was an increase of 44,232 people. Our daily mail deliveries of documents to be recorded in the earlier years went from being a handful to sometimes in the later years, being carried in by the tub full.

When did we ever start talking about there being an "Old Delaware County" as opposed to just Delaware County, anyway? For me the answer is very simple. It's when Polaris came into the picture. Until then, downtown Delaware had about everything anyone in the county would need. But when those 44,232 more people came to live in Delaware County in the 1990s, everything changed. It changed where you got groceries, where you ate out, where you bought your clothes, where you went to the movies, where you went to school or church, where you bought your cars, as well as where you went to see your doctor. We had only 67,482 people living in the whole county in 1990, but by adding 44,232 more, in the next 10 years, it definitely was not "Old Delaware County" anymore.

Joys and Memories of
Horseback Riding

The first time I saw her was when she came to lunch at our house
with another young girl from the barn. I asked her how old she
was, and she said, "10." With that answer, I went inside and
got her a blank journal and told her that I give all 10-year-old girls a
journal because it's the perfect time to start keeping the story of their
lives.

And so began a friendship that has lasted all these past 13 years.
During that time, while coming to our farm to ride, she has gone
through public school as well as four years at Ohio Wesleyan University.
She has a job now and still manages to come up to ride any chance she
gets. Her name is Sarah, with an "h."

I've written articles about James and his pretend horse, so I want to
let you know that he lives in Florida and has a good job with the Coca-
Cola Company. He had come to the farm for several weeks when he was
only 9 and came back to stay the next summer when he was 10. He will
be 45 in April, and we have been in touch every year since we met him.
It's always been interesting to keep track of James.

And I won't forget Katie, who "wanted to ride a real horse." I told
her dad that I could make that happen. She was in our lives from the time
she turned 5 until she was 13, and then she moved away. We missed her
coming to the barn after school to help do the feeding. But we'll never
forget the years of watching her learn to ride. I knew she had learned a
lot when I went to see her have a lesson one day. She rode the horse clear

to the other side of the arena, stopped, got off of the horse all by herself and walked it back to where we were sitting.

Before we met Sarah, we had met another 10-year-old girl who had come with her dad to the barn a lot. She was being homeschooled and this was a part of her lessons. She became a jumper. Well, the horse did the jumping, but she was on its back. George went with her to a horse sale in Delaware, for her to buy a horse. They sat there all day, through many horses being sold, but none was just right. That is, until close to the last one. It was everything they wanted in a horse. Most importantly was the fact that the price was right.

She had saved her own money to buy herself a horse and got one whose name was "Just Like Sonny." She went on to college and graduated, and now she has her own farm where she teaches people, young and old, who want to learn how to jump. I always thought they should make a movie of her life, and she would be perfect to play the lead. If that ever happens, you will know it's her, because her name is Charlotte.

We also had a boy who wanted to be a jockey, but grew too big to be able to meet the weight limits. Now he has a job working mornings at a harness horse stable and has school in the afternoons. His name is Gestin.

Now, we have all kinds of young people coming to take lessons and ride. Once, George was going to go up a 12-foot ladder, halfway up the outside of the barn, to replace a broken door. It's the door you open to load the hay into the mow. He had to fasten the hinges to the outside of the barn siding. I was afraid he would fall with nothing to catch him except the ground. I had my cell phone in my hand to call 911 if he did, but I was too afraid to even watch him. So, I asked Kora, one of the very good riders, as well as a hard worker, to stand there with me in case I needed her. She is 15 and very grown up. All went well, but you never know what could happen when you are up that high on a ladder and trying to hang a new door on the outside of a barn.

The word retire has been sneaking into George's vocabulary lately more than ever. For years, the only time he ever took off was just one day a year to go fishing with his Uncle Sonny. We always had a picnic at Aunt Mary's, and then George and his uncle walked Millcreek, that is over by Bellepoint.

George partly retired once, back in 2004, when he quit racing harness horses at Scioto Downs, Northfield, and in the fair circuits. But I am looking forward to the day when he completely retires and doesn't have to be up and over to the barn by 7 a.m. every day of every week. I'm looking forward to when he doesn't have to make and put hundreds of bales of hay in the mow every summer. Also, when he goes to get, and take back home, the Amish horseshoe man who has to spend a whole day at the barn every 10 weeks, shoeing and trimming the feet of about 10 horses.

I will also be glad when he doesn't have to get a truck and trailer-load of sawdust from the Amish sawmills about every six weeks. And last but not least, when he won't be worrying about the weather and needing to catch every forecast on TV to know when the horses can be outside or have to be kept in their stalls all night. Being in all night results in a lot of cleaning of all the stalls the next day. There is no way I can include all the work he has that goes with having his stables. But it is all worth it when we realize how many children have gotten to ride a real horse.

Many Happy Memories
of Central Avenue

My memories of Central Avenue in Delaware come from when I was living on East Central Avenue and attending the fifth and sixth grades at East School.

The house I lived in with my siblings and parents was on a corner where there is a drive-through now. Every time we drive past that corner, these many years later, I think of the fun times we had there, playing games like "kick the can." All the neighborhood kids came to our house to play because we had the street light on that corner. Others came over from Milo, Annette, and East Winter Street to play, too. Lots of fun outside, summer and winter with snowball fights or running races on Estelle Street. Our house didn't have a garage, so our dad just pulled his car off the street and parked it in the side yard near the sidewalk to our back porch.

We have an old picture of five of us siblings and one niece all bunched together to get in one picture while sitting on the steps of said porch. We also had a front porch facing Central that served as a place for several neighbors to come over to listen to our radio one summer night, to hear a famous boxing match. I think it was either Joe Lewis and Sugar Ray Robinson, or Rocky Graziano and Jack Dempsey.

I doubt if there are any kick the can games going on at that corner today, with all the endless traffic on Central Avenue, day and night, summer and winter. To walk to school we had to go up the street to where the railroad crosses East Central Avenue. That's where most of Delaware came out to see Dwight D Eisenhower in the back of a train on his campaign for president of the United States, when he stopped for a few minutes while passing through town.

What happened to our wonderful memory filled neighborhood? Also, what happened to the big old brick East School, later named Conger Elementary, that was there when I went to school for those two years? The growth of the population of Delaware city is what happened.

Back then is when West Central Avenue kind of ended at the old Jane Case Hospital, now known as Grady Memorial Hospital. Not much of anything was further on west of Grady, not even sidewalks, that I remember. Now look at what happened! Every foot of the whole East and West Central Avenues seem to be under construction, somewhere all the time. Recently, we had reason to travel several days in a row from Sandusky Street west to the hospital. Day after day, we waited in line while large pieces of the street were being dug up and filled in.

While at a yard sale at one of the houses on West Central, I asked the owner how she liked living there. She said that now there are constant sirens from EMS vehicles passing by, day and night. There was a tearoom on West Central for several years, in a house that used to be the home of a friend of mine. I had lunch in the tearoom at noon on the day my office was being moved from the old courthouse to the new Hayes Building. It was a very dark, rainy day. I didn't realize at lunch that day, how much I would miss that old wonderful old homey atmosphere of the old courthouse.

I have watched as many big West Central Avenue houses have been sold, fixed up, and sold again. Every house that had friends of mine living in them is still known to me by their names. For instance, Ufferman's house, Wolf's house, Spring's house, as well as some of my teachers' houses, are now all owned by someone else. None of the people I knew then are still living, or still living in those same houses anymore.

The railroad overpass on West Central has had its share of accidents of out-of-town trucks getting their roofs peeled back like a can opener as the drivers try to drive under the overpass, but to no avail. A picture of the wrecked truck usually ends up in the next day's Delaware Gazette.

There aren't many other streets with such growing pains as the entire Central Avenue has now. It's one of only two, the other being William Street, that takes you from the east corporation line of town to the west corporation line. I guess the part most heavily traveled might be West Central Avenue because of the stores like Kroger, as well as the hospital and doctors' offices. It is also heavily overburdened with so many huge trucks, as well as cars. I wonder what can be done as the Delaware County population continues to grow?

Visiting the Dentist
Over the Years

Yesterday, I had a capped tooth break off, so now I have to make an appointment to see my dentist and have him look at it to see what needs to be done.

Dental appointments have always seemed to be something no one wants to make. I know I used to be like that, because so many of the people I knew had complained about the pain they had, or were scared of the pain, they were sure they would have.

As a kid, my dental appointments all came after major damage had been done, and I would need extensive work by the dentist. I remember my dad telling the dentist to "go ahead and put out, because it will have to come out, sooner or later, anyway." So, by the young age of about 12, I had had several teeth extracted. But when the day came and I was out of high school and working, and had my own paycheck, I started going to a dentist for checkups. My dental appointments were my responsibility, and they slowed down the loss of anymore of my teeth that may have needed work done on them.

I remember when I was in school, a lot of my friends had to have braces. I felt a little left out, because I didn't get to have them, too. I didn't need them because my teeth were straight. How lucky for me, and at the time, how stupid I was for wishing I was one of the gang who had braces. That goes for glasses as well. I didn't need glasses, but all my friends were getting them and I felt a little left out there, too.

Eventually, I ended up with the dentist I have now and have been going there every six months for the past 20 years. He has never once mentioned the word braces. So, I never did get to have those braces I wanted so badly. But the day came when he started talking about a partial. How was that going to work? I found out a lot about how they worked when I had to have a second partial, as well. Now I find myself at the place where I have a broken tooth and I have to have a consultation. What is he going to say? Is there any hope of saving it? Will a new cap be made to replace the tooth that is practically all gone? I don't want to try to second guess what it will be, so I will have to wait and see.

One thing I do know is that when I was much younger and would see any elderly lady come out from having some type of work done by the dentist, I felt sorry for her. I assumed that she was in a lot of pain and any treatment would have been horrible for her, especially if she was frail. But now that I am older than most of those elderly ladies were then, I have been fortunate to never have been in much pain.

I still remember the day I took my mother to a dentist to have the remainder of her upper teeth extracted. This was her last step before being ready for dentures. She was only in her mid-50s at that time. What I remember is that she never complained. She never was a person to complain anyway, but going through what she did, would be grounds for complaining, if there ever was one.

Since it was late in the afternoon when we got back home, I was wondering what we were going to do about supper, because at that time there were six of us in the house to be fed. But she went right to the kitchen, put on her apron, and had supper on the table as soon as our dad got home from work. No one would have ever guessed what she had been through just a couple hours earlier. Sitting here now, with a large part of one of my teeth in a small plastic container on my desk, is nothing like what she went through. As I pick up the container and take a closer look at the piece of tooth with the cap, I just see that maybe, just maybe, there is a chance that it could be glued back in place. But, as I look a little bit closer, I guess for that to happen my dentist would have to be a magician.

Paying dental bills is usually a big problem for someone who has no dental insurance. And in some situations, people who have insurance find that they are still having to pay a large part of the bill, since some dental insurances don't seem to pay very much.

Once I figured out that since I didn't have dental insurance during my earlier years, I have spent an excess of $7000 of my own money on dental bills. How much in excess, I don't even want to know. Ironically, not too long ago, when George and I were having lunch with a friend and were talking about our teeth, the friend said to me that I should just have all my teeth pulled out and get it over with. I don't want to do that. Not after all the money I've spent for my past care.

So, I'm ready for the news, good or bad. Knowing that after the consultation, I will probably have to wait a period of time before it can be taken care of, means I won't get to have it done until after this article is sent to the newspaper. So, I will hold the thought that whatever the diagnosis turns out to be, it will be a good one. Wish me luck!

Finding the
Perfect Quote

———————

Recently, I had reason to be searching through my quote books for the perfect quote that fit for a couple who were soon to be celebrating their 60th wedding anniversary. Of the five books of quotes I have collected over the past 20 years, I found one that I thought would be perfect for them. (#17 was for cousins Bill and Barb Brake.)

During the search for this one particular quote, I decided that the following would be good to use for this week's article. I'm sure that at least one of them should strike a chord and speak to you.

"You cannot do a kindness too soon, for you never know how soon it will be too late." Ralph Waldo Emerson

"There is more hunger for love and appreciation in this world than for bread." Mother Teresa

"Light tomorrow with today." EB Browning

"Feeling gratitude and not expressing it is like wrapping a present and not giving it." William Arthur Ward

"When someone gives you something, it's not really yours until you say thanks." Unknown

"Not all readers are leaders, but all leaders are readers." Harry S Truman

"Take care of your friends, because there will come a time when you're not much fun to be with and there is no reason to like you except out of a long-standing habit." Garrison Keillor

"The fruits of the spirit are: love, joy, peace, patience, kindness, goodness, faithfulness, gentleness and self-control." Galatians 5: 22

"High school is closer to the core of the American experience than anything else I can think of." Kurt Vonnegut, Jr.

"Diplomacy is to do and say the nastiest thing in the nicest way." Isaac Goldberg

"A fanatic is one who can't change his mind and won't change the subject." Winston Churchill

"It takes your enemy and your friend working together, to hurt you to the heart; The one to slander you and the other to get the news to you." Mark Twain

"Once, during prohibition, I was forced to live for days on nothing but food and water."
W.C. Fields

"We judge ourselves by doing what we feel capable of doing, while others judge us by what we have already done." Henry Wadsworth Longfellow

"You will always have in your life what you desire others to have in theirs." Gloria Steinem

"Love is born with the pleasure of looking at each other, it is fed with the necessity of seeing each other, it concludes with the impossibility of separation." Jose Marti

"Beautiful young people are acts of nature, but beautiful old people our works of art. Eleanor Roosevelt

"You are only young once, but you remember it forever." Liberty Heights movie

"We only see in a lifetime a dozen faces marked with the peace of contented spirit." Henry Ward Beecher

Thanks for taking time to read these wonderful quotes. I hope that some of them spoke to you as they first spoke to me.

Watch Out for
Table Saw Blades

J ust when I thought we were going to have a nice peaceful supper at
our daughter's home, my husband, George, decided to saw some
boards to use for a fire to toast some marshmallows.

However, in one second, everything changed, and we found ourselves calling the EMS, because when he was using his table saw, the
blade cut into his hand. Blood everywhere. Getting out the paper towels came next to keep as much of the blood under control as possible.
And just then, we heard the EMS coming up the street. The driver and
other persons began the task of seeing what could be done for him. As
they looked at the injury, it didn't take them long to tell us that they
will be taking him straight to Riverside Hospital, because it is a case
for an expert to either sew it all together, or amputate the necessary
part.

Watching and listening to what all was being said seemed like it
couldn't be true. Just a couple of minutes ago, weren't we having a family
dinner? How could everything go wrong so fast? And speaking of fast, just
that quickly he was put in the ambulance and left the rest of us standing
there to figure out what we would do next. We had to decide who would
drive, and how quickly we could get ready to leave.

Riverside Hospital is a long drive through roads being under construction and highways being congested. I am thankful for our son-in-law,
Loren, for being the one to get us there. All the way there I kept thinking
about how in just one second, that accident had changed our lives.

Parking in a parking garage is one thing, but remembering where you parked, and finding it later, is another. I read somewhere that you should take a picture with your phone so you can find your car more easily when you finally get to go back home. But, no time to stop to do that.

Finding Room 19 in the emergency area was not as bad as I thought it was going to be. That's because it was late in the evening, and no one was on duty at the front desk. We were supposed to use one of their phones to call a certain number that was listed. But just that quickly, an angel of a lady walked up and told us what door to open and which way to turn.

And just that quickly, we saw him. He was wearing a hospital gown and had a bandage on his hand. Some smaller injured places on his hands were overlooked by the enormous loss of what the table saw had done to his left index finger. But he looked great. He had been in the sun and had a farmer's tan. His doctor's name was Michael, and looked very young to have so much knowledge of a hand injury. The main talk centered on the decision as to whether to amputate, or sew it up and hope it heals. X-rays were taken and showed where the saw went into his finger, but not totally through it. Soon, because it was George's decision, the doctor took him down the hall and sewed it up.

It was after midnight by the time we were told to take him home and get some rest. And in the morning we were to call to get an appointment with a hand specialist.

So, we took him home, with a prescription for antibiotics, a couple of copies of the X-rays, and other important looking papers. The trip home was so much better than the trip down because the construction crews had all gone home for the night. So, it was smooth sailing as we headed north. It was about 1 a.m. by the time we got home. Just eight hours later, we called the specialist, and she wanted to see him at 12:45 p.m. that very afternoon. So, we were soon on the road again to go see Marlo O. Steyn, MD, whose office was at the south end of Sawmill Road in Upper Arlington.

It turned out we had been to that same medical building years ago, so all went well with finding it. After the specialist looked at his hand, she and George had their discussion as to whether to leave in the stitches or amputate. Since George wanted to save it, the deciding factor was "you can always amputate later." So, we were to go home and come back to see her in 12 days to have the stitches taken out. The main thing we talked about was that "it could have been much worse." He is to get some rest, change the bandage every day, and definitely stay away from any saw, especially, his table saw.

What's My Line?
On YouTube

My thoughts for this article go back a year ago when I first found YouTube on my computer and watched "Britain's Got Talent."

Deciding to watch some of those contestants led to finding two brothers from Wales who sang as a duet, one tenor and the other, a baritone. Check them out at "Richard and Adam" because their voices are great! That led to watching more of BGT for the next several weeks. When I noticed the small pictures that were along the right side of the screen, I chose a couple of other topics to see. One was about "Long Lost Families" and had very interesting stories. I began to think that my computer could read my mind, because it kept showing me other pictures of other topics I was interested in. How could that be? After all, there are hundreds of topics I am not interested in, and none of them were shown!

When I saw they had just one picture of the old "What's My Line?" show, I jumped at the chance to see it. After watching just that one, the next time I turned on the computer and found YouTube, I found several more of the "What's My Line?" programs. I got to see a lot of the very young famous people from my past, such as Jerry Lewis, Bob Hope, Roy Rogers and Gene Autry.

And, the next time I turned on my computer, you may have guessed it, almost every picture down the right side of the screen was from "What's My Line?" So, now I am hooked on it. Everyone should enjoy these shows today, especially if you don't mind seeing them in black and white. Since there isn't much I care to see on regular TV, YouTube has opened a whole new world of entertainment, plus the fact that there are basically no commercials!

Mostly the people who would enjoy the "What's My Line?" shows would be the older crowd who watched TV in the 1950s and 1960s, when these programs were aired live. I enjoyed these shows back when they were first broadcast from 1950 until 1967. We stayed up late every Sunday evening from 10:30 until 11 p.m. to see them. I was getting to see Dorothy Kilgallen, a young journalist, Arlene Francis, and actress, and Bennett Cerf, a book publisher, as well as the moderator, John Charles Daly. And, they usually pick different comedians as a fourth panelist, to keep things extra entertaining.

Just as I was about to turn off my computer one evening, a flash came across the screen that Dorothy Kilgallen had been murdered! Well, that stopped me in my tracks! Why was that soft-spoken, intelligent panelist murdered? Along with that flash was a book title: "The Reporter Who Knew Too Much," by Mark Shaw. I knew then and there that I had to find that old book to read. When I asked at the Delaware Library, they said it was in! Really, after all these 50-some years later, they still had that book? I was wrong in assuming that it was written at the same time as Ms. Kilgallon's death. It was recently written in 2016! What could have interested someone about a murder, 50 years ago, to be writing about it now in the 21st century?

Come to find out, it had to do with the assassination of President John F. Kennedy! And, that she, Dorothy Kilgallen, was the reporter who knew too much! Wow! She was murdered because she knew too much about the investigation of the assassination of JFK. There was even a quote by Dorothy Kilgallen on the back cover of the book: "If the wrong people know what I know, it could cost me my life."

I have not yet finished reading said book, as I am writing this article. It would be impossible for me to even begin to write about the reasons given of why the writer, Mark Shaw, believes that Ms. Kilgallen's death was a homicide. So, I will stop here. If you are interested in finding out why that well-known journalist was murdered, get the book and be ready to relive the events around November 22, 1963 when our president, John F. Kennedy, was assassinated.

Who knew that when I first ran onto YouTube, it would lead me to wanting to find out more about that young journalist that I enjoyed watching back in my high school days, who seemed to always be on the panel of "What's My Line?"

Thoughts on
Pre-planning a Funeral

I never thought I would write anything pertaining to pre-planning a funeral, but since my husband and I recently did that very thing, I thought I would give it a try. I don't tend to be gruesome about it, because it wasn't gruesome at all.

It all began when we went to church to hear a presentation by a representative from a local funeral home. Mostly, we learned about the importance of having your plans already in place, so that other family members won't have to plan it at the time of your passing. Waiting until then leaves too many decisions to be made in too short of a time. This reminds me of an article I read comparing planning a funeral in a matter of hours to planning a wedding over a matter of weeks or months. So many of the same things had to be decided, such as finding a place for each to be held, as well as the announcement in the newspaper, and deciding on flowers and food. Another point that was presented by the speaker was the cost of funerals going up every so often, and the benefits of paying ahead.

Our meeting at the funeral home went very well. We were asked several questions about what we thought of either cremation or a regular burial. Maybe you have never thought much about either one, but when it comes down to it, your wishes will be addressed, whatever they may be.

Once that decision is made, then you go down the list of questions which pertain to the type you have chosen. If you choose cremation, you don't have to decide on nearly as many points as you would for an open casket. For this, the cost is much less. One of the most interesting things we found was that they have a two-compartment urn, that's for the ashes of two persons, not just one. At the time of the first spouses passing, his/her ashes would be put in one of the compartments, and the urn would not be buried until the passing of the second spouse. Then, at that time, a plot at the cemetery will be prepared, and there will be a burial of both spouses, in the urn, with just one headstone for both. And, of course, the expense will be much less than a casket for each, and the need for two plots.

One important point that I have thought about in the past, pertains to having food for family and friends. It pertains to where to have the food, and how to get it there at the time of the funeral. We have attended funerals lately that have had a catered meal right at the funeral home after the viewing hours, while others have had carry-in food at their church after the burial. Also, they would discuss the service itself and your wishes would be carried out in a very professional manner. For men who have served in the military, they will need a copy of their discharge papers in order to provide the benefits offered because of having served.

Also, if the passing should take place while the deceased is out of state, or at any distance from home, the funeral home offers a plan to transport the deceased back home. Paying ahead would mean that the costs would be much lower than the cost would be if you had to pay full price at the time of the passing. And all of those transportation plans would be carried out by the funeral home by professionals.

Ever since we completed the plans for our funerals, we have been at peace with the whole situation, knowing our family will not have to take care of so many necessities at the last minute.

Learning More
About Horses

T he weather is finally not too hot, not too cold, or not too wet, but just right, so, I got to spend some time at the barn over these past two days. It all started when I knew that our friends from church wanted to bring their two grandsons to the farm to ride.

Plans were made for them to arrive about 15 minutes before feeding time at 4 p.m. The grandparents brought their grandsons, Cody and Adam, who are preschool and elementary school age. George wanted them to have the experience of brushing and feeding the horses before riding one of them. They were ready and willing to do anything that George suggested for them to try. It was great for me to just watch their activity as they were learning something new, every minute they were there.

The brushing lesson went very well, and then he had them go with him to fill the feed cans and put them in each of the stalls. We all stood out of the way and watched as the horses came running in, single file, and headed directly to their own stall, to happily have their supper. It didn't take long for all of them to eat their food and run right back outside again. All, except for a horse named "Trobby."

Trobby is a 30-year-old retired racehorse that George raced back in the early 1990s. It seems that all the kids who have ever come to the barn have always loved Trobby. So, we put a smaller-sized saddle on her for Adam and Cody to use while riding. Then George led them to the outdoor arena. We couldn't use the indoor arena because it was being used for 4-H riding lessons at that time.

First, Adam was put up on the horse and George led him two times around the outer edge of the arena, and then the same for Cody. Just when they thought their riding was over, George told them he would lead them around the arena one more time. While this was going on, I was watching as both the grandparents were taking a lot of great pictures for them to show people the wonderful experiences the boys were having. All the fun was over way too soon, and they lovingly led Trobby to the back gate and turned her out to pasture for the night.

The above all happened two evenings ago, then last evening there was a "Ride Out" at the farm. I wanted to be sure to see what that was all about. I'm not sure why they call it a Ride Out, but the horses are definitely out of their stalls, and someone is riding each of them. The riding took place both in the indoor arena with the "Horsemanship" that was going on, and in the outdoor arena with all the jumping that was going on. I went around and talked to most of the 4-H members when they had a few minutes to spare. I got to talk to Trent, Emily, Haven, Grace, Ava, Rene, and Cora. One boy and the rest were girls, who ranged in ages from 11 to 17 years. They all told me the names of their horses, such as Wrangler, Ritz, Stella, Shadow, Pirate and Cisco.

When I asked them what type of riding they liked the best, almost all of them chose "Barrel Racing," over trail riding. I'm guessing they like speed. However, one of them told me about liking "Slow Barrels," so maybe it's not all about the speed. They all told me the amount of time they have been riding, and it ranged from six months to "all my life."

The most interesting part of our conversation was when I asked them what they like to do with their horses besides just ride them. The variety of answers were from "liking to hang out with friends who want to talk about horses," to "liking to learn more about the horse." One answer was just two words, "grooming and grazing." The girl explained she likes to walk with her horse while it's grazing. Another said she likes all animals and enjoys watching them. Another said she likes to bathe them. Also, one likes to draw horses, because she likes drawing. And the one I remember most was when one of them said she has a miniature horse and takes it to nursing homes for the residents to see.

During all my conversations with the aforementioned 4-H members, I noticed how very well spoken they were and how serious they were in their answers. During the time I was at the barn, I realized that they were all practicing what they were to do at the 4-H Horse Show during the Delaware County Fair, which is usually held during the third week of September. And, that it was all being done under the instructions of their 4-H advisor, Naomi Derwent. With all their good instructions, I am sure that by the time the fair gets here, they will all know what they need to do to be a winner!

Ways of Remembering

One day last week as I left the house to take my usual morning walk, I realized I had not written down the time I left the house. I write down the time every day, then, when I get home, I can figure out how many minutes I had walked. My goal is to walk my planned route in 26 minutes.

So, as I looked at the clock in front of our church, it was 9:52. So, I needed to remember the" 52" part. But how? Several different ways came to mind, and then I decided to use the year 1952. And during the walk, I would try to remember anything I could from the fall of that year. It was my junior year at Willis High School, and the memories I recalled were a good way to spend the time during the rest of my walk. The following are just some of the things I remember about that year of 1952:

1. Black and white TV. Better to have black and white for the next 20 plus years, then none at all. Then, somewhere around the mid-1970s, everyone seemed to be getting color TV, but we still had black and white. That's about when our 3-year-old daughter, Carolee, took her paint set and used the brush to paint our TV screen a big variety of colors. And when I walked in the room, she said, "Look mommy, color TV!"

2. I will never forget the big house on North Sandusky Street where all our family lived. My family, at that time, included our

parents, and all my siblings, a niece, and our brother-in-law, recently home from the Navy.

That was the only part of our lives when we had 10 or more people sitting down together for meals at our kitchen table. That's when one day one of my siblings said to me, "You talk too much." I still remember those four words.

3. I remember the bedroom I shared with my two younger sisters. It was at the front of the house and next to the bathroom. I remember that bathroom because the next house our parents moved us into didn't have a bathroom.

4. I remember my job after school every day of my junior year. I was asked by the Ditslear family in Delaware to babysit their two children from after school until they got home from their jobs at 5:45.

I was paid 35 cents an hour. My job was not only to babysit Roseanne, 6, and John, 8, but to "pick up the house" and fix their supper. There was always a note on the kitchen table telling me what to fix. Mostly some kind of meat with potatoes and other vegetables, as well as a good dessert, just so everything was done by 5:45. Unlike our family, they ate every meal in their dining room, so had to set the table as well.

5. I remember singing in the choir at the First Presbyterian Church. Choir practice was every Wednesday evening at the church, that's how I got to know other families who needed a babysitter, so got some evening babysitting jobs also.

Those five things are about all I remembered on my walk that day last week. But I did remember the number 52, so when I figured how long I had walked, it turned out that I did the whole route in 27 minutes. I am now reminded of a line by some doctor who said, "You need to walk your dog every day, whether you have one or not." Well, I don't have a dog, but I walk it anyway.

Downtown Delaware
Lookin' Good

W hen I was in downtown Delaware early this October 9th morning, I decided I wanted to take a close look at the Rutherford B. Hayes statue. When I was still across William Street from it, I knew I had to get closer, because it blended in with the dark color of the awning of the pizza place behind it. So, I hit the "cross" button on the post and waited my turn to get a better view.

I was surprised that it stood so high off the ground and how dark of a color it was. I felt like I was a tourist in my own hometown while staring straight up to see all I could see. What a great gift for downtown Delaware! It's the icing on the cake! After seeing it up close from all four sides, and then stepping back a bit to take it all in, I knew I would have to come back again soon to get an even better look. If you stand at the same spot as I did, you can see the fire in the fireplace inside the Amato's Woodfired Pizza place on that corner. It didn't take me long, as I was walking back north across William Street, when I said out loud, to myself, "Downtown Delaware is lookin' good!"

Flowers are everywhere. On the northwest corner of William and Sandusky streets, looking west, I saw tons of flowers for as far as the eye could see so, I had to walk in that direction to see all the beauty that was growing up as far as the William Street United Methodist Church. I ended my westward walk when I approached the amazing rose bushes in full bloom that line the walkway of the church. And for the first time, as my eyes followed the line of roses,

I saw a large church bell at the end of the walkway. It made me wonder if it had been a part of the original sanctuary that had burned on that bitter cold snowy night of January 30, 1971.

When I got back to Sandusky Street, I headed north to see all those inviting eating places that are set up along the sidewalk. There are also some new shops that I had not yet seen. Too bad there wasn't time for me to sit down at one of those tables and have a hot cup of coffee. As I looked down at the sidewalk, I realized this is the same place I had walked several thousand times during my growing up and older years.

Traveling the rest of the downtown streets brought more beauty than I had ever seen there. The flowers and the big pots of plants have taken over the town. The displays in the windows seemed more bright and colorful than I remember. What a wonderful October morning it was! It reminded me of the famous scene from the "Wizard of Oz" when the whole screen turns from black and white to full color. Wow! I have to say it out loud, to myself, again: "Downtown Delaware is lookin' good!"

Quote from
My Mother's Book

The following is an exact quote from a page in the book my mother wrote about her life. I've given her a bound 8x10-inch book of blank pages when she was 72 years of age. The entire book is written from her memories of her life, since she had never kept a journal. The book has made its rounds to each of her seven children to read. One of her grandsons has her book at this time, and found a page she had written about the evening of my birth. As a gift for my birthday, he typed the page and printed it with a superimposed picture of both of our parents, Earl and Carolyn, in the background. This is a copy of that page:

"On a Sunday evening, October 11, 1936, I knew it was time to send Earl to get the doctor, old Dr. Gantt, who was to come when our next baby was due. So, about dark, after Earl had got the milking done, he drove in and got the doctor and brought him out to the house.

"This doctor didn't know where we lived exactly, also he said he could not drive after dark. Then Earl had to drive to pick up the young woman who was to come and do the nursing job. She was Jessie, who did that kind of work for a living. Earl and Jessie didn't get back until it was almost over, so there was no nurse there to give me anything for pain. Anyway, this old doctor didn't believe in giving ether, but it wasn't so bad, and soon a baby girl arrived around 9 p.m.

"Jessie then took over. They weighed her on our household scales, said she weighed 7 1/2 pounds. She didn't open her eyes until she was about three days old, and I was scared that maybe she was blind.

"So, we were so happy when we found out she could see then, and was healthy. We got Carnation milk by the cans, and I found out how to dilute it to feed her by the bottle. She started soon to gain weight and stayed a fat healthy baby."

The setting for the above words about that October evening was a farmhouse in the eastern part of Delaware County on Justamere Road. At that time, the house had no running water or electricity. The summer months preceding my birth happened to be one of the hottest on record for Ohio, and that it reached over 100 degrees for several days. Since she had no way to cool the house, my mother and her three young children, ages 11, 8, and 3, spent a lot of time sitting in the cool woods next to the house.

Several years ago, my three older siblings and I went looking for that house. All we knew was that it was near Sunbury. Eventually, while driving around the countryside, our oldest sister recognized the woods and then the house that is still standing. So, I got to see the house I had always wondered about and imagined being born in that upstairs, while my older siblings were playing downstairs.

One of the reasons I was happy to have a copy of her words is that there are parts I didn't know about. I never knew how much I had weighed at birth, or if the doctor really made it to get to her before I was born. I had heard about the fact that my eyes didn't open until three days after I was born. And I am pleased to know that she was only in labor for a couple of hours on that October evening.

As time passes and we all get older and older, the more special it is to see her words on paper. Especially since the entire book is in her own perfect cursive handwriting. This article has been written by my mother's fourth child, Kay E. Conklin.

Mom's Mind Was 'Sharp as a Tack'

This is a continuation of the article I wrote last time about my being born at home in a farmhouse in eastern Delaware County back in 1936. My parents and three older siblings we're living in a house that had no running water or electricity. My dad did the farming, but by the time I was two years old, his health was so bad that he had to get a man to help with all the chores. The man didn't have a home, so he moved in with us in our home. He was given their bedroom, and they had to sleep on a roll-out daybed in the living room.

When the sheep were having their lambs, and the hired man would not get up at night to check on them, he was asked to leave. A week after he disappeared, mom discovered that the man had stolen all her treasures. The treasures consisted of two watches, the old-fashioned kind that are pinned to your blouse, as well as our dad's class ring and a valuable teapot filled with her keepsakes of her trip to California in 1909, when she was six years old. The teapot also contained a small bag of gold!

With no help to do the farming, our dad had to give it up. I was two years old when we moved into Centerburg to rent half of a double house. The rent was $100 for a year, to be paid in advance. When we moved it to that house, we took along a cow and some laying hens, because there was a small barn and pasture behind the house. Mom had nearly 400 cans of vegetables, fruit, and meat, that she had canned the year before, as well as the potatoes she had already raised. This was a better house in that we finally had electricity and running water for all our needs.

Just five months after they celebrated their 50th wedding anniversary, our dad died at the age of 74. Previously, he had suffered 8 years of having a form of dementia that caused him to lose most of his memories. Mom took care of him at home every day until the day he died. Once he looked right at me and asked where his little girls were, and there I stood, one of his daughters, but now a grown woman he didn't know.

Mom lived to be 83 years old, but since she was bedfast, she had to be in a nursing home for the last 16 months of her life. The nursing home was in Johnstown, which was the town where she had grown up, so was content to be back "home." Her mind was as "sharp as a tack." You may not have realized that she had a severe hearing loss ever since she was a child. All seven of her grown children were with her that whole day when she died at St. Ann's hospital. She had just asked us a question that we couldn't quite hear because she spoke so quietly, and just that quickly, she was gone.

A few years ago, while at an arts festival, I saw a huge painting that had a background of many brushstrokes of various shapes and types of white paint that completely covered the canvas. Painted on the canvas are words I have never forgotten. I feel it's appropriate that I add those words here, since I am describing my mother's passing. The words were: "The last thing she heard was the sound of angel wings filling the air"

All Kinds of
Friends

———————————

Hopefully, everyone reading this article has someone in their life who has been a really good friend. I have heard that if you can count at least three people as your friends, you are very fortunate. When I think of friends, I realize there are different kinds of friends.

Living in the same area all of your life allows for lifelong friends. Friends from church come to mind. Since you are fortunate to be seeing them every week, little by little those friends can grow into lifelong friends.

If you eat at the same restaurant every day and see the same people at their same tables, they can become friends, too. It's nice to have friends at lunch who consider themselves as a "Lunch Bunch."

My sisters and I enjoyed being part of a lunch bunch of OWU clerical staff back in the 1980s. Also, my son-in-law has his lunch bunch, who like to get together at a Wendy's and talk about farming.

You may get to know a lot of people who come under the headings of "friends of your siblings." When I was grocery shopping recently, I noticed a woman in the next aisle over, and I thought I knew her. So, I waved and said, "Hi." But when she started to walk toward me, I realized that I didn't know her at all! But, she kept walking toward me and I had to say something, so I said, "I'm sorry, I thought you were someone I knew." And she said, "you do know me." And in my head, I said to myself, "No, I don't."

But, just that quickly, as she told me her name, then I remembered her as working in the same office with one of my sisters. Right away she asked how my sister was. So, knowing they had been good friends, I told her it would be her birthday the next day, and we were having a party at her place, and she should drop by to surprise her.

We have all known of friends from our days in school. One of my friends has lifelong friends from her days at Jones Elementary in Massillon, Ohio. She is such a Perry Como fan that they all came down from Massillon several years ago and had a Perry Como birthday party for her. She was president of her own Perry Como fan club, back in their school days together.

I am fortunate to still have four good friends from my days in Delaware City Schools. Over the years, we have gotten together at various places. The last time, and it may be the last time, we had a get together for almost a week, at a house on Lake Huron. We celebrated the fact that we had all just turned the big 80.

Friends from work seldom remain friends, because once you leave a job, their friendship usually fades away. I am reminded of the title of a book, "You Can't Go Home Again" by Thomas Wolf. I have found that you can't go back to the office again, either. Someone else is in your chair, doing your job, and you soon realize that there is no room for you there anymore.

Friends come in all ages. And my first real job just out of high school, I worked with a lady who was 22 years older than me. She was the very nice person who took me under her wing and taught me everything I needed to know for my new job. She also taught me the ins and outs of the politics that ran the place.

Her name was Ruth Scott, and I have always wanted to write something about her. Everyone who starts a new job should have a "Ruth Scott" to meet them at the door the first morning. Ruth passed away a very long time ago, but I will never forget her friendship. If anyone reading this remembers Ruth, I would love to hear your memories of her.

Every once in a while, if you are fortunate, an old acquaintance can become a good friend. I have a good friend who is a writer, who I've known for almost my entire adult life. And we have lived just a block away from each other. Our friendship grew when I realized that she needed someone to get her mail from the post office last winter when we had all the ice and snow. So, I started getting her mail for her, and once she started talking about writing, we haven't stopped yet.

Be sure to let your friends know how much you appreciate them, whether they are old or young, lifelong or new, near or far. I doubt if the "Ruth Scott" of my life would ever believe that, 60-some years later, in 2020, I would be writing about how she "took me under her wing" and made my life at work such a good place to be.

It is with tears in my eyes that I sit here typing my memories of Ruth, who taught me how to order from a menu, always have a good time no matter what I had to do, and to not let it bother me when people made fun of me because I didn't drink or smoke. This paragraph about Ruth is example of how long a good memory can last!

I hope everyone has lots of good memories of lots of good friends you have had over your lifetime.

Take Time to
Share Good News

It all started on the first day of 2020. I received an e-mail from Mary Rose, and she had listed three things that were good news.

She said she had: "Lots of sunshine, a raisin bagel for breakfast, and soft cats to pet." In reading those wonderful words, I realized that I, too, had a "cinnamon bagel," so I decided to send that and some other positive thoughts back to her.

Then the next day, she sent me another couple of good things that had come into her life, and I returned a couple more good things of my own.

We have continued to write back and forth each morning about the good things that happened yesterday, and it has become a routine we have kept up for the entire month of January, as well as everyday so far in February. What a joy it is to know that Mary Rose has so many good things come into her life!

Mary and I met about 25 years ago when she was working at the Delaware Gazette, and she came in my office at the courthouse to get the deed transfers from the previous week. At that time, she was still able to walk. But after a period of time, she became confined to a motorized wheelchair and was no longer able to pick up the deed transfers.

A couple of years ago, she and I decided to enter a contest that was mentioned in "Good Housekeeping." It was to write a 3000-word essay about our mothers.

Neither of us won, but it kept us adding more and more to our stories in order to hit the 3000-word mark. Without that inspiration, we may never have written such a long story of the lives of our mothers. Now, each day, we are finding some good things that happened the day before and writing about each of them.

Maybe you could find a friend who would like to exchange only the good things that happened to each of you. Most people seem to forget the good things and only remember the bad. Maybe we all need to dig a little deeper to find the good things.

While on my computer recently, I came across a few minutes of an old Paul Harvey radio show. He was telling about a newspaper that was founded on writing only positive stories. It sounded good to me. However, the newspaper lasted only 14 weeks.

Some of you may remember Paul Harvey. He had a one man mostly positive news show and was on various times for five or 15 minutes, he always ended his programs with a long pause then the words: "Good day!"

This past Christmas I received a very nice glass jar with a lid on it. Inside was a printed note that said: "When something good happens to you, big or small, write it down and place it in this jar. If you're not having a good day, take some papers out of the jar and read about the things you're grateful for."

There was also a quote that had been added: "The secret to having it all, is knowing you already do."

Maybe you know someone who may benefit from having such a jar for their own. If so, get a glass jar, copy the above note, and give it to them.

It is such a wonderful feeling to know that Mary Rose had 31 good things happen to her already this past month. And with adding in the ones for February so far, she has had 50 good things that she has experienced. Thank you, Mary Rose. Everyone should be so lucky as to be in touch with a positive person like you!

I will sign off with my thought for today: "Be the person who makes something good in someone else's life, so they, too, will have something to remember that was good in their yesterdays."

Being on the Ballot

I t's March now, and since time flies by very quickly, Election Day will be here before we know it. I've been thinking about writing about the fact that my name has been on several of the ballots of Delaware County.

The very first time I ran for office, I lost. It was 1976, and I was at a place in my life when I had a lot to learn. So, when I had the opportunity to work as a secretary at Ohio Wesleyan University, I jumped at the chance. That's because while working there, I was allowed to take one class of semester. So, I did that for the next 12 years and graduated from OWU on May 8, 1988. Also, in that same month of May in 1988, I ran for office again.

I, again, ran for the position of recorder and I again took the necessary steps to do so. I filed for office in the Delaware County Board of Elections, campaigned as much as possible while still working full time, and I was on the ballot May 3, 1988, which just so happened to be five days before my graduation. What a busy week that was!

Putting campaign signs up all over the county can be a pain. You walk lots of miles, climb lots of steps to get in front of doors, and you hear lots of barking dogs as you set foot on the registered voters' property. If someone comes to the door, they may spend more time trying to control their dog than listening to what you want to tell them.

It's too bad that a lot of elections are won by whomever has the most money to spend for mailings, which are very expensive. Because the county of Delaware has been growing profusely since I ran, now it is almost prohibitive to think of going door to door.

When the polls closed on that Election Day in 1988, I went in the front door of the old courthouse and found the hallway was filled with people standing in clusters, or watching as the number of votes were being shown on the wall. They had to use a slide projector back then. Someone from each of the precincts carried in their results to be added to others already on the wall. With a glance, I could see the votes changing as the evening went on, and it looked like I was doing very well. As I got close to winning, I remember thinking, "Could this really be happening to me?" This was the primary, and since there was no competition in the general election, the winner at that time would be the new recorder for the next four years. When all the ballots had been counted, I had won.

At that moment, since the recorder's office was right there on the first floor, I got to go inside the office that I hadn't seen since I had worked there a very long time before. I saw the same desk and chair I had used back in the 1950s and 1960s. Right away, I knew I wouldn't be sitting there anymore. I would have to sit at the elected official's desk, and I immediately remembered the responsibility that went with that desk.

When you have any amount of control over other people's lives, it is a big responsibility! You have to enforce the rules, whether it means everyone's sticking to the work to get it done every day, or following the sheriff's orders about which door was to be used to come in. Or, if you need to hire a new employee, you may have to choose from several, who all need the job whether it's for money, or because they need to get away from a bad situation in their present job. And you have to get everything done perfectly, because if the name on the deed or mortgage is not spelled correctly, it will never be found in the right place in the index.

One of the first things I was told was by an assistant prosecutor who said, "You can have no mistakes in this office!" So, I spent my 16 years of being recorder doing the checking of everything, every day.

What a busy day I had on that May 3rd Election Day of 1988. It was exhausting! Working full time at OWU and getting ready for their graduation, which was to be mine, too. Voting that morning before work, and then seeing my name on the ballot; walking across Sandusky Street on the way to the Brown Jug for lunch and almost getting hit by a truck; having a photographer come in to take my picture for the next day's paper in case I won! And being at the courthouse all that evening, watching the votes come in and seeing those numbers that were put up beside my name on the wall.

Those numbers changed my life forever thereafter.

Together Is
the Best Place to Be

Because we have to stay home today, as I write this on March 27, it is unlike any other day I have ever lived through!

Today, I have been wondering where all the people have gone! Years ago, my life was filled with a lot of different people. People who are my family, my friends, people I heard stories about, people who appeared on the TV screen and made me laugh, people who did the news and I would recognize their voice anywhere, or even those little children who ran around in my house, or played on the swing set and ended up in our home movies.

Where have they gone?

Where are those teachers I had in all my school days, the elementary ones I feared, the high school ones I admired, and the college ones I never got to know, but intently listened to, while in their classrooms?

Where have all the people gone that I used to see on the streets who always said, "Hi Kay?"

Where are the shoe stores where people used to help me find shoes that fit? Where are the people who worked at places like the News Shop, where they had things you were interested in? You remember, places where you could find records, magazines, newspapers, and birthday cards.

Where are those stores we used to call the "Five and Dimes?" I guess they are now called dollar stores. Where is that bunch of attorneys who used to come to the old courthouse and file endless numbers of documents? Or that OWU lunch bunch who met each day at that big table in the back at the Brown Jug? And, if it was your birthday, Ed Wolf would sing happy birthday as no one else ever could.

How did I miss their exit from my life? Did I ever get to say goodbye to them? Did I give them a hug and wish them well? I don't remember. I just know that now, they are gone.

No one comes down the street and up on my porch like they used to. Did they move away one day when I had a cold and stayed on the couch under warm blankets with my cup of hot tea? Or was it when I retired and spent my time babysitting a couple of little girls named Kailey and Katie, or did tutoring at the school down the street? All I know is, they are gone!

I would love to have them all back, even if only for one day! One day so I could tell them how rich they made my life. Just one day, so I could say that I'm sorry for the time I may have made fun of their hair, or when I thought I was too busy to stop and talk.

They're gone now! Some are gone forever, and I feel sad because so much time passed when I had the chance to hang on to them a little longer. Others, who are gone during this relatively short period of time, are self-quarantined in their homes. One day they were here, and now they aren't.

With everything coming to a stop right now, and everyone having to stay in their homes, we have a lot of time to remember those days that flew right past us. Think about the people who helped make our lives richer than they would have otherwise been.

Think about all the good things we can do when this period of self-quarantine is lifted. I look forward to the day when we will all be free again.

I've said this before, but it rings true now, more than ever before: "Together is the best place to be."

Search for Farmhouse
Worth the Wait

Recently, I got to see the room in the house where I was born. I had always been told that I was born in an upstairs room of a farmhouse, while my three older siblings had to take care of themselves and stay downstairs. Those three older siblings had also been born at home, each in a different one.

Since I had always wanted to see where I was born, the four of us got together to see if we could find all four of the different houses. By lunchtime that day, we had found the houses of the three older ones, and next it was my turn. While ordering dessert, I asked them where we should be going next to find my birthplace. And, to my surprise, none of the others had a clue as to where the house was located. After all, they were only 11, 8, and 3 years of age when I was born. However, I knew the name of the owner of the farm we lived on, so that was a start.

As the waiter brought our desserts, he got in on the conversation and suggested we go down the street to an insurance office, and maybe someone working there may know where the said farm was located. And sure enough, we hit the jackpot! A guy there knew about the farm, that was Ross Beard's farm, and he drew a circle on the map on the wall, and said, "It's right around in here, somewhere."

So, with those words running around in my brain, we headed for that place on the map. We found a stone road about where the road should be, so drove on it for a while and came upon a farmhouse that was right beside a woods. And as soon as my older sister saw the woods, she knew that the house beside it had to be the farm we were looking for. She remembered having to walk past that woods to get to the corner to be picked up by the school bus. And when we got closer to the farm, we noticed the name on the barn. It said, "Beard Farm," so we knew for sure that it was the right one. But when we stopped and knocked on the door, no one was home. We tried again, about 10 years later, but no one was home then either.

As my older years set in, I lost interest in seeing the house. After all, in this day and age, who would ever open their door and let me come in? But, this past May 30, when my husband and I were in that area to put flowers on my parents' grave, he asked me if I would like to try one last time to see if I could see inside the house where I had been born. And, without thinking, I said, "Yes." So, he turned the car around and took another road north and found the house.

Again, no one was home. However, as we were driving away from the house, a car passed and we watched as it pulled in the driveway. Finally, someone had come home!

Hoping I looked presentable, I walked up to the door, and it was opened by a young woman with a smile on her face and I quickly said something like, "I just wanted to see your house because I was born here 84 years ago." And, she welcomed both of us inside. And with that one short step across the threshold, I was standing in the kitchen of the house I had longed to see. It was like a dream. Immediately, I was thinking of my mom having cooked supper for the five of us at 6 p.m. and right then, going into labor. And my dad having to leave to go get the doctor because the doctor didn't drive. Then I told the owners of the house that I was born in one of the rooms upstairs, and they insisted that we go upstairs to actually see both rooms to be sure to be in the right one.

So, upstairs we went. Only now, while I am writing this story, did it ever occur to me to wonder how my mother survived at all. After all, there was no electricity or running water in that farmhouse! And by the time I was born at 9 p.m. on October 11, 1936, it would have been dark outside. My poor mother.

Somewhere in my photo albums, I have a picture of the house that was taken during the time we lived there. I need to send it to the present owners. Maybe that would take away any uncertainty as to whether or not I really had been born there, so many long years ago.

Sunday Dinners
Hold Special Memories

While growing up with my six siblings we always had a Sunday dinner that was the best meal of the week. I miss our Sunday dinners we had in the dining room. That is if we were living in a house that actually had a dining room. That's when we seemed to use our manners more than we usually did while eating at the kitchen table.

You remember things like not putting your elbows on the table, not chewing with your mouth open, or even not kicking each other under the table! I don't remember ever having a Sunday dinner that we didn't have a "meat and potatoes" type of meal, as well as mom's homemade pie or cake. But it isn't the food that I miss. What I miss is the noise!

When all my siblings and I lived at home with our mom and dad there were anywhere from seven to nine of us seated around the table at every meal. You can imagine the noise when everyone wanted to have their say. I remember many times when I was told that I talked too much. We were supposed to wait our turn to say something, but a lot of the time some of us just couldn't wait that long.

With our mother, the rule was, "If you can't say something nice, don't say anything at all." So, I always tried to, but that didn't always come easily. For instance, all the talk about the time our dad brought one bicycle for all of us to ride. And everyone wanted to have their turn riding it.

When my brothers each had a paper route, you know who got to have the bike then.

It seems that mealtime was the only time we were all congregated together in one room. That changed in 1951, when we got a TV set.

With the passage of time, the number of siblings at the table became less and less. Being the middle child, there were still siblings at home when I got married and moved into my own home. I was told several times how much quieter it was when I wasn't there.

Recently, I got an e-mail that one of my brothers is having a birthday lunch downtown. We always invite all of our siblings when that type of occasion occurs. And at this time in our lives, some of our nieces and nephews join us, too.

I'm looking forward to that gathering, because, by now, you know it isn't the food I'm looking forward to, it's the noise!

Saying Goodbye to
My House Full of Memories

Watching my old house being torn down is not an easy thing to do. From the moment the jaws of the backhoe took the first bite out of the corner of the roof, to the time it literally pulled down the last remaining wall over the accumulated trash, I watched our old house be disintegrated in front of me. All those pieces of siding, flooring, roofing, windows, bricks, and glass came down and disappeared into the rubble that accumulated ahead of them.

The noise is different from any other noise I have ever heard. The sound reminded me of chains clanging together along with heavy weights falling.

Layer by layer of roofing was stacked in a pile, and all I could think about is how great that type of standing-seam roofing had been, because it lasted the entire 61 years we lived there. I had to stand way back from the backhoe because the operator could swing that entire "grabber" around in a circle to put the pieces of the house right where he wanted them to land. Then I began to cough. And once the air was heavy with dust, I should have left, but I couldn't pull myself away from the house that had been an important part of my life. Sooner than you can imagine, I saw an opening which ran from the front of the house to the trees in the backyard.

During the entire day that I watched my past residence become trash, I thought about how good it always felt to have this house to come home to, whether it was after being away on a vacation, or just coming home from my walk. I thought of the importance of the furnace when, on the bitter cold days, we would get home and the first greeting from the house was the warmth I felt as soon as my foot touched the kitchen floor. Many times, I know that I said, out loud, "Thank goodness the furnace is still running!"

Or, on those hot summer days when we kept the house all closed up and had a couple of fans running to keep it cool, is when I appreciated the trees outside that gave so much shade that it kept the temperature at a comfortable level. Especially the tree that we planted out front when my mom died, because as it grew bigger and bigger, it shaded the entire front of the house.

Lots of pictures were taken. One of the great ones showed the pile of rubble with a center opening where you can see the red, white, and blue of the American flag waving from across the street. Or the one showing a lot of boards having been thrown in every direction which amazingly formed a frame for our old piano, sitting in the middle. Yes, our old upright piano, that had seen its better day, ended its life in the jaws of the backhoe. Before these tons of trash get hauled away, I hope to go over and see if I can find a couple of those 88 keys that might be left on the ground.

And while I was thinking of those piano keys, I missed it when the hot water heater was tossed out near a hedge. We had only three different hot water heaters during the entire time we lived there. Each time we got a new one, the person who put them in was very surprised that the old one had lasted so long. And now that I think of it, I am surprised that our house, itself, lasted so long.

We knew it was in its last years as far as most of it went. Most of the floors, upstairs and down, as well as the stairsteps, were squeaking from strain of not just our 61 years there, but of the previous 50 years before we bought the house. This also applies to the various windows that refuse to open. And a note about the hot water heater: it was tossed inside the bathtub so it could be hauled away. Several other smaller trucks have come and gone, taking some various pieces such as the roof, or the foundation.

Everyone knows that saying about "One man's trash being another man's treasure."

As the time passes and the sounds of the chains clanging and the motors roaring begin to run down, I am aware that soon it will be completely gone.

Nothing will be left that even resembles the home I lived in since 1959. No red front door, no brick porch with the trellis, no double-car garage, rec room or patio that George had built all by himself. In the following days, I hope to have a chance to dig through the safe places looking for the three things that were lost over our years of living there. They were George's billfold, his cell phone, and one of our remotes for the TV.

I am pleased when I remember that we will always have the home movies that were taken. I have been asked if I had any tears over this destruction, and all I can say is, "Not yet."

Back When
Neighbors Neighbored

For a while now, anytime I heard the word neighbor, I thought of the Mr. Rogers show and the song "Won't you be my neighbor?"

But recently, when I learned of the passing of my longtime neighbor, Evelyn, I think of her. She had been my neighbor since 1959. At that time, she and her husband and their three growing boys, Bob, Kenny, and Gary, lived right next door. A row of hedges is the only thing that separated our driveways.

When we were seeing about buying the house next door to her, and because George and I worked every day, we needed someone to unlock the house for the inspector from the bank to go inside to examine it, to see if they could loan us the money we needed to buy it.

So, I knocked on her door and asked if she would do that as a favor for us, and she said she would be glad to. We got to know her family and she got to know ours. She talked me into joining her bowling league. She also baked us beautiful birthday cakes as well as sharing vegetables from her garden.

I remember after I got home from taking our older daughter for her first day of kindergarten, my house felt too empty. So, I went over to Evelyn's, and I ended up staying there all afternoon until school was out.

Evelyn spent her later years in a nursing home, and her house sat empty during that whole period of time. When we sold our house recently, and it was being torn down by the new owner, he asked me what I always called that house next door. I told him "Evelyn's house." So, he said that he would call it Evelyn's house, too.

While at the funeral service for Evelyn, I was asked to tell some of my memories of her. I was honored to be asked, especially because all three of her adult sons were there, I wanted them to know how good it was for us to have been a part of their growing up years. I remember going with Evelyn when she took Gary to the airport when he had to leave for the Army. Also, we attended the wedding when Bob married Nancy. We remember the times they went water skiing with us. And I didn't want them to forget the summers when we all used plastic holey balls to play a homemade version of miniature golf, out in their own backyard.

A while back, when her youngest son, Gary, came back one last time to see the house he had grown up in, we saw him there, so went over. I hope he and his two older brothers remember some of the good times they had when they grew up next door. And we want them to know what a joy it was for us to have them for our neighbors.

Sharing Good News
with Dear Friend

I want to write about Mary because I haven't heard from her for several months now. We had a custom of sending emails of only "Good News" to each other every day. She sent me just one sentence of some good news about something she had happened to her, and then I answered with one sentence of some good news about something that happened to me. And after that continued for several days, we decided we should keep it up.

An example of some of her "Good News" sentences to me consisted of one as simple as she "finally got my calendar changed." Also, another was that "CVS sold me two stamps for two cards I had purchased there." A funny one was when she said she ate "Bumblebee Stew in downtown Delaware," and a very nice one was that her sister had "brought me a container of Peach Ice Cream."

I know I sent her back my "Good News" every day, but I can't remember any of them right now, so I'll have to look them up. My computer tells me that some pieces of good news that I sent to Mary are as follows: "I got home from the library without falling down in the mud;" "I boiled all the eggs in one pan, making all the Easter eggs the same color-- green." Also, I wrote that I had "just read the last page of the book "Remember" by Lisa Genova," and last, but not least, was that "I found my bracelet that was engraved: 'IT'S ALL GOOD' that came from a fundraiser for Doug Missman."

So, that's some examples of the emails that went back and forth between us every single day for a couple of years. But then, without notice, her e-mails stopped! However, since I wrote the above, I got a note in the regular mail that stated she's in a nursing home. I need to add that Mary has been wheelchair-bound for most of her adult life, and that most people in nursing homes do not have access to a computer to send e-mail.

Knowing that she liked cats, I ran across a wonderful nonfiction book of cat stories that was written by a veterinarian. So, I got it for her and mailed it to her at the place mentioned on that one note.

I first met Mary when she came into my office to get some information that she needed for her job. She's a wonderful writer and used to have a column in the Delaware Gazette. She also writes poetry. My favorite poem of hers has to do with the dried leaves blowing around in the breeze, looking like baby birds running around. So, when I see those dried up leaves being blown around outside, looking like baby birds, I think of her poem.

I am aware that Mary and I exchanged "Good News" every day for at least two years. With 365 days a year, it means that in two years, each of us came up with 730 things that fit under the heading of "Good News." We decided that everyone could benefit from coming up with their own piece of "Good News" every day.

So, Mary, if you are reading this article in the Delaware Gazette, you can call it my "Good News to you" for today.

Who Knew Youth Baseball
Could Be So Fun?

I 'm aware that there have been baseball teams for young children for a long time. However, I never saw one of their games until this summer. We have a cousin whose two grandsons are now playing on baseball teams for children. One is on a team of four-to-six-year-olds, and the other is in the next older group. Their games have turned our quiet summer afternoons and evenings into grabbing a folding chair and taking off for the baseball field.

There is never a dull moment for us in watching these baseball games. It only took the first game for us to be hooked and not wanting to miss any future games. These games are made possible because their parents do all the work. They are the pitchers as well as watching over the bases and guiding the little ones as to whether to run or not. The adult pitchers do a great job in teaching them how to hit the ball. Most all have a good swing.

What amazes me is the smallness of these players who are able to hit the ball and make it go out into the field. That has to take a lot of practice before the children could possibly do half as well as they do. There are both boys and girls playing in these games. Usually the boys outnumber the girls, but the girls can hold their own. Some girls have pink helmets, which helps to identify them.

Last week was the last game of the season for the children from four to six years of age, and awards were given out. These awards consisted of frame certificates with their names as well as descriptive words as to their playing. They also received a trophy with their name on it and a group picture, as well as a picture with just the player and their coach.

One of the entertaining parts consisted of two of the younger ones running into each other while trying to catch a fly ball, and then "kind of wrestling" as to which one got to throw the ball to home plate. While they were wrestling, there were a lot of people in the stands yelling, "Throw the ball! Throw the ball!"

Another fun thing to see was how they spent their time waiting to get to run from one base to another. As boredom sets in, some sat down on the ground and started playing in the dirt with stones they found.

It has been the best sports entertainment I have had all summer, bar none. I found myself saying that these games should be on TV. There was never a boring moment at any time during the entire games. Watching them be pitched to is amazing. While watching them run from base to base, you might find them running on out into the field without stopping at the designated base. I can't wait until next year to see them play again.

There are a lot of growth spurts between a 4 to a 6-year-old, so there will be all kinds of new abilities. I never knew they could possibly bat and run as well as they do. When I asked a 4-year-old what he likes best about playing, he said, "Hitting." That's the best answer I could have thought of myself. Good luck to him and all the players in their future years in baseball. And, I do believe in the famous line, "There is no crying in baseball" because of what I saw, it was all cheering and laughing.

Thanks to all those parents who get out on the fields and make these experiences happen for their lucky kids. We can't wait until next year to watch them play ball again.

Cards, Concerts and Christmas Greetings

I t isn't every day that you receive a very unusual Christmas card. But this year I did. On the very first day of this month of December, I received a very nice Christmas card in the mail.

Right away I knew who it was from because of the return address. It was from the young couple who invited us to their home, when I knocked on their door last May and asked if I could come in and see the room where I had been born. Since we hadn't been in touch since then, I was pleased to see that we were remembered by them.

When I looked at the front of the card, I saw a nice outdoor scene. It was of a white house and a red barn in the country with the words "Merry Christmas." And as I laid the card down, I said, "Wouldn't it be nice if it was a picture of their own house and barn?" And immediately I picked it back up and looked at the house and saw a great similarity. So, after about five minutes, we decided it had to be the house I had been so happy to find and got to go inside seven months ago! And George was sure it had to be the same red barn as well. So, I sent them a letter asking if it was their house. And we got the confirmation that it was! What a wonderful card to have for Christmas! I ended up sending copies to all my relatives.

That takes care of the card part of the headline, and now for the concert part. Since we live in Buckeye Valley Local School District, and are senior citizens, we are pleased to be invited to a concert at BV each year just before Christmas. It was held on Friday, December 9, at 9:30 a.m. at the high school auditorium.

In past years, they had a sit-down lunch served by the students. But this year it was a breakfast of fruit, sandwiches and desserts. As we filed in the door, we found we were in line to pick up the food of our choice and go inside the auditorium and be seated by the students.

First was the choir, with their wonderful director, singing some great Christmas music. That was followed by the orchestra, which filled the entire stage, all dressed in black and white. When the band director spoke, he was filled with joy to be able to play for the audience of senior citizens. It is pure joy to get to see and hear live music just for us from all of the wonderful students who sing and play instruments so well. Every senior citizen is invited to come, and I hope they have another concert next year and that everyone will come to BV to enjoy it as much as we do.

The above stories of cards and concerts make me feel that it's really Christmas. Previous years I've encouraged all readers to attend a Christmas candlelight service on Christmas Eve. Singing all the favorite Christmas hymns, being in a candlelit sanctuary while everyone's candle is being lit, and singing "Silent Night," is Christmas for me. If you haven't already made plans to go, find a church that has one and be sure to be there.

Merry Christmas to everyone.

Night's Stay at
Old Campbell House

Sometimes, things that happened years and years ago surprisingly pop back into your head.

That happened to me yesterday. This situation I thought of happened about 15 years ago, just as I walked out the front door of the bank on north Sandusky Street in downtown Delaware. I was about three steps out onto the sidewalk when a young woman approached me.

When I first saw her, I thought she was one of the OWU students from my days of working there. She was very well dressed and seemed happy to see me. However, when we got closer, I knew I had never met her before.

Immediately, she told me her story. She said she needed $25 to get a room at the motel, the old Campbell House on South Sandusky Street so she and her two young children could stay inside for that night. Otherwise, they would have to sleep in her car. And that her mother was going to be in Delaware the next morning after driving here from Florida and would give her the money she needed. I remember that it happened during the week between Christmas and New Year's.

As she talked, she kept glancing across the street at a light-colored parked car that was facing south.

I have never had a stranger ask me for money before, so I wasn't sure how to handle it. She said she needed to find a person who looked like someone she could trust. I think that meant that I wouldn't yell at her for even asking.

I believed her story, so I gave her the money. She asked me where I lived so that she could mail it back to me, but I said, "No, that's not necessary."

Then things changed. She asked me where I was going. I pointed to the antique store a couple of doors down. And that's when she said she would like to go there with me.

That's when I decided that if she had two children waiting alone in her car, the first thing she should do is to go check on them. I didn't see her glance across the street again.

But there was no stopping her, so when we got to the antique store, I opened the door and she followed me in.

She said she needed to see if they had shoes that would fit her son. And right away we saw some high-top infant baby shoes on top of one of the cases.

As soon as she picked them up, I said that I had to run, so I left without looking back. My car was up the street facing north, so I knew she couldn't follow me. I never met up with her again.

I have always wondered if her story was true. Or was she going to ask me for more money? Or did she really have two children who may have been in that car?

I'll never know, but I can always be glad that if it was true, she and her children didn't have to sleep in her car that cold December night.

Siblings Joined Forces
to Tour Graceland

Keeping a journal for the past 50 years has its advantages. That's because I found one of my "portable journals" that contained the four-day trip I took with my six siblings to see Elvis in October 2003. When I talk to friends about that trip, I usually get remarks something like, "I would never survive a trip of any kind with my siblings!" Or "With my three, no way."

When we all got together for the trip to Graceland, the five sisters drove a van, while the two brothers flew down and met us there.

Our first meal together that evening was at a nice place called "Dale's" which had been recommended by our room clerk. Our waitresses name was Nancy Ann, and after she got our seven orders, at the suggestion of my younger brother, we all got up and traded seats.

He must have done it someplace before and wanted to see what would happen if we did it. She did very well getting us served correctly, and no one said a word. The next day when we went there again, we had the same waitress and when she saw us, she said, "Oh no, not you again!" I remember one of us jokingly said, that's what our mother always said. That day was Elvis's day, so we had an early morning. We all travelled together in our van to Graceland. We went in on the left side of Elvis Presley Boulevard with Graceland on the other side of the street. We parked beside the Heartbreak Hotel and passed the Lisa Marie jet to get to the main entrance. It only cost $20.70 for our entire group at senior citizen rates. Elvis's music was playing all the time we were there.

The tour was crowded, and it was hard to see the inside of the house. Lots of mirrors and gold and velvet and other opulence filled the rooms. Enclosed stairways were all lined with mirrors. In the basement was a jungle room filled with stuffed animals. The carport was filled with his cars, motorcycles, golf carts, horses and an old swing set. Outback was a memorial garden place where Elvis, his twin who died at birth, parents and grandmother, are all buried. Lots of fake flowers were circulating around a very small waterfall.

The original racquetball court was filled to the ceiling with his pictures, clothes and awards. The rooms had carpeting on the walls as well as floors. It was a much smaller house than we thought it would be.

Elvis had a row of three different television sets because that is what he had seen our president do. We were told that the kitchen was always open because people came there to eat at all times of day and night. In his bedroom, he had a big round white bed with a radio built in the headboard.

We also toured his museum of cars. We saw the big beautiful pink Cadillac convertible that he had gotten for his wonderful mother. After the house tour, we took a shuttle to see the little drugstore that had been turned into "Sun Records" where Elvis had recorded his very first song. On the night before we left for Nashville, we had dinner at Dales again. We asked for Nancy Ann to be our waitress. No, we didn't change seats, we enjoyed our meal and left her a very large tip.

Birthday Memories,
Parties Live on Today

Growing up with six siblings meant we always had lots of birthdays to celebrate together. However, in the recent past, our two older sisters died.

They were in their 90s, and their names were Ginny and Marilyn. When Marilyn's birthday came up this past May, her children got her siblings altogether for brunch and celebrated her birthday anyway. We spent a couple hours just sitting remembering the good times we had with her. Then in June, when it would have been Ginny's birthday, her children got us all together again to remember the years we had with her as our oldest sibling. I enjoyed it because it was a time to talk and laugh together for as long as the restaurant allowed us to stay.

My memories of our childhood birthdays were to have supper, and the one with the birthday got to pick what mom would make for dessert that night. My choice was banana cream pie. And, we had a special plate that the birthday "kid" got to use. That plate would be at our place at the table when we sat down. With seven kids and only one special plate, it was a problem as to who got to have the plate when we all got married and left home.

I was lucky one day when I was at the DPS Antique Store in Delaware and saw enough of those same plates to buy, so now, each of us has our own.

This year, for our birthdays, we have been meeting at Bun's at noon. They will put tables together for us, and we can sit and talk as long as we want.

Our younger brother has already sent out word that he wants us to meet for lunch at Bun's on his birthday this month. The majority of my siblings are now in our 80s, with our youngest sister still being in her 70s. Mostly, we bring birthday cards that make everyone laugh. And if we can find any old pictures of the birthday person, we can laugh about what we look like back in the day. It's too bad it wasn't possible for our parents to live long enough to celebrate with us.

"No one knows what the future holds, so we have to live for the day and enjoy every minute of it." The previous quote is one that wrote itself. I could say that because it wasn't on the screen when I left the room, but it was there when I came back in just now. If that can't be true, then it must be my forgetfulness taken over. Whatever it is, do as it says. Enjoy every minute!

Music, Flowers
and Funerals

Having just returned from a friend's funeral made me think of other funerals I have attended in my lifetime. I remember the very first one when I was only 5 years old, and my parents took me with them to my grandpa's funeral. I still have vivid memories of all the flowers I saw there. They seemed to go from the floor to the ceiling. There were flowers everywhere at that funeral home.

It was in 1941 that grandpa died. I wasn't aware of what they were talking about when they said he would be going to heaven. I remember assuming that heaven must have been that place with all the flowers that went from the floor to the ceiling. Since no one explained the difference, that confusion stayed with me for a very long time. So, for years, whenever people talked about heaven, I thought it was a room filled with flowers.

Another part of funerals is whether or not they have music. A long time ago, one of our previous ministers asked that our church choir learned to sing the sing the "Hallelujah Chorus." He said he wanted to be sure it would be sung at his funeral.

I was very glad to have learned to sing it. It's a rather difficult song to sing, and I was surprised, and pleased, when one of the classes at our elementary school had it memorized and sang it at a Christmas program several years ago.

"Amazing Grace" is a familiar hymn that is often sung at funerals. It was especially meaningful to me when everyone sang it at our son-in-law's funeral back in 2006. That may have been the first time I heard the new words for the fourth verse. The new words at that time were:

"When we've been there 10,000 years.
Bright shining as the sun
We've no less days to sing God's praise
Then when we first begun."

There's no question as to the fact that by the time you get in your 80s, you have given thought as to what you want your own funeral to be like. You can go to the funeral hall and plan the way you want everything to be, and they will see that your wishes are carried out.

Speaking of funeral homes reminds me of something I was told by a lady at work. If my memory is right, she told me that her husband had died when their daughter was only 3 years old. And a long period of time later as they were driving past the funeral home where his funeral had been held, her daughter looked at the building and said, "That's where my daddy lives." That was a very sad story.

While writing this above part of this article, I searched out well-known hymns to play. I found that "Amazing Grace" is recorded by II Divo as well as the Gathers and others, and the hymn was written by John Newton who was born in 1725 and died in 1807. And it has had 67,642,047 views. Check it out for yourself, I think you'll like it.

Paying for Electricity Is
Money Well Spent

I just finished paying my electric bill for this past month, and I was comparing the cost of this month's bill from other bills in the past.

It made me think of all the service we receive for each month's payment. For instance, during a storm this past month, our electricity went out completely. It was in the late evening, so it was pitch dark in our home. The first thing we got out was a flashlight and that led us to go looking for candles to light.

One of the great things we found was the battery-operated globe that sits on our table for nice lighting during breakfast. At the time, I was wishing I had about 10 of them to turn on. It ended up that the electricity came back on around 4 a.m. By then, we had found four flashlights and had lit one big candle. And I had found the extra batteries if they became necessary.

Those several hours without electricity made me appreciate having electricity more than ever. Someone once said that if your electricity goes out, go outside and get your solar lights and bring them inside. What a great idea. They don't give off a lot of light but it's better than none. We only had a few solar lights at that time, but recently purchased 12 more. After we put them outside last evening, I said the lighting in our yard makes it look like Christmas. We also have a wishing well in the front yard that is lit with two solar lights. And just today, we put up a new solar light on our flagpole to light up the flag.

Then our conversation about electricity reminded me of how much a flashlight helps. For several years there has been a young boy who walks past our house all alone before daylight to get to the school bus which is at the school down the street. He has his own flashlight to get to the bus.

Another light bulb that helps a lot is inside our refrigerator. You know something is wrong if it's not lit when you open that door. Also, our night light in the bathroom helps a lot.

Years ago, there was an article in the paper about how much it costs for each light bulb to burn. All I remember is they said that one bulb would last a very long time if you didn't turn it on and off very often. That must apply to the house across the street because their TV is on all night every night. It's noticeable because the TV is directly across from their large living room window. In the summer when we are sitting outside, it's like being at a drive-in movie when we were younger and watched the cartoons.

One of the very nicest lightings of a tree I have seen is about half-a-block away. If I stand at one of our windows and look through the trees, I can see a small Christmas tree on a porch that is lit year round. It's a beautiful sight at 3 a.m. when I can't sleep.

One more light I remember being glad to see was when I was a teenager and babysat evenings. I was glad to see that our porch light was still on when I got home.

Our daughter has a sensory light in her yard that turns on as soon as she drives up her driveway. It would be nice if everyone had a sensor light for when they come home after dark, it would be money well spent.

At this point, I have to say that I feel my money for our electricity has been well spent. Maybe when I pay my bill next month, I should include a thank you note with my check.

Memories of Dear
Sister Will Live On

Her name was Ann. It was really Edith Ann when she was born on January 14, 1942. Our new little sister was blonde and very pretty. Her name of Edith was added on because Edith was the name of our mom's mother. And it was the day of her mother's funeral, and our mom wasn't able to go.

One of my first memories of her is when she was about 5 years old and swallowed a nickel. She said she did, and mom believed her, so they spent a lot of time checking to see if she passed it, and finally it was recovered. That nickel has been talked about a lot over all the years since. We often wonder where it is today.

She was always noticed as different from the rest of her six siblings because she was a blonde. The only blonde in the house. No curls, but braids mostly. She was a very pretty girl.

When she got to high school, she was a cheerleader and also the homecoming queen. She also had the lead in many of the plays. One was when she was Mama in "I Remember Mama" in a Delaware theater group. She had the lead in a couple of musicals in high school and sang very well.

Later in life, after her marriage and the birth of two daughters, she and her husband had a house built in Delaware. It was a very nice house, with a basement for having lots of parties. We have pictures when we were all down there for a big Thanksgiving dinner. She liked to talk about dancing on the table, but I never did see her do it.

Eventually, she got a job in the registrar's office at Ohio Wesleyan University and worked there until she retired. While there, she talked me into applying for a job in the education department. I was very glad to get hired and, thanks to her, I had the opportunity to take classes.

While both of us worked those years at OWU, we met for lunch every day at the Brown Jug. When our sister, Jean, came to work at OWU, she joined us for lunch, too. Then other staff from OWU started joining us. That's when the owners told us that if we were going to eat there every day, they would give us our own table in the back. Lots of good memories for all of us from those days. Especially every time Ed Wolf sang "Happy Birthday" to one of the group.

During that time, Ann's marriage came to an end, and there was a divorce. That's when Ann bought her own smaller house up on Pennsylvania Avenue. Her two daughters went on to graduate from OWU because Ann had worked there long enough for them to get to go to tuition free.

Eventually, Ann's health began to fail, and she had to retire. After too many surgeries, she had to give up her home and moved to Saint Michael's. That was followed by having to move to the Sarah Moore nursing home. And as her health continued to get worse, she had to have constant nursing care. We knew it was becoming extremely bad when hospice came on the scene. Then, sadly, last month on August 3, she died. She was not alone because her two daughters and one son-in-law were there with her. Sorry to say, Jean and I had just left 10 minutes before. May Ann rest in peace.

This article is dedicated to all the nurses and staff at Sarah Moore for their care of Ann Lee, during the year she was with you. Thank you!

Not Enough Time
to Thank Former Teachers

I t isn't every day that I get inducted into the Delaware City Schools
Hall of Fame, but since I did last week, I want to write about some
of the things I had planned to say.

I was told I would have to give a speech that could last only five minutes. So, I sat down and started writing about my favorite teachers during
my years in the Delaware City School District. I got carried away and I didn't
stop writing until I'd written about all my favorite teachers in both elementary and high school. Of those, I chose four of the best ones and planned to
use them in the speech. So, I had my daughter time me, and I started in. Just
as I finished the first one, she told me that my five minutes were up. No way
could I only talk about one, but my five minutes were up. Rules are rules, so
I decided I would choose just Mr. Conger of my fifth and sixth grades at East
School. The school is now called Conger Elementary because it was named
for him long after I had left to go on to Willis High School.

I had several reasons to choose Mr. Conger. First was because he was
nice all the time. And it helped to get to know him since he was my part-
time teacher in the fifth and then again in the sixth grade. Nothing else
comes to mind about the fifth grade, except he seemed to be always just
talking to us. I remember him talking about the pictures of presidents that
were on the wall. And also, it is important to let you know that he also had
us memorize the western states.

So, the next year, when the sixth grade came, I was prepared for
something in class one day. He asked if there was anyone in the room

who remembers memorizing the western states, north to south and east to west. When he asked that question, my hand went up in the air. I didn't know that no one else had raised their hand. So, I remembered him saying, "Kay, stand up." So, I did, but my heart was pounding. I was going to have to prove that I had a right to put my hand in the air. Then he told me to name the states in question. So, I said, Montana, Wyoming, Colorado, New Mexico, Idaho, Utah, Arizona, Nevada, Washington, Oregon, and California. When I finished, Mr. Conger said the nicest things about me being able to do that. It was something about how great it was that after one whole year, I was able to recite all those states. I wonder what he would have thought if he knew I had remembered them after 74 years, since that happened in 1948.

The next teacher I wrote about was Mr. Felts, the Willis High School math teacher. He was so good that I wanted to become a high school math teacher just like him.

The reason I liked his class so much was because the answers were in the back of the book, and he gave open-book tests! How good can it get? When I did my homework, I knew it was right because I had checked it in the back of the book. If my answer was wrong, I worked on the problem until I got the correct answer. And as for open-book tests, he always said that in life you can look up the answer to any problem you have. You just have to know where to look. The example I like to use is that if you need to know how much air to put in the tire of your car, just open the driver's side door and it will be pasted in the edge of the opening.

When I ran for the office of Delaware County recorder, I was out campaigning and went to his house. That was 1988 when I had been out of high school for 34 years. When I knocked on his door, his wife answered and he saw me and said, "Come on in, Kay." Getting to speak to him as an adult, I asked him why I ever took all those classes of algebra, geometry, and trigonometry? I had never used any of them. He said, "Those classes taught you to think." He added, "You must have thought a lot about running for office before you filed, didn't you?" Yes, I did. He was right. I thought a lot about running before I actually did. Thinking about it must have helped because I won and spent four terms as Delaware County recorder before I retired.

I am glad to have the opportunity to write about two of my favorite teachers in the Delaware City School District. Maybe in the future I can write about another one, for instance, Mrs. Hearn.

Pictures Help
Remember Good Times

For a week now, I have been thinking of what I could write for this week's article. Earlier today I thought of writing about going to the cemetery, but decided against it. So, I went through my quote books to find something to put here that someone else had written. And this is one of the things I found. It was written by Robert N. Test (1926-1994) that is about organ donation at the time of death.

"When my life has stopped, do not instill artificial life into my body by use of a machine.

1. Give my sight to someone who has never seen a sunrise.

2. Give my heart to a person whose own heart has caused nothing but pain.

3. Give my kidneys to one who depends on a machine.

4. Take my bones, every muscle, every fiber and nerve in my body and find a way to make a crippled child walk.

5. Explore every corner of my brain.

6. Take my cells and let them grow to help a speechless boy or a deaf girl be able to speak and hear.

7. Burn what is left of me and scatter the ashes to the winds to help the flowers grow.

If by chance you wish to remember me, do it with a kind deed or word to someone who needs you.

If you do all I have asked, I will live forever."

Above was a quote from my quote book I filled back in 2011. This past Christmas, I was given a bulletin board for my office, and I have been putting special pictures up, one by one. Now I have 10 pictures. Two of my sister Ann, who died this past August. The pictures each show her when she was younger and full of life. I wanted a good picture to take to the nursing home to put up on the wall so that the nurses could see how she looked when she was well.

Another is of our mother, on her 80th birthday. Everyone was sitting around a big table in my dining room from the house across the street. Ann is standing beside her and has just placed the birthday cake in front of mom for her to blow out the candles.

I want to add that I have a very old black and white picture of the seven of us "kids" when we were young back in 1945. In that picture are my two older sisters who died in the past six years. Their names were Marilyn and Ginny.

To end this article, I would like to use a quote that showed up and I don't know who said it, but it speaks volumes to me: "There will come a time when thoughts of your loved ones will bring a smile to your face before it brings a tear to your eye."

Remembering
Mrs. Hearn

D uring this past month I have been doing a lot of thinking about my teachers from my years in elementary and secondary schools.

I have already written about Mr. Felts and Mr. Conger. One of the others I have thought about is Mrs. Hearn. She was in the classroom and also doing school plays we had back in the 1950s. She and other teachers wrote the script and music for a production of "Delaware Diary." I wish there had been videotapes back then, but no such luck. So, I will stick to mostly parts of her classroom.

Anyone who knows her knows that she was very strict. Very strict! And because of that strictness, a lot of students weren't very happy to be in her classroom. My first memory of her was when we were practicing for the "Delaware Diary" in the evenings. I was only late once, but that once was enough. She was so mad at me that she didn't even want to be the person to bawl me out for being late. So, she told one of my classmates to bawl me out for her.

My interest in Mrs. Hearn's teaching goes back to the day she asked if any student in the class wanted to come to an informal class after school in her room, and we would write and read short stories. I was in my sophomore year of high school and had the free time, so I went. I was excited when I got there and found that she had arranged about 8 or 10 chairs in a circle and was already sitting in one of them. The famous line, "If you build it, they will come" applies here because all the chairs were filled from the first day on.

Next was the fact that she would laugh. I don't ever remember hearing her laugh in the regular class. So, we were off to a good start. One by one we read our stories and the whole class talked about them. She seemed so happy and relaxed to do that. I only remember one sentence. A girl named Katie had read one line in her story that went like this: "My dad is so dumb, he doesn't know the difference between 'red' and 'red-red' lipstick." I think what bothered me was that she would refer to her father as "dumb." I don't remember anything that I had written, but i remember how nice it was to feel relaxed in a classroom with Mrs. Hearn. Here's where I need to give her a lot of the credit for my enjoyment of writing these short articles I have published since my first one back in April 2016.

I need to comment about something that happened some 25 years later. It was when we had our class reunion at the Campbell House and while some of the guys were out in the hall, they met up with Mr. and Mrs. Hearn coming in the front door. They decided to invite them to come in to see our class.

When she got in, she started calling a lot of students by name. My memory is of her talking to Connie and Ron about the play they were in called "Arsenic and Old Lace."

It felt good to see my classmates make over her at that time in her life. Three cheers for great classmates!

I have to add this last thought. Mrs. Hearn's classroom had a small stage in it. Just one step up, and you were on the stage. During one of the classes, she had each student in the room walk across the stage. Up one side of the stage and down the other. As we finished, one by one, she told us what was wrong with our posture. She told us to imagine that a string around our chest was pulling us straight up. So, every once in a while, when I'm out walking, I can hear her voice saying, "Kay, stand up straighter!"

Thanks Mrs. Hearn!

Memories from Graduation
Day Back in 1954

Most people can remember something about the day they graduated from high school. For me, lots and lots of things have stuck in my mind.

So, I decided I would see how those memories look on paper.

It was Thursday, June 3, 1954. When I woke up that morning, it was light outside, and I looked around the room and was reminded that I was staying at the home of a friend of mine named Judy. Since my family was living in Morrow County at that time, she had asked me to stay there so as not to miss any of the parties and practices for our graduation that evening. I knew immediately that she and I needed to be ready very soon to be on our way to an 8 a.m. senior breakfast at Buns Restaurant's upstairs dining room.

We were both seniors at Willis High School and were meeting the rest of our class there. It was a four-block walk that we made in time to be served a wonderful breakfast, which included a dish of fruit of pineapple, bananas, and strawberries on a plate with eggs, bacon, and toast. I think all 105 members of our class were there. Back in the 1950s, Bun's Restaurant had an upstairs dining room. To get to it, you had to enter from a door on West Winter Street and walk up a steep narrow set of stairs that took some strong leg muscles to get all the way up.

With breakfast finished, we all headed south on Sandusky Street for Gray Chapel on the grounds of Ohio Wesleyan University. We were to practice marching in, and then up on the stage to receive our diplomas that very evening. It was announced that the 14 students who made-up a group to sing a new song called "You'll Never Walk Alone" by Rodgers and Hammerstein, would have to be there an hour earlier than the others. Since I was an alto in that group, I was concerned because that was shortening my time to finish making the dress I had to wear that evening. I should never have procrastinated so long in getting that dress finished!

When Judy and I got back to her house, her family was leaving to take her shopping in Columbus. That left me alone in their house to get my dress finished. But first, I had to pack up my suitcase so that my parents could pick it up before the graduation ceremonies. Then, I started working on my pieces of already cut-out white Dotted Swiss material. Things went just fine until it was time to iron it. Using someone else's iron is when the problem began. As soon as the iron touched the finished dress, it burned a hole the size and shape of the iron right through the front of it! The rule was for all the girls to wear white dresses under their cap and gown. And there I was with the chimes of the clock striking 2 p.m. and no other white dress to wear.

As I looked over the leftover material, I considered sewing it all into one big piece and then cutting out another top and using that. Since nothing had to match, I gave it a try, and it worked! It's a good thing because there was no time to run back to Uhlman's to buy another $1.00-a-yard of Dotted Swiss.

Judy and her family had not returned, so I left early enough to walk to pick up my cap and gown and put it on over my patched dress before anyone saw it.

After I had been given my diploma, I started looking over the audience to see if I could find my parents so as to know which way to go to meet them.

It all worked out well. They had successfully picked up my suitcase, too. Everything went well except for one little question. When my 12-year-old sister, Ann, went in to pick up my suitcase, they asked her what my family was getting me as a gift for my graduation. It had never been talked about, so she told them she didn't think I was getting anything. However, when we got home at the farmhouse, there were three wrapped packages on the kitchen table. It turned out that I received three white purses from three different people. I guess that when asked what I needed, my mom must have told everyone in the family that I needed a white purse.

When everyone else had gone to bed, it was a long time before I got any sleep. It had just hit me that my life, as I had known it for all of my past 10 years, was over. Our family moved to Delaware at the beginning of my third-grade year. During those ten years, I had never left the Delaware City School system. However, I didn't belong there any longer. I didn't have a job. I had no money, so I wouldn't be going to college. I didn't even know how to drive.

I had no way to go anywhere. All I knew was that somehow, some way, somewhere, I would find a job. My dad told me that I didn't have to worry about finding a job right away "Because once you start to work, you never stop." And he was right.

Moving on Following
Loss of Loved One

<hr />

His name was Nick.

He was my nephew's son.

He had a smile that really did go from "ear to ear."

Whenever we were both at the same place at the same time, he hugged me.

When he hugs you, you know you have been hugged.

The last time he hugged me was at my sister's funeral.

It was so strong, my glasses turned sideways on my face.

He was a little over 6-foot tall.

I took his picture while he was sitting in my living room.

With a smile like that, I just have to take his picture!

He was very pleased when I gave him a copy of it.

Mostly, we ran into each other at hardware stores.

He always spotted me before I spotted him.

You would think it would be the other way around since I'm only 5-foot-4.

He recently gave me a card of his business he had started.

I was glad for him to have his own business now.

Earlier this year we all met to celebrate my sister and his grandmother's birthday.

She had died last year, but we still wanted to celebrate her special day.

When we met, he was with his wife and carrying his baby daughter.

And what a lovely baby she is.

And on that day, he told me that he would be coming to see us.

And I said I will be looking forward to that day.

But that day never came.

Just a week ago now, I got a very sad phone call.

My niece tried to tell me that he had died.

I couldn't understand who she said it was.

So, she had to say it over several times.

I guess I just didn't want to hear it.

She didn't tell me how he died, just that he did.

This past week there was a gathering in his honor.

Before we got to the building it was in, we could see the parking lot was filled.

So many cars, so many people!

Family and friends who cared about him.

If he only knew how much people cared about him.

Maybe he would still be smiling his smile and giving those big hugs.

But now, we have to go on without him.

His name was Nick.

Some Losses Are
Harder than Others

I t's hard for me to believe, but I began the journey of writing articles for the Delaware Gazette back in July 2016! While I was leafing through the first of the old journals, I ran across the story titled: "The things I have lost."

It was summer when I was inside a friend's car and she hit my car while it was parked in my own garage and demolished it from front to back and from top to bottom. It was my new white Chevy Malibu. Our police chief said he had never written-up a report on a car being totaled while in its own garage. So, that was the first of many losses that began the year of 2016.

So, my topic for this article will be some of the things I have lost in just the past six years.

My biggest losses were three of my sisters as well as one great nephew and one niece's husband. Their names were John, Ginny, Marilyn, and Nick.

Another loss was the house I lived in from the day we got married in 1959 until we sold it in 2020. I lost it because we needed to downsize, so we bought a smaller place across the street.

The new owner tore down our eight-room house, so nothing is left of it. I can't tell you how many times I have looked across the street expecting to see that white house with a red front door still standing there. But it's gone.

I've also lost some of the clothes I was wearing in old photos I've looked at. Recently while going through some of my photo albums, I became aware that the outfits I had on were gone. I know I would have never given them away, so how did they disappear? My guess is because as I was packing, I was putting good clothes in one bag and old clothes in another. And then I got them mixed up and I ended up with my old clothes, with my better ones having been given away. We even made a trip to Goodwill to see if we could find any of them. No luck.

All of the horses we had at the farm are gone now. I'm not sure where they went other than they may have died by now. Their names included "Tango Tag," "Sweet Georgia Kay," "Bubba" and "Bevis." For me, a big loss was not getting to be at the farm when children came to ride in our indoor arena. And then go to the horse shows and see them win all their ribbons, especially the blue ones. A couple of the girls have continued into adulthood with having their horses at their own or another horse farm. But mostly the children have all grown up, and we no longer own the farm.

So, losing three of my sisters, a great nephew, and a niece's husband, my new car, the house I had lived in for 60 years, my better clothes, horses and kids who came to ride, all add up to an overall big loss that happened to me since 2016. I should add that I have lost a lot of my hair and more of my hearing and some of my eyesight.

Writing about loss is a little too depressing for me today, so I got out my journals to see if I could find something to at least bring a smile to my face. And I chose this one sentence by our youngest daughter when she was three years old. She handed me her little book and said, "Talk to this page." And sure enough, I talked to that page and a whole lot more pages and I've been smiling ever since.

Old Pamphlet Brings
Back Memories of Delaware

Y ou never know what you may discover when you are looking for something else. I set out to find my "birthday book" that has a record of family and friends birthdays.

Instead, I found a pamphlet titled "Welcome to Delaware, Ohio." It looked rather old, but interesting. It didn't take me long to start reading it. Who knows what interesting things I might find out about my favorite subject, "Old Delaware?" Since I am one of those people who always opens a book from the back first, it was there that I found a list of all the businesses in Delaware that contributed to making the printing of this publication possible. I couldn't find the exact date it was published, but it was in the 1970s, which is 50 years ago now!

First, I enjoyed reading the names of familiar places where I would have shopped, but are no longer here. For instance:

Bennett-Brown Funeral Home which is now Snyder-Rodman Funeral Center.

The Delaware County Bank on the corner of Sandusky and Winter is no longer there.

Del RX Pharmacy is no longer at the corner of Sandusky and William.

The First National Bank, where I got my first checking account, no longer exists.

Grays Shoes is gone.

Grief Brothers Corporation is no longer on Pennsylvania Avenue.

Independent Print Shop is no longer at 9 East William Street.

New Method Cleaners, a company with a new method of cleaning, is gone.

People's Store, the best place that had the best sales, is gone.

Sullivan's Western Auto store run by Mr. Sullivan and his son, Bill, is gone.

U. S. Store, that wonderful downtown grocery store that is needed now, is gone.

Wilson's CJ of Course that had the best clothes is gone.

L&K restaurant, where everyone wanted a toasted pecan roll, is gone now.

There are a lot more establishments that are gone, but I only listed the ones that were familiar to me.

The second page from the back of the pamphlet is about the climate of Delaware County. It was interesting to quote just one of their sentences. "Past weather records indicate an average year will have 100 clear, 118 partly cloudy and 146 cloudy days, with average mean temperatures of 28 degrees in January and 73 in July." Sounds like a great place to live.

As I looked through the pamphlet, I found a page of pictures of downtown in the 1970s, and just seeing the signs on the outside of the buildings brought back memories, memories and more memories. They included the Treasure House, the L&K, People's Store, the Nectar, First National Bank, and even the words Billiards and Famous Foods. It reminded me of a song from that era titled "Downtown." If you are like me, you remember some of the words of that song, so I looked them up, and here are the first several lines:

"When you're alone and life is making you lonely, you could always go, downtown.

When you got worries and all the noise and the hurry seems to help I know, downtown.

Just listen to the music of the traffic in the city, linger on the sidewalks where the neon signs are pretty.

How can you lose? The lights are much brighter there. You can forget all your troubles, forget all your cares.

Go downtown, things will be great when you're downtown, no finer place for sure downtown, everything's waiting for you."

There are a lot more lines to that song, so if you want to read them, just search "Downtown" on your computer. Enjoy.

This pamphlet I just ran across has one small paragraph that I would like to quote that was written in the 1970s, that fits very well for today:

"Right now, Delaware still offers the 'best of both worlds'-- the quiet of tree-lined streets and familiar faces and business establishments plus the services of a modern city enhanced by convenience of a major city— Columbus-- 30 minutes away. It's 100-year-old brick homes find appreciative owners and diligent restorers, but new homes and apartment complexes are also springing up in many sections of town."

So, I'm glad I found something I wasn't expecting to find. Remember this one line: "Go downtown where all the lights are bright, downtown's waiting for you tonight, downtown you're gonna be all right now!"

Some Memories
Remain Vivid

Several years ago, I decided to write some poems about growing up with all my siblings. I decided to give the poems to them as Christmas gifts that year. Before my time ran out, I had written 13 poems about different subjects from how we were living before World War II ended, and then afterwards. I had nothing to go by, except the memories that I have carried during the years that the seven of us were living at home with our mom and dad.

The poem I have chosen is about the "blackouts" that happened while WW II was going on. As I look back, this took place when we were living together in a house in Galion, Ohio.

"There was something called a blackout when no lights were allowed to be lit.

It was so airplanes couldn't see us, and our town would not be hit.

There was something called a blackout that happened during WW II.

It cost me a lot of worry at our home at 225 Grove Avenue.

When the radio announced the blackout, I would sit in the dark and stare.

I searched the sky for an airplane that I hoped would never be there.

I worried that our neighbors might fail to turn out their lights.

I worried about a number of things; I worried both days and nights.

I worried that we'd run out of tokens; I worried that our rations wouldn't last.

I worried that mom worried about sugar and everything else now passed.

Did anyone else worry about blackouts? I may have been the only one.

My older siblings knew it was only a test, the younger ones were just having fun."

The above poem is what I remember most from when World War II was going on. I was worried more than anyone else in our family because I didn't know it was only a test. I thought there really were airplanes flying around, looking for cities to bomb. The house across the street never did turn out their lights. I sat on the floor and noticed that we had a design in our carpeting that resembled a swastika. Having that design scared me as well as everything else. I never did point out the swastika to our mother.

I didn't want her to worry more than she already was. No one else seemed to be worried. While our dad was reading the newspaper, the boys were listening to a story on the radio and the older girls may have been making fudge out in the kitchen, while the younger girls were probably sleeping. They let me do all the worrying.

Driving Drunk Can
Change Lives Forever

I t all began the very same minute that a man named Mr. Carr was heading west on the highway with the blinding sun shining in his eyes, and our nephew, Rick, was heading east on his motorcycle to go home. And just as Mr. Carr started to make a left turn, he and Rick collided, and Rick was hit head-on and thrown to the ground where he died instantly.

That evening my phone rang at home, and I was told that the Clark County Coroner's office was calling for George Conklin. When I said he wasn't there, the officer asked if I was Kay Conklin and if so, for me to give George a message that "Richard Conklin had been killed in a motorcycle accident."

My first thought was that I didn't know any "Richard" Conklin, so why was he calling me? Then it dawned on me that Rick always rode his motorcycle and his name was really Richard. Oh, NO! So, I called our daughter and asked her to go over to the barn and tell her dad what had happened. What a shock! Then we had to find Rick's grandparents and tell them the bad news. Such terrible news!

At that time, our nephew was 37 and had a bike shop in Clark County. His own father had died from cancer when Rick was only 10, and his mother was now living in Texas. He was like a brother to our daughters. He loved his bike and graduated from the "Harley-Davidson School for Mechanics" out in Arizona. He was a friend to a lots of bikers, and they called him "Pup." This accident happened back in May 2004.

Rick was the type of person who didn't hold a grudge. He didn't hate, and he saw the best in people. He gave everyone his unconditional friendship. He lived life to the fullest and passed away doing what he loved, riding his Harley!

Going back to the time of the accident, Mr. Carr was at that very spot on the highway because he was going home from an anniversary party where he had been drinking.

He was under the influence of alcohol. We didn't meet him until the day of his sentencing for vehicular homicide at the Clark County Courthouse. When he and his wife arrived, they looked very frail and seemed to have to help each other walk as they entered the courtroom. They look as sad as anyone I had ever seen. At that time, he knew the law said that if you were driving drunk and caused someone's death, you must spend eight years in prison. He was 72 years old at that time.

The majority of our family did not want Mr. Carr to have to spend the next eight years in prison. Therefore, our daughter, Carolee, read a letter to the Clark County judge asking him not to send Mr. Carr to prison. She knew that Rick would not have wanted him to spend the last part of his life in prison. Sending Mr. Carr to prison is not going to bring Rick back. Mr. Carr suffers enough just knowing what he did and having to live with it.

I have to add the quote from the judge right after Carolee finished her speech. He said, "Well, the world hasn't gone to hell in a handbasket after all."

Mr. Carr will have to follow a lot of other rules that were set up by the judge, such as giving up his driver's license and not leaving the house other than to go to the doctor or to church. As he ended his other rules, he made it very clear that Mr. Carr would not be sentenced to prison at all. Thank you, judge!

Two Jury Rooms: One in Delaware, One on Big Screen

T his is a story set in two different jury rooms, from two different places, and at two different times. One of them was for a jury that I sat on, with the other being in a movie I saw on TV.

I'll start with the jury I was a part of back in the 1960s. I was a juror in the case of a young man who was being tried for selling drugs in Delaware, Ohio. When the time came for us to be sent to the jury room, we had barely gotten seated at our place at the table when one of the male jurors loudly said, "We all know he is guilty, so let's vote now and get it over with so we can go home!"

I was shocked that he had said it and have never forgotten those words during all these years since. I didn't feel comfortable enough to say anything, but the others did, and we ended up having a rather long period of time in that jury room. We even had to have an explanation by the judge as to what was meant by part of the terms used. It was explained to us that if the defendant had given another person the drugs, it was the same as selling the drugs to him. And, since the defendant admitted giving away the drugs, he was found guilty.

During the trial, we had not been told what the punishment would be if he were to be voted guilty. We didn't know if he would spend a few months in jail or a few years in prison. But later, we found that he would be spending a few years in prison. I never felt good about anything that happened that day in that jury room, but the part about being found guilty had to be done.

I will now write about the other jury room which was the location for almost the entire movie titled "12 Angry Men" that I had never seen until two weeks ago.

I had known about the movie ever since it came out in 1957. It starred Henry Fonda, Lee Cobb, and ten others who were well known back then. My reason for writing about both of these two court cases is that the movie also had a man in it who said something very similar to what was said at the time I was on jury duty, "We all know he's guilty, so let's vote now and get it over with so we can go home!"

At the time I thought I was hearing those words said, for a second time, I was not paying as close attention to the movie as I should have been. This "12 Angry Men" movie was being played on Turner Classic Movies which plays all the old black and white movies every day and night, year round. As for the jury room itself, since it was set back in the 1950s, there was no air conditioning, so the jurors "suffered" all the time with the "high temperature" in the room.

On the first vote, it was 11 for guilty and one for not guilty. Henry Fonda's character was the one vote for not guilty, and eventually, he changed the minds of 10 of the other 11 jurors who had first voted "guilty" to now vote "not guilty."

But, when it came to the 12th juror, their good acting abilities showed through, and Fonda was able to finally convince Cobb to change his vote to "not guilty" also.

Now, back to the Delaware County courtroom. At the end of the day and having found the young man guilty of selling drugs, I was not comfortable walking down the long winding steps and out the front door of the courthouse with all the others involved in the case. Mainly, all these rather "scary" young men and women who were there wanting him to be found not guilty. Back in the 1960s, we called them "hippies." As I went down the street, I knew I had to do something if I didn't want these young people to ever recognize me as being one of the women on the jury. So, as

I passed a beauty shop, I decided no one would recognize me if I went in and had my long hair cut off. So, I did.

How Buying Our
First Home Came to Be

T his story took place over 60 some years ago. It all began on a regular day when I was still single and living with my parents and siblings. We had just finished supper when someone knocked on the front door. When I opened it, there stood two young high school girls. Their names were Bev and Reg. They asked me if I would like to come to their church and sing in their choir. When I had lived in Delaware, I had attended the Presbyterian Church and sang in their choir for about eight years.

So, I walked on down the street to the Methodist Church and went in and ended up singing in their choir. That's where I met my husband, George, in 1957. By November 1958, we had gotten engaged and had set a wedding date for January 1959. That was the first time both of us had a two-week vacation from our jobs, so we could have a honeymoon.

As soon as everyone in church knew about our engagement, one of the older couples met us at the door after the service and wanted to talk to us. The first thing they said was, now that you are engaged, you will be needing a house for when you get married, and we want you to buy our house. What? They want us to buy their house? Buy a house already? How could we ever do that?

When I went back to work the next day at the Delaware County Recorder's office, a man named Mr. Black, who handled the filings for the Sunbury Savings and Loan, came in our office to file their new transactions of property. After I had taken care of everything he needed done, I casually mentioned that I had a chance to buy a house. And I laughed at the idea. I wasn't even married yet, but Mr. Black invited us to the bank to discuss the opportunity. One thing led to another and the next week we found ourselves going back to the said bank. This time the potential seller went with us. We had an appointment with Mr. Black and another bank official. George and I had the perfect schedule for the transaction. We were to give them the selling price, which was $7000, at the closing, and then they could have their new house finished and move out by February 1, 1959.

Our new home had three rooms downstairs and three bedrooms and a bath upstairs with a front porch and an extra room for laundry and storage since it had no attic or basement. And there was a single-car garage off to the side of the property. There were nine large trees, with room for swing sets, a picnic table and a sandbox.

Just as we were signing the mortgage for our new home, we discussed the fact that George was four months short of being 21 and that meant that he could not sign a real estate mortgage. That little fact stopped us in our tracks of getting to buy the house before we got married. But, since I was 21, Mr. Black suggested that I buy the property as a single woman, and it would be put in my maiden name at that time. If we had been married, we couldn't have bought the house, but since I was single, I was able to put the house and mortgage in my name alone. So, when we left the bank and got our papers filed at the recorder's office, it was ours, but only in my name. What a surprise ending to getting the house that we lived in for the next 60 years. On November 14, 1958, I was a single woman who owned a home.

As I am writing this article, our older daughter has come home from Florida because it's George's birthday. He is now 85.

Good Titles on Books
Can Draw in Readers

I know I spent a lot of time at our library just reading titles. Before I ever take a book off of the shelf, I have read the title and had become interested in what the book could be about. When I saw the title of a certain new book, I couldn't put it down without opening it up. The book is, "For You When I Am Gone" by Steve Leder.

Each of the 12 chapters of this book asks a different question for the reader to answer in their own minds.

I have picked a few of the questions and will be writing the anonymous answers that were given to him.

One of the titles is, "What makes you happy?" And one of the answers is: "Happiness really is togetherness. It is who, not what, we have that makes us happy, and so often happiness is in the most ordinary moments with the ones we love. Tell the people you love about those moments great and small when happiness filled your heart because of them."

A second title is, "What got you through your greatest challenge?" And what are the answers is: "Don't be afraid to ask for help. There are plenty of people out there who want to help you and can help you. It makes them feel good to do so."

A third title is, "What do you regret?" And one of the answers is: "A critical message of my ethical will is having humility and wisdom to admit we never know how much time we or our loved ones will have on earth. Act as if there may be no second chance because there may not be and don't risk the heartbreaking regret of not showing up."

A fourth title is, "What is a good person?" An answer is: "I've learned that people will forget what you said, people will forget what you did, but people will never forget how you made them feel."

A fifth title is, "What is love?" And one of their answers is: "Love is unconditional. When you love someone, you accept them for who they are, for better or for worse. Saying you're sorry, even if you're not sure how you really feel. Love is just a feeling you don't have to think about it-- you just feel it. If you have to think about it, it's probably not love."

And the sixth title is, "How do you want to be remembered?" And one of the answers is: "Just remember me at my best. Laughing, smiling, listening to the music I love. And passionately engaged in my work and witness to love and serve others."

This covers half of the chapters, and you may want to pick up the book to read the other half of the questions that were asked.

Great Memories from Times Shared with Nephew

Whenever I answered the phone, and it was my nephew David, he would say, "Watson here!"

He was my nephew who had been in my life since he was born when I was in junior high. His mother and my sister, Marilyn, had to stay in bed for the first week after his birth, and I had gone to her home and helped her get through that period of time. Mostly doing all the running up and down the stairs.

Having him as a nephew has kept our lives interesting. He was stationed in Germany while in the U. S. Army. I remember the day he came home because that's when our dad died, and we were all at the funeral home that evening. And while I was standing up front, he walked in the room. To me, he looked exactly like Tony Orlando. He had matured a lot during his time in the service.

After George and I retired, he often called us to go somewhere with him. He would pick us up in his shiny black car and when we left, I never knew exactly when we would be getting back home. Last fall, on the last nice day of the season, he appeared at our door one morning and said, "Come on, let's go. The leaves are beautiful, and we need to go out and see them." Eventually, he drove us to where George had built a cabin that someone destroyed. It was the first time we got out of a car and walked along the road to see the creek, as well as what was left of our three acres of beauty we had called our "Cabin in the Woods."

I should be writing about the trip we took to Florida when we stopped to eat at a Cracker Barrel, and I was looking around at their stuff, and out he stepped from behind the other aisle and said, "I think you should buy that Kay!" I was shocked to see him there. I didn't know he was in Florida, let alone in the same place we had picked for supper. He and our daughter, Cathy, had arranged that big surprise.

While recently reading an old journal, I ran onto the time he rented a small bus and took all his aunts and uncles to see the houses we had moved into and out of in our growing up years. Before lunch, we saw the four houses where the oldest four of us had been born. They were all in the areas of Johnstown, Centerburg, and Sunbury. After lunch, we found the houses where we lived when the remaining three were born in hospitals.

I have lots of other stories of my nephew but need to have some closure and write about the phone call I got in the very early morning on this past May 11. That's when I was told that David had died. They found him sitting in his chair in his home.

There had been no warning, that I know of, that this would happen to him. I guess it was his heart. Just six months before that, his son had died. His name was Nick, the same Nick I wrote an article about on November 30, 2022.

The following were some words that were written about David in a handout at his funeral.

"He believed that every morning was a gift from God of a brand new unused day that we needed to make the most of, knowing that we have more yesterdays than we have tomorrows."

I know I'm going to miss my nephew, David. Especially when the phone rings and I know I will never hear those words again, "Watson here!"

Journals, Swings and Premonitions

C ould you tell me what happened in your life on Thursday, July 21, 2011? How about on Monday, May 2, 2011?

I started keeping a journal back in 1970. Before that, I was just putting a few words on the kitchen calendar. But since I wanted to be serious and keep a real one, I used a small book and gradually ended up using 8"x10" notebooks, which I still use today.

Now, I fill an entire lined, spiral notebook on both sides of each sheet with what is going on every day. I decided I would check my own journal and see what I had done those particular days and found that July 21, we had a church supper, and I had served food to the 80 people who came to the free meal. Then I checked May 2 of that same year and found that I picked up my sisters, Jean and Ann, and went to our sister Marilyn's home to play cards and have lunch at Perkins Pancake House.

I encourage everyone to keep a journal. You never know when you may wish you had.

As for swings, I am writing about porch swings. We have one on our front patio. That particular swing dates back to 1948 when it was on the porch of my parents' home on North Sandusky Street in Delaware. I remember crowding on to that swing and making it go as fast as possible before hitting the porch railing. As heavy as it was, it got moved from house to house and ended up here. That's because no one else wanted it. It's a great place to sit.

I enjoy looking at porches on homes as we pass in our drives around the country. I remember seeing a porch with not just a swing, but a couch, a floor lamp, and two other overstuffed chairs. It looked like an outdoor living room. With all the subdivisions and smaller homes, I rarely see a porch swing or even a comfortable chair because the porches are so small. And the row of homes all look so much alike, I wonder how children can find their own home when they are walking home from school. You can have a swing that seats three or even four that costs anywhere from $100 to $1000. I'm glad we ended up with the same swing that our parents may have paid $5 for back in the 1940s.

My third subject is about premonitions. Last evening, I had a premonition that I should call my old friend today. Her name is Mary. We met at junior high at Willis in Delaware back in our school days. I remember a slumber party she had. When she gave me my invitation, I thought it said she was inviting me to a summer party. But, in conversations with other girls in our class, I found that it really said a "slumber party." Not knowing what it was, I had a lot to learn. She had a playhouse, so a perfect place to have a party.

Our friendship went from those days up to now-- which spans a time of 75 years. Shocking! We have met at class reunions, but I hadn't been in touch with her for years. So, I got out my address book and dialed what I hoped would still be her number. And it was! She was shocked that it was me. I'm sorry to have to say her husband died last evening and here I was, out of the blue calling her at noon today. Her husband was a nice guy named Jim. I'm so glad to have had the premonition to call at the time I did.

Having three different topics to write about I didn't know which to choose, so I chose them all. Would you like to have kept a journal for the past 50 some years? Do you have a swing out on your porch? If you have premonitions, do you follow them?

Many People Deserving
of Blue Ribbon

Have you ever won a blue ribbon? For those who haven't, I haven't either. The closest I came is when I had perfect attendance one year when I was on a bowling team. And that was a whole lot of years ago.

If you come to my house, you might find three blue ribbons. One is George's and the other two are still in the box they came in when I bought them several years ago.

Yes, you can buy them at a place called the Ribbon Factory, and it's just on the west side of town. I got the idea of buying some a couple of years ago when one of my brothers-in-law retired, and I wanted to give him a blue ribbon for all the work he had done for so many years.

It was suggested to me, recently, that I write about the others I had chosen to give a blue ribbon. I think the second one was to a lady I worked with at the courthouse. She had been making copies of documents for people who needed them. Making the copies isn't the hardest part of the work, it was the lifting of very heavy books down off the shelf and opening them to take the page out and putting the page back again. And then putting that very heavy book back up on the shelf. That was also very hard since the books were in one room and the copy machine was in another. And I never heard her complain once. So, now, years after we each retired, and I had that box of blue ribbons, I thought she should have one.

Right now, I am reminded of another person I gave a blue ribbon, and that was the man who always rings the bell for church every Sunday morning. He even brings a big bell with him if we have church outside at the Oxford Township Hall picnic area. He brings it in the trunk of his car and rings it from there. What a great job he has done for all the years I can remember.

I would be remiss if I didn't give one to his wife, as well, for her 30-some years of teaching our Sunday school class. It's the place to be every Sunday except in August when we have a month off.

Next comes to mind is my husband's chiropractor. He has kept George out of pain for more than the past 20 years. George has a regular time for maintenance, which is every six weeks. And, Dr. Thomas kept both of us out of pain when we both had shingles. So, he definitely deserves a blue ribbon.

If I can add another two people to my list of blue ribbons, it would be our two daughters. They have been there for both of us every step of the way. Especially during this period of our lives now, when we may have need for their help.

This isn't every one of the people I gave a blue ribbon, but I need to stop now for the lack of space. George thinks I should keep one for myself, since I have earned it by writing these articles for the past seven years. I have passed my seventh year, and in April I began my eighth.

So, if anyone reading this knows a person who deserves to have a blue ribbon, for whatever reason, just come to the RB Powers Company at 118 West High Street in Ashley and buy them one. It makes a fun gift.

Children of the 1930s:
'The Last Ones'

T he story with the above title and author is something I found recently with all my old papers. I don't know where it came from or how I ever got it, but it appeared just at the right time.

From the beginning to the end of reading it, I knew I wanted to use it for the Delaware Gazette. It was written for the "Children of the 1930s," and I am one of them. And so, for those of us who are still left, it speaks to us loud and clear.

If you have any connection with the 1930s, read and enjoy, because he is talking to you.

"Born in the 1930s, we exist as a very special age cohort. We are the "last ones." We are the last, climbing out of the depression, who can remember the winds of war and the war itself with fathers and uncles going off. We are the last to remember ration books for everything from sugar to shoes to stoves. We saved tinfoil and poured fat into tin cans. We saw cars up on blocks because tires weren't available. We are the last to hear Roosevelt's radio assurances and to see gold stars in the front windows of our grieving neighbors. We can also remember the parades on August 15, 1945: VJ Day.

We saw the "boys" home from the war, build their Cape Cod-style houses, pouring the cellar, tar papering it over and living there until they could afford the time and money to finsh it.

The lack of television in our early years meant, for most of us, that we had little real understanding of what the world was like. Our Saturday afternoons, if at the movies, gave us newsreels of the war and the holocaust sandwiched in between westerns and cartoons.

Newspapers and magazines were written for adults. We are the last who had to find out for ourselves.

As we grew up, the country was exploding with growth. The G. I. Bill gave returning veterans the means to get an education and spurred colleges to grow. VA loans fanned a housing boom. Pent-up demand coupled with new installment payment plans put factories to work. New highways would bring jobs and mobility. The veterans joined civic clubs and became active in politics. In the late 1940s and early 1950s the country seemed to lie in the embrace of brisk but quiet order as it gave birth to its new middle class.

Our parents understandably became absorbed with their own new lives. They were free from the confines of the depression and the war. They threw themselves into exploring opportunities they had never imagined. We weren't neglected but we weren't today's all-consuming family focus. They were glad we played by ourselves "till the streetlights came on." They were busy discovering the post-war world.

Most of us had no life plan, but with the unexpected virtue of ignorance and an economic rising tide, we simply stepped into the world and went to find out. We entered a world of overflowing plenty and opportunity; a world where we were welcomed. Based on our naive belief that there was more where this came from, we shaped life as we went.

We enjoyed the luxury; we felt secure in our future. Of course, just as today, not all Americans shared in this experience. Depression property was deep rooted. Polio was still a crippler.

The Korean War was the dark presage to the early 1950s and by mid-decade, schoolchildren were ducking under desks. China became Red China. Eisenhower sent the first "advisors" to Vietnam. Castro set up camp in Cuba and Khrushchev came to power.

We are the last to experience an interlude when there were no existential threats to our homeland. We came of age in the late 1940s and early 1950s. The war was over and the Cold War, terrorism, climate change, technological upheaval, and perpetual economic insecurity had yet to haunt life with insistent unease.

Only we can remember both the time of apocalyptic war and a time when our world was secure and full of bright promise and plenty. We experienced both.

We grew up at the best possible time, a time when the world was getting better not worse.

We are the 'last ones.'"

The above ends the article I had saved that was written by Carl Peterson.

I hope it spoke to all of you who were born in the 1930s, as it spoke to me.

Trip to Old Church
Brings Back Memories

There is always a first time for everything. This past Sunday was the first time for us to go to church and find no one there. I remember when I went to church and the door was locked. I soon found out that it was Saturday, not Sunday, so I went back home.

But last week was different. George and I drove in the church driveway to a totally vacant parking lot. We realized we had missed church the week before, because of being ill, so missed out on whatever was going on. We headed back home, and on the way, George asked me where I would like to go.

In a second's time, I said I would like to visit the First Presbyterian Church in Delaware.

My reason was that I had grown up going to that church and have often thought about going back to visit. I had only been back inside it twice in the last 60 years. Once to a wedding and the other was when the public was invited to sing along with the choir when they sang the "Hallelujah Chorus."

So, we headed for Delaware and arrived right on time. We noticed some of the people going in a side door, and when George suggested that we follow them, I said that they were in the choir and go that way to get to the choir loft, and we needed to go to the front door. But, I was wrong. They were on their way to an elevator that had been added since I had left there. Someone came and invited us to use the elevator, too. We entered the sanctuary from the front and were given a program and settled in for some of my memories to take over.

Growing up there meant my years from seventh grade through two years after high school. Getting to sing in the choir meant that I always got to sit in the choir loft.

The memory of the Christmas Eve service filled my brain. Back in the 1950s, Mrs. Peeples was the organist as well as the choir director. And on Christmas Eve, when the program upstairs was over, she put together a party for the choir on the lower floor where the Sunday school classes met. She always transformed the entire large room by having lighted candles on all the tables. The places to sit had lovely glass place settings. Along with a lot of other good food, she served what she called "figgy pudding." I never have found out what it was, but it was really good!

Over the many years I went to that church, I served at a lot of dinners down there, but it never was as lovely as when it was lit with candles for our choir's Christmas parties.

After last Sunday's service, we were greeted by a lot of very nice people. When I told them I had grown up there, most seemed surprised. Probably because I had already moved away from Delaware before any of them had first come there. I was there when Reverend Campbell first came to be the minister. And I babysat their three children. I babysat on Sunday evenings over supper time and the children always had tomato soup with popped popcorn on the top. It was a long time before I realized that all ministers do not serve their children tomato soup with popped popcorn every Sunday evening for supper.

As we left the church and walked out into their new front entrance, I looked back at the winding stair steps that I remember so well. At this age of my life, I can't imagine everyone climbing those stairs. And as we were heading toward our car, I looked back one more time to admire all the stained-glass windows that I had always thought were so beautiful in my growing up years ago.

Thanks to all the people who made George and me so welcome to an important part of my past.

Dealing with Effects
of Alzheimer's

My article for today is about a friend of ours. I will not be using his real name, so we'll refer to him as "JR."

George and JR have been friends for a lot of years. If it hadn't been for their horses, they probably never would have met. In the horse business, you get to know a lot of people, and JR became one of his very best friends.

I haven't written about the horse farm for a very long time because we sold it and no longer have any horses to write about. Thirty years ago we met JR when he came to our farm with one of his neighbors. He didn't come to ride, he just came to be a part of the world of a boarding stable with lots of horses, a racetrack, and an indoor arena.

He had his own full-time job, so before his retirement, he only came on the weekends. But when he retired, he started coming almost every day. He had his own farm with a couple of horses, but he liked being a part of a bigger riding and racing stable. They helped each other make hay every year, as well as building fences at each of their farms. JR. had Tennessee Walkers, which are show and riding horses, while George had both riding and standardbred racehorses.

After years passed, JR started forgetting how to do certain things. For instance, which door to open on his truck, or how to get his seat belt fastened. That was followed by him not doing much driving at all.

He was allowed to drive to our house to sit and talk to George, but not allowed to travel any more than the mile to get here. But, after a short time, he wasn't allowed to drive at all. That led to the word "Alzheimer's" coming into our daily conversations with his wife.

Eventually, George started taking him to lunch a couple of times each week. That was to give JR's wife a break from him following her around the house wherever she went. JR liked going to the same place and having the same food every time they went. He wanted French fries, a cheeseburger with pickles and onions, and a Coke. First, he ate the French fries, one at a time, and then the pickle, and then the onion, and then the cheeseburger back inside the bun.

After lunch, George always took him to either Lowe's, Menards, Delaware Hardware, or TSC for him to look around while George purchased whatever he needed for our garden.

One time at Menards, he wandered away, and George had to get the employees to help find him. When they started to look for him, he had been at the back of the store, but by the time they found him, he had wandered clear up to the front.

Eventually, JR had to be moved to a place for Alzheimer's patients. After a few weeks, we were allowed to go see him. We found him standing near some other people, and when he saw us, he came to greet us, and walked us to his room. It was almost lunchtime, so the employees invited us to have lunch with him there. He was served a very nutritious meal and George is glad he no longer had to have this that same cheeseburger and Coke he had always eaten when George had taken him out to lunch.

When it was time for us to go home, we explained to him that we had to leave. The three of us were standing in the hallway in front of his room, and as we started walking away, our final words were, "We'll be back." And standing there alone, just outside his room, he very quietly said, "No you won't."

Aunt Mary Sure Does
Love Horse Racing

Everyone should have an Aunt Mary like our Aunt Mary. She is my husband George's aunt. She is now 97 years of age.

I use the word "age" rather than the common word of old because she is not old in any way whatsoever. Last September we went to the Delaware County Fairgrounds with her for every day of horse racing. We were there for as many as 20 races each day. She has her own box and shares it with members of her family. She has spent her entire life learning about horses because her dad, Charlie Norris, raced horses from the 1940s until he was in his 80s.

We go to visit Aunt Mary whenever possible. A big part of any time spent with her is talking about races, and the horses her dad raced, as well as those that George raced. They discuss the differences that have taken place in the last 50 years.

They know the drivers as well as the owners. At the races, you will always see a racing program in their hands as well as a pencil to write the place each horse finished in their race.

If you go to the races, you will find that everyone sits in the same spot every day. There are a lot of friendships that take place because of that arrangement. I, myself, like to look for the people who are there every year that we never see otherwise during the year. We may not even know their name, but we feel a friendship when they are cheering for our horse, and we are cheering for theirs. I have seen many people come up to see Aunt Mary in her box every year.

George and Aunt Mary talk about everything imaginable that pertains to racing. Recently, they discussed the different colors of racing outfits worn by different drivers. George wore orange and brown with a certain design on the shirt and helmet. Every driver is different. I guess that helps everyone pick out who is who. And that reminds me of a famous man with the name of Roger Huston. He is the announcer of all the Brown Jug races, along with others at Delaware. He has a very distinctive voice. In fact, earlier this baseball season, at the Liberty High School ball field, the announcer of the game sounded exactly like Roger himself. Aunt Mary suggested that maybe it was him, since he does more announcing than just at the Brown Jug. That is quite something when you realize that those players were only around 8-to-10-years old.

I also learned about how horses, as well as their drivers, can get hurt while racing. After all, they are running at 30 mph and can get hurt by falling or having one bike run into another bike. Aunt Mary had two brothers and four nephews and one great niece, who also raced horses, so she did a lot of worrying about so many of her racing family.

We have always tried to attend the All-Horse Parade that the city of Delaware has each year before the fair. You can find Aunt Mary sitting on North Sandusky Street with all her family. We are lucky that North Sandusky Street has a lot of shade.

It won't be too long now before the beginning of the next Delaware County Fair. And, as we have seen at the fairgrounds, they are working on the grandstand. I think they call it "updating." You can tell they are doing extensive work on the grandstand, and perhaps even modernizing the restrooms and the stairs. That would be great for Aunt Mary to continue to get to attend the races in September. I heard someone say they were even putting in an elevator. That would be great. I believe that Aunt Mary has already purchased her box seat tickets, so she doesn't want to miss it.

So, if you can attend the races on any day, you could come to the part of the track that is the finish line, look up to the main level, and you might see Aunt Mary and her family cheering on the horses they are familiar with.

It's coming fast, so hope to see you there. I'll mark her chair with a sign that says, "Aunt Mary."

Intel to Change
Johnstown Forever

T he first time I saw the words Intel and Johnstown in the same sentence in the newspaper, I wondered what was going on. I know lots about Johnstown, but what does this word "Intel" mean? I thought it might be an abbreviation of the word "intelligence." However, when the word Johnstown pops up, I think of the fact that my parents were born there and my mother lived there until she married my dad and moved away. However, her siblings stayed, so we visited there often. A quick scan of said article told me that Johnstown was going to have 1,000 acres of their land be a part of a $20 billion computer chip manufacturing facility. Reading about that type of business made me think about the large number of people who would be moving into the area to work there. With all of that going on, my first thought was of the many children who would be coming and adding to the schools in the Johnstown system. Ever since reading that first article, there has been a lot written about what is going on in Johnstown, Ohio.

Since the newspapers had more stories, we decided to drive over and see what that area looks like now. Since it will be 2025 before it's done, it might be interesting to watch it all grow. We knew exactly how to get to Johnstown because of all the trips for family reunions as well as when my mom was in the nursing home there.

So, we took off for Sunbury, knowing to take Route 37 east right on into Johnstown. When we stopped at a gas station, we asked how to find Intel. The directions were simple. We were told to go to the first stop light, turn right, take that road until you can turn right again, and follow that road until you see it.

Following their directions, we drove right to the place that looked just like the pictures of it that had been in the newspaper. The roads we were on used to be two-lane roads but are now rather messy three-lane roads. And just that quickly, we found ourselves on a road filled with a mass of huge trucks, both in front of us and behind us, for as far as we could see in either direction. As we first began on this long road, we noticed several large white buildings off to the left. They must be for the huge number of people who will be working for Intel.

When we thought we had seen enough, we decided to start for home. It seemed unnecessary to turn around and go all the way back where we came, so we chose to exit when we saw a sign that said, "New Albany." We thought we were going into New Albany. However, there was a roundabout section and we found ourselves on back roads that had no road signs at all.

This is where I got worried about ever getting out of the unmarked countryside. All we had to do was to find Sunbury again, and we would be on our way back home. But Sunbury wasn't about to be found. At that point I was glad it was still daylight and that we had a full tank of gas. And that the roads were clear with no snow insight. But there were no road signs anywhere to let us know where we were. I was hoping to find some of those places with houses only on one side of the road, with the other side belonging to Intel.

But no luck on that either. A note about those houses on only one side of the road. In tonight's paper, one of the owners of one of those houses tells how difficult it is at this time to get his house sold. They are concerned as to what future places they will be able to move to. They want to stay close to where they are now. Mostly because of being close to the rest of their family.

After too much time on unmarked roads, we saw the word that meant we were going in the right direction. It was a huge red and black water tower off in the distance with the word "Johnstown" written on it! What a relief! By heading toward the sign, we had to get in another of those long lines of huge trucks. It didn't bother me that we had to stop and start every few feet all the way, as long as it led us toward home. We found ourselves right in the heart of downtown Johnstown again. This time, for just a flash, I got to see the house where my dad was born back in March of 1900. Before it got dark, we found Route 37 and happily headed home.

I'm glad we went. All I know is that Johnstown, Ohio, will never be the same as it was before Intel came to town.

Growing Square Watermelons Becoming New Trend

The first time I heard of a square watermelon was one night when I had my computer on and noticed a lady hanging watermelons from a high fence, after wrapping them in old T-shirts and dish towels. She had them hanging so as not to sit on the ground. That wasn't new, but just that quickly, before I had a chance to turn it off, she started talking about "square watermelons."

She was telling how to grow them so they will turn out square. Nice thing to know, so we decided to try it in this spring's garden. We had never had time for much of a garden because of too much work to do at the horse farm.

We like fresh corn on the cob. So, if you plant a few kernels every couple of days, you have corn ripening at different times, so we have lots of fresh corn on the cob every few days over a large part of the summer.

As I type this, our corn is already gone, the stocks are cut off, and leaning against the garage and about to be tied around our flagpole as a Halloween decoration.

We did have cucumbers this summer, but instead of being green, they turned out yellow. But they tasted just as good as any other cucumber. Well, as long as you put them in a bowl of the right amount of vinegar, water, and sugar.

And, can't forget the red raspberries. Last year we were given about five plants to transplant, and they had a small number of berries. But this year, those plants multiplied, and we had to stake them up because we have two or three times more plants with hands full of berries every day. Lots of fun to go out and pick and eat all of them before getting back in the house.

I see I've left out one important fact. It has to do with how you can plant a watermelon to get it to be square. The reason for the fence is so the vines won't grow out into the yard. They will intermingle in the fence. And the fence is 5-feet-by-16-feet in order to be big enough for six to eight plants. First, you build a box that is 8-inches square by 12-inches deep. It has to be open at the bottom enough for the rainwater to run out. When the watermelon is about the size of a softball, you place it in the box, and be sure to water the vine often. As it grows, it becomes flat on all four sides. When you know it is ripe, you take the screws out of the box to save it for another year.

When people have heard us speak of "square watermelons," they are usually very surprised and interested. One lady was in front of us in the line at the grocery store and heard the words "square watermelon" and turned around and asked us to explain what we were talking about. Then, just a couple of days ago, a maintenance guy came to check to see if our furnace was OK, and when we told him about what was growing in our garden, he followed us outside to see what a square watermelon really looks like.

The TV show left out how to cut a square watermelon, so I guess we will just have to figure that out for ourselves.

Take Me Out
to the Ball Game

The following is a song about baseball that I had memorized years ago. I read somewhere that it was written in 1908, and that they used it in games when they have their seventh-inning stretch.

"Take Me Out to the ball game, take me out with the crowd.

Buy me some peanuts and Cracker Jacks. I don't care if I never get back.

Let me root, root, root for the home team. If they don't win, it's a shame.

For it's 1-2-3 strikes you're out. At the old ball game."

This has been a summer of baseball at our house. I have watched more baseball on TV and gone to more baseball games of children than ever before in our lives. It is all coming to a close very soon, so I thought it is a good time to write about the sport.

First, we have been attending baseball games played by children around 5-to-6-years old. We love every minute of every game. Whether they are at bat or running between bases. I like watching when the players are out to catch the ball and how they can keep their foot on the base and stretch out enough to catch the ball on the end of their glove. I appreciate the work done by the parents of the players. How dedicated can they get? They stand by each of the bases to encourage the runners to run or stay where they are. They keep statistics on what's happening from start to finish. Their season finishes soon because it gets dark earlier and earlier as fall sets in. And the players must go to school the next day.

Now, I would like to jump ahead to professional baseball. My first thought is about something I heard about 20 years ago when someone said, "October is the saddest month because that's when baseball season ends." I never thought about it being a sad month at all. I thought it was the most beautiful month because of the colors of the trees. But this year is different. I am more on the side of those who will miss seeing baseball games almost every day.

Next, I have chosen one of the professional players to write about. It all started when every time I walked past our TV, I kept seeing the very same player on the screen. That went on about four times before I stopped and asked my husband who that player was on the screen every time I walked past.

He said his name is "Jose Ramirez." And that started a series of statements as to what a good player he is. Between what he knew, and our older daughter told us, I have learned a lot about Jose. The following paragraph is about his life and his years of playing baseball.

His name is Jose Ramirez, and he is from Boni, Dominican Republic. He is 31 years of age and is 5-foot-9- inches tall, which is short for a pro baseball player. A year ago, he signed a seven-year contract for $141 million. That's about $20 million a year. Wow!

He has had 1,327 hits, 216 home runs, and 202 stolen bases. Five times he has been on the All-Star team, and four times he got the Silver Slugger Award for hitting. He is a switch hitter meaning he can hit from both sides of the plate. He rebuilt a youth baseball field on the west side of Cleveland named "Jose Ramirez Field." He buys equipment for the kids in the Dominican Republic.

He started out as a shortstop and now plays third base. He will be playing for the Cleveland Guardians through the 2028 season.

If he hadn't been on our TV screen every time I walked from my computer to the kitchen, I'd never would have learned anything about him, and so much more than I ever knew about baseball. Good luck to the Cleveland Guardians!

Making Sure There's a
Beginning, Middle and End

My questions for today's article are: Where do these articles come from? How do these words get from my home to yours? Where does it all begin?

For my part, it begins the first day after the previous article appears in the newspaper. Using last week's article as an example, how did that story about baseball find itself printed on a page of last Wednesday's Delaware Gazette?

To put it in words, it begins in my brain when I ask myself: "What can I write about next?" I try never to write about something I have already written about, so it usually takes a long time to come up with something new. I already have over 200 articles stacked on my shelves here at home. I have articles about the horse farm, deaths of my family and friends, our new gardening experience, and many other topics. (I have to stop and enter here that we just heard the news that our friend JR died last night. I had written about him this past August 23.)

Since articles are supposed to have a beginning, a middle, and an ending, I think I will call the previous two paragraphs my beginning for this article. Now comes the middle.

Just this week, I found an article from the Marysville Journal-Tribune that I would like to quote here. It was originally written by a 72-year-old grandfather to his grandson. They are anonymous, but it is about a grandson asking his grandfather, "What was your favorite fast food growing up?" And the grandfather answered, "We didn't have fast food when I was growing up." Then, he asked where he grew up, the grandfather said, "It was a place called home. My mom cooked every day, and we sat down together at the dining room table, and if I didn't like what she put on my plate, I was allowed to sit there until I did like it. Then I had to ask to be excused from the table."

Then he added that his parents never wore jeans, set foot on a golf course, traveled out of the country, or had a credit card. There was no TV until he was seven years old. It was, of course, black and white. And there were only two stations, and they went off the air at 10 p.m. after playing the national anthem. The test pattern came on then.

Pizza was not delivered to his house, but milk was. So was bread and doughnuts from the Omar man.

There were no movie ratings because no movies had profanity, violence or almost anything offensive.

The grandfather also knew about headlight dim switches on the floor of the car, using hand signals in the car for turn indicators, and party lines on telephones. He remembered coffee shops with juke boxes, metal ice trays with levers, and washers with hand-cranked ringers to get the water out of the clothes. He had been born before polio shots, frozen food, contact lenses, pantyhose, air conditioners, and dishwashers. The grandfather concluded, "In my day, grass was mowed with a push mower, coke was a cold drink, pot was something your mother cooked in, and chip meant a piece of wood."

And today, my closing thoughts are that I have no idea what happens after I hit the "Send" key after finishing my article and sending it on to the editor of The Gazette. All I can guess is that he checks for mistakes that need correcting. Also to see if it has a beginning, a middle, and an ending that makes sense. Would you believe that the endings are as important as the beginnings?

The next time I see my article is when the mail is delivered in the mailbox. We don't have "paper boys" any longer. Years ago, we had a very nice delivery paper boy. His name was Harold. He told us once that if he was short one paper for him to deliver, he always shorted us and gave it to the last person. He said that he knew that if George didn't get a paper that day, he wouldn't be mad at him. We miss having Harold around.

One last thought about my articles. They include my picture and I think I should tell you that the picture was taken over 10 years ago, when I was much younger. It was a part of a snapshot. I cut off the other person and sent my picture to The Gazette. At that time, it was the only picture I had with my hair being the same color as it is now.

I will stop here because I have a beginning, a middle, and this is the end.

Old Stairway
Brings Back Memories

O n November 18 of this year, when I opened the Gazette to page 6A, the first thing I saw was a decorated winding open staircase with beautiful Christmas decorations going from the floor to the top. Then, I noticed an inside door at the end of the hallway. Within a few seconds I was surprised because it looked exactly like our stairs on North Sandusky Street from the house my family lived in for five years from 1949 to 1953. It had to be it! That house has been in my memory ever since the day we moved there.

We had previously been living in a very small house on East Central Avenue. The Disbennett Realty man knew there were eight of us living in that very small house, so he came to my dad and told him about a nice big house on North Sandusky that would be great for our whole family. And, he was right, so before we knew it, we were moving across the Central Avenue bridge to the north side of town. And that very nice open stairway was the first thing I liked about it.

As I looked at the picture, I thought I saw the same door to the underneath of the stairs, and that door led to what looked like a small closet. We had a table that sat outside the wall that we called our "telephone table." My claim to a quiet place in the house was to take the phone into that little open space, pull a string that turns on the light, shut the door, and sit on the floor to talk to my friends from school. Being that that happened back in 1949, I am happy to have that same "telephone table" in my living room today.

I can also see the door that led to the dining room and then on to the kitchen. Then late that night, I realized that it may not be where we lived those five years of my life. So, I phoned someone who I knew would be able to find out the address of the home. And, sadly, I learned that it was not from our home on North Sandusky, it was from a home on West Winter Street.

My reason for wanting to see that exact stairs again is my memory of something that lasted only for a few seconds just after we put up our Christmas tree in our living room. It happened when it had just gotten dark, and I was upstairs, changing my school clothes to my old clothes. I heard someone call me from downstairs that supper was ready. At our house, when supper was ready, you better be there before all the good stuff our mom had made was gone. So, about halfway down, I saw one of the most beautiful sights I had ever seen. It was our living room. The only lights on were our newly lit Christmas tree and from the brand-new TV set. Everyone else was out in the kitchen ready to eat. But I had to stop for those few seconds. I just stood there, on those stairs, looking at the beauty I had never seen before. Even the muffled voices from the kitchen sounded wonderful.

Both my parents and three of my sisters are now gone. But after all these many years, I can still see the beautifully lit living room and hear the muffled voices of all my family when I think of standing about halfway down that lovely open stairway. Both of my brothers have now seen the same picture in the Gazette, and both agreed with me and immediately said that the photograph had to been taken from our wonderful home on North Sandusky Street some 75 years ago. I may have to check it out for myself.

Popular Christmas Song
Brings Back Memories

66 "I 'll be Home for Christmas" is the title of a song that seems to have been running through my mind since the year 1945, when it was first sung by Bing Crosby. I first heard it when our oldest sister had a phone call from her husband, who happened to be in the Navy and was stationed in California.

When her husband wanted to call her, he had to call the lady across the street because we didn't have a telephone. So, he called the lady and she came over to the house to get Ginny so she could talk to him. He had a nickname of "Bud."

I was still in elementary school but got to go with Ginny and sit in the lady's kitchen while she talked to Bud on the phone in the living room.

The lady across the street had a radio on while I was there, and I heard the song, "I'll be Home for Christmas." And then when the war was over, it was the perfect song to be singing because now it meant that the servicemen would get to come home. And every year since, I have been reminded of how great it was back then when World War II was over.

During that time, my whole family was living in one house on Union Street. There were 11 of us then, my parents, Bud and Ginny and their daughter, Donna, and the rest of my five siblings and me. That was the year of my fondest memories of Christmas as a kid. We were all giving little gifts to each other. Things like a candy bar, a balloon, crayons, and even a spool of thread for our mom. Everything was wrapped in the paper we saved from the comic section of our Sunday paper. I could still see all those gifts under the tree that Christmas morning.

Since Bud had a nickname, I think he wanted everyone else to have one, too. He gave me the nickname of "Mopsy."

Mopsy was a comic strip of a girl whose hair was a mess. And mine must have been a mess because he took up a collection to see that I got a haircut and a perm. Other nicknames I remember were "Dingbat" and "Chope."

Because of having to spend a lot of time in the water of the Pacific Ocean, Bud wasn't well in his later years and was only 57 when he died.

If you do not know the words to "I'll be Home for Christmas," you can put the title in your computer and bring up either Bing Crosby, Elvis Presley, or Frank Sinatra to sing it for you. And just yesterday there was a commercial on TV using that very same song. That was almost 80 years after it had been written.

Here are the words that are very well known at this time of the year:

"I'll be home for Christmas,
You can plan on me.
Please have snow and mistletoe,
And presents on the tree.
Christmas Eve will find me
Where the love light gleams.
I'll be home for Christmas,
If only in my dreams."

Wouldn't it be wonderful if everyone in the world would get to come home for Christmas this year! If that could happen, it would be the best merry Christmas ever!

Life Involves Adjusting
to Changing Times

Recently, I have become aware that I am not keeping up with the changes that go on every day. Of course, I've blame it on my age. I have been spending some time thinking of the changes that have been occurring during my lifetime. Big changes like having fourteen different addresses in the first 22 years of my life.

1. My life changed when I was 10 years old and got to help my older brother with his paper route. His route was the entire length of East Central Avenue, and I helped him by taking all the side streets. He paid me 5 cents a week to help him. One of my customers on one of the side streets paid him an extra 5 cents a week to have the paper put inside her storm door. I'm the one who got off my bike and put it in the door. Later, when I was older, I realized where my 5 cents came from.

2. Our lives all changed when we moved to the 300 block of North Sandusky Street in Delaware and had a bigger house with more room for everyone. We had a dining room big enough for all our family to sit around one table. What I have missed, since then, is the noise of nine of us at the table. After George and I got married, we rarely had more than four people at one time.

3. Another change was when I turned 14 and got to babysit for 35 cents an hour. When I babysat with four children, from 7 a.m. to 11 p.m., I got a whole $5.00 bill.

4. When I started to drive, there were filling station attendants who not only pumped your gas, but cleaned your windshield and checked your oil. Then the day came when you had to pump your own gas, and no one cleaned anything for you.

5. Getting groceries started out just telling the person who stood behind the counter what groceries you needed, and then they got them for you. Later, we could take a cart through the whole store. Now, you can phone them in and have them delivered to your kitchen door.

6. As for money, I started out getting an allowance that was $2.00 a week when I was a senior in high school. However, the majority of it was for my lunches. Then when I got my first job, I got a real paper paycheck that I deposited in the bank myself. That was followed by "direct deposit," and it has been direct deposit ever since.

7. As for the style of clothes, when I was a lot younger and working outside the home, I had more clothes that were in style. However, since the day I retired, style has gone out the window. To me, being comfortable is the most important thing.

8. As for libraries, from my seventh grade in school until today, except for a very short period of time, I have lived close enough to a library to walk to it. Hard to believe, but true. I am at a

point in life now when walking to the library is also where I walk for exercise.

9. A big change along the way has been our mail delivery. My grandfather delivered the mail back in the early 1900s using a horse and wagon. Back in the early 1950s, we had mail delivered two times a day-- morning and afternoon. Later, we could have mailboxes out at the edge of the street where the delivery person could put it in our box while sitting in their car.

With the Delaware Gazette cutting back delivering to just two days a week, it will take a while to get used to it. For the past 60-plus years, we have had the Delaware Gazette delivered to our house every day except for Sundays. The paper was always delivered to the homes I have lived in, until the time it started to come in the mail. Back in the past, when we had a delivery man put the paper on our porch, sometimes we didn't get a copy.

For a lot of years now, I have known that someday there wouldn't be any newspapers printed anywhere. It is too much of a waste of trees in our environment. What I didn't know was that it was maybe taking place in my lifetime. When I went to our mailbox earlier this week, it was totally empty! Not a card, or a bill, or magazine, or letter from a friend or relative. Not even the newspaper that I could always rely on. Just one of the many new changes I'm going to have to get used to!

Riding in Elevators
Can Be Scary for Some

Ever since I can remember, I have had a fear of getting on an elevator. Back in the 1950s, when I had a dentist appointment in the office above the bank on Sandusky and Winter, I had to ride an elevator to get there. I'm not sure which floor it was on, but just one floor up was too much.

This would have been at a time when there was always an operator running the elevator. That was not as scary as when I had to get on one by myself.

When I first began work at the courthouse, an elevator had just been added because a person in a wheelchair had recently been elected to office. I never rode it because I believed in walking for exercise in those days. I use that as my excuse anyway.

There was a time much later when I was working at OWU when I was told that I had to go to Columbus and meet in an attorney's office that was on something like the 16th floor. It was around that high of number anyway. I know I dreaded it from the day I found out about it till the day we had to go. I didn't have to go alone, there were two women from the office that went as well, and they got me through that scary experience.

And now for my most recent experience with an elevator. This past Friday we set out for Delaware with the main reason of going to the Gazette and dropping by to meet the editor. I have been sending articles to the Gazette for six or seven years now, but I had never met this editor.

I thought I knew exactly where to go because of seeing a sign in the PNC Bank stating to get on the elevator and go to the second floor. So, as soon as we walked in the east door of PNC and saw an elevator, we pushed the button to get up to the second floor. I dreaded getting on, but with my husband there to open the door and talk me through it, I got on with him.

It was small which is not what I hoped for. As soon as the elevator stopped and the door opened, I stepped out as soon as possible. But we weren't where we should have been. We were in an empty area on the second floor of the bank and really didn't know where we were. We walked the hall and looked in all the rooms, but no offices had anyone in them except one way in the back. We asked about the Gazette, and he told us that they had moved from that area a long time ago.

Next was to find the stairs to walk back down to the first floor and after what seemed like a lot of looking, we did. And within minutes, we were outside again and heading home.

I don't know how I became so afraid of elevators. I think it has a lot to do with something called claustrophobia. After all, I have never enjoyed getting on an airplane. Or, maybe it has something to do with that first ride in an elevator when I was on my way to my dentist appointment. Who knows?

Fond Memories of
Progressive Mothers Club

The question about when I was going to join a "Mothers' Club" was asked to me by my husband about a month after our older daughter was born. I told him that you must wait to be asked to join one of the clubs. This was back in the 1960s when everything in our village was still new to me.

He knew about Mothers' Clubs because his own mother had always gone to Mothers' Club meetings. It wasn't long until I was asked to join the Progressive Mothers' Club. At that time, there was a total of about 15 members, and they met on the third Thursday evening of each month.

They met in each others' homes at 8 p.m. and sometimes talked until near midnight. Almost every meeting had a different topic for discussion that had to do with being a mother. It's also a good way to get to know a lot of other people in your community.

Over the years that I went to the meetings, the club shrunk down to about 10 members. We had officers and everyone took their turn to fill those spots. Sometimes we had guest speakers, but other times the members themselves chose a topic to speak about. We learned a lot from each other, especially about what was going on in our school system.

When we were all beginning to get much older and we didn't want to meet in the evenings, we decided to go to different restaurants in the area, have lunch, and then just sit and have informal meetings afterwards. Once when we planned on eating at Buns, members decided to first come up to see what my office was like at the courthouse. That didn't work out so well because by the time the last ones got to my office, the first ones had already started to eat their lunch at Buns

Over the years while I was still working at the courthouse, the Mothers' Club disbanded.

I knew exactly when because I had been too busy to attend any of the last year's meetings. But I am certainly glad that I had those 40-some years to spend time with those wonderful women. Getting to know about their children growing up and being parents themselves would not have happened in any other way. I wish I had made a list of all the things I learned during our time together.

Maybe I could have learned to knit or was it crochet? Or how to fix the best stew, or even what cleaner was the best for your good silverware. Maybe if I had taken notes, I could fix a good chicken dinner for my husband, but he doesn't like chicken anyway.

Some of those women's names were Edith, Margie, Lyn, Mary, Vera, Betty, Evelyn, Twila, and Gayle.

Thanks to them for inviting me to join their Progressive Mothers' Club back in 1960. Maybe they had something to do with the fact that just last year, I was given a sign that hangs over my desk that says, "I love that you're my mom."

Valentine's Day Trip
Brought Back Memories

V alentine's Day is always kind of fun. The fun started when we were all in elementary school and exchanged little cards. That's how it was at the school I went to, anyway. It can be good, or not so good, depending on if you received a Valentine from the right person. That's the way it is while you are in elementary school anyway. It's different when you are an adult and have had a spouse for a lot of years.

In my case, being married for as long as we have, it's usually a given to get one.

So, yesterday when George asked me what I would like to do for the day, without thinking, I said that I would like for us to go up to Galion. I lived there while in kindergarten, first and second grades. Those three years of my life certainly must have had a lot of meaning to me because I enjoy going back as much as possible. So, that's where we went.

It was about 11 a.m. before leaving for the 45-minute trip. Before having lunch, we drove around to look at the houses that I had lived in back in the 1940s. One of the houses is completely gone, one is totally unlivable, and two are livable. The last house that looked most livable looked empty yet had a porch full of bags of groceries and a whole gallon of milk. The neighbors next door were sitting outside, so I went over to ask what he knew about the house. In turn, he asked me where I went to church. When I said it was the Ashley Community Church, he was very pleased to know we each had the same minister over the past years.

Our lunch was at "Granny's Kitchen," which is on State Route 61, at the east edge of town. Great place to eat. We found out that the original owner was still there. I was supposed to get a side of carrots, which was forgotten, but when the waitress realized it she gave me a container with the carrots to take home. Plus, the fact that they made sure we had a senior discount.

As we were leaving, two different ladies mentioned how much they liked my purple raincoat. I told them I have been wearing that same purple coat since back in 1988.

When we lived there, my dad worked at a place called the Galion Square Market. And, I have always remembered the one time I walked by myself to where he worked. What I remember most is what happened when my mother walked downtown alone on a cold day right before Christmas. Our two older sisters must have been at home to take care of us younger ones. Mom had lost her hearing as a child, so barely ever left the house. But she wanted to buy a new white shirt for our dad for Christmas. And when she found a store and they had the right shirt, and she went to pay for it, she was a penny short. And the store employee would not let her have the shirt until she brought back that needed penny. So, she walked clear back home, got the penny, and walked clear back to the store, got the shirt and walked clear back home all alone, in the cold.

I never thought to ask her what year that happened. If it was the last year we had lived in Galion, it would have been December 24, 1943.

This year was a great day for Valentine's Day. No snow, just sunshine all day. It was a day of meeting a lot of friendly people, including our waitress at Granny's Kitchen. We told her that we hope to come back again before next Valentine's Day. But what I don't think I will ever forget is about the time mom had to walk an extra trip home and back just to give the store one more penny for the cost of a shirt for a Christmas present for our dad.

Recalling Memories from a
Day Seven Decades Ago

At about 5 a.m. Friday, when I couldn't get back to sleep, I realized that I remember a whole day from 70 years ago! I remember where I lived, what I wore to school that day, where I had lunch, and so forth for the entire day. Wow, it's shocking to me that I can remember that far back!

First comes where I lived. I was living on Mason Court in Delaware at the home of a family I was babysitting for during my senior year at Willis High School. I had been babysitting two elementary school children the year before, and rather than move to a farm in another county with my parents and siblings, I was asked to live with the family and still cook supper and take care of the children. So, during my senior year, I did just that.

As for what I would have worn to school that Friday, in the second week of November of 1953, I would have worn my cheerleading outfit. If we were having a home football game, we would have worn our white cheerleading outfits, and if the football game was an away game, we would have worn our black. I need to add that I did not own these two cheerleading outfits. They were given to us to wear during the year we had been elected and had to be given back to the school when the year was over. I remember the disappointment I felt when I had to give mine back.

As for lunch that day, I ate in the school cafeteria. Being it was the last day of the week, I would have had just enough money to pay the 35 cents that lunches cost back then. The best part was getting to have chocolate milk on Fridays, and not having to drink the white milk.

In the extra time after students ate, we had time to do one of several things. One thing to do was to pay five cents each day of the week and get to watch 1/5 of a good movie in the auditorium. The other option was to attend a necessary meeting.

As a cheerleader, we had to plan for the pep assembly which was held each game day. The assembly schedule included introducing the coaches, singing some songs with the pep band, and introducing any new cheers. The whole idea was to get the students to want to attend each of the school's games.

As for after school that second week of November, I would have gone back to take care of the children I babysat and fixed their supper by the time their parents got home. Then find a ride out to the football field, which was a long way down a side street off West William Street. I saved all my homework to be done when I got back to my parents' home for the rest of the weekend.

I chose to write this article about another day in my life because a lot of readers commented on the fact that I could remember everything that happened on my graduation day. Mostly, they remember about my having to make my own white dress to wear for graduation and when I thought it was done, I tried to iron it and I put a big hole, the size of the iron, right on the front of it, thus having to make it over. I don't remember any such things happening on that second week in November of 1953, but it's the fact that it was a whole 70 years ago that is a shock to me!